SAVING SIN CITY

SAVING
SIN CITY

WILLIAM TRAVERS JEROME, STANFORD WHITE,
AND THE ORIGINAL CRIME OF THE CENTURY

MARY CUMMINGS

PEGASUS BOOKS
NEW YORK LONDON

Saving Sin City

Pegasus Books Ltd
148 West 37th Street, 13th Floor
New York, NY 10018

First Pegasus Books hardcover edition May 2018

Interior design by Sabrina Plomitallo-González, Pegasus Books

ISBN: 978-1-68177-746-7

10 9 8 7 6 5 4 3 2 1

Printed in the United States of America
Distributed by W. W. Norton & Company, Inc.

TABLE OF CONTENTS

PROLOGUE   *vii*

1901

1 "THE JUDGE WITH THE AX"   *3*
2 PASSION SPARKED   *11*
3 A DIFFICULT LAUNCH   *21*
4 ON TOP OF THE WORLD   *29*
5 GOO-GOOS AND GRAFTERS   *41*
6 SOARING CELEBRITY, SOARING DEBTS   *53*
7 A HERO ON THE HUSTINGS   *59*
8 "MAD HARRY"   *67*

1902

9   INTO THE FRAY   *77*
10 PASSIONATE PLAYMATES   *83*
11 "THE KING OF GAMBLERS"   *87*
12 ERRANT EVELYN   *93*

1903

13 CHARLIE'S FOLLY   *101*
14 HEADING FOR TROUBLE   *105*
15 THE DODGE-MORSE TANGLE   *111*
16 THAW UNMASKED   *115*
17 JEROME'S SECRET   *123*

1904

18 SPIRALING DOWNWARD   *129*
19 DEATH IN A HANSOM CAB   *133*

20 EVELYN ASCENDANT 137
21 HARD WORK AND HEADACHES 141
22 KEEPING UP APPEARANCES 149

1905

23 CORPORATE SCANDAL AND A CAUTIONARY CASE 155
24 COMING TO TERMS 159
25 "THE BIG SPIDER" 165
26 A SHOPPING SPREE 171
27 MORE CHALLENGES 175
28 PARADISE LOST 183
29 ANOTHER PROBE, A NEW HERO 187

1906

30 GATHERING SHADOWS 191
31 A HIGH-WIRE ACT 195
32 JUNE 25, 1906 201
33 BEFORE THE STORM 207
34 A DISCREET FAREWELL 213
35 THE PRESS POUNCES 215
36 GIRDING FOR BATTLE 219

1907

37 *PEOPLE V. HARRY K. THAW* I: THE PRELIMINARIES 225
38 *PEOPLE V. HARRY K. THAW* I: "THE ANGEL CHILD" 233
39 *PEOPLE V. HARRY K. THAW* I: JEROME, THE INQUISITOR ... 241
40 *PEOPLE V. HARRY K. THAW* I: CLOSING ARGUMENTS 253

1908

41 *PEOPLE V. HARRY K. THAW* II: A "PROPER VERDICT" 261
42 FINISHED AT FIFTY 271

EPILOGUE 275
WORKS CITED BY CHAPTER 283

PROLOGUE

What is the chief end of man? To get rich. In what way?
Dishonestly if we can, honestly if we must.
—MARK TWAIN

If the people want blackmailers and other criminals vigorously
prosecuted without fear or favor, they will elect Judge Jerome.
—*NEW YORK HERALD*, NOVEMBER 3, 1901

I n the early evening of January 4, 1901, a crowd is beginning to form
around 871 Fifth Avenue, the palatial residence of one of the city's
richest and most powerful men. They have come out on this frigid night
to catch a glimpse of the diamond-draped women and men in swallowtail
who are expected at William Whitney's society ball, though it will be hours
before any of the guests arrive. A celebration of the formal debut of his niece
Helen Barney, the party is also an occasion for Whitney to unveil his splendid
new home, one of his friend Stanford White's most lavish creations. For the
gawkers outside, a broad span of wrought ironwork over the main door offers
a meager but tantalizing view of the mansion's green onyx vestibule aglow in
the light of three immense bronze chandeliers.

As darkness descends and their numbers increase, Captain Titus of the
25th Precinct keeps a watchful eye on the crowd, ready to leap into action at
the first sign of rowdiness. Then, at precisely 11:00 o'clock, the hour named
on their invitations, the guests begin to arrive. As the *New York Times* reports
the next morning, the "flash of the carriage lamps and the clang of the
motor gongs" alert the sidewalk spectators that their patience is about to be
rewarded. There are gasps as Caroline Astor, unbent by the weight of her

magnificent diamonds, glides toward the entrance like a majestic battleship lit up for the night. When the stunning Cryder triplets are sighted wearing identical "frocks of white lace over white satin," excitement reaches a pitch that has Captain Titus on the alert.

Many of the four-hundred-odd guests have come straight from the opera. Passing through splendidly decorated gates acquired by White from an Italian palazzo, they mount a marble staircase to be greeted in the salon by Whitney, his sister Lily Barney, and her daughter Helen. Lily is resplendent in velvet and brocade, Helen demurely radiant in white mousseline de soie, but the one from whom each guest is craving some sign of special attention is Whitney himself—tall, suave, and heartthrob handsome. Profiled in a recent *Times* magazine, he is described as a man "of distinguished appearance" standing over six feet, "straight and vigorous as a West Point cadet . . . a staunch and generous friend, and a liberal-minded and public-spirited citizen."

The transformation of what had been a rather undistinguished residence into this treasure-filled palace fit for a doge has required what the *Times* discreetly termed "a large amount of money and time." Others are more specific, citing $2 to $3 million (roughly $65 million today; currency in 2018 is worth roughly twenty-six times what it was then) and nearly five years under construction. Whitney, who has abandoned a promising political career to make his fortune, lacks neither time nor money. While still in his forties he has turned his back on idealism and entered a period of frenetic financial gain. After helping to bring down the Tweed dictatorship in his days as a reformer, when, as New York's corporation counsel, he successfully contested the Tweed regime's fraudulent claims against the city, he has made peace with the corrupt Tammany machine, which still controls Manhattan's Democratic Party. A pragmatic move, it has enabled him to all but corner the city's transit system with franchises awarded to him by his Tammany pals. In league with the wily Thomas Fortune Ryan, he has spearheaded the creation of the Metropolitan Street Railway Company and its holding company and has been watering stock and emptying the profits into his pocket. It is rumored that he has obtained virtual control of Tammany Hall and acquired a fortune of some $40 million.

Whitney's ruthless tactics and questionable ethics are surely no secret among those in his social orbit but among his peers his transgressions are largely ignored, if not envied. He remains a society favorite, popular with men, adored by women. It is a small world whose denizens are members of the same clubs, use the same bankers and lawyers, hold neighboring boxes at the opera, and attend the same balls in a city awash in money and fast becoming the financial, entertainment and manufacturing capital of the country.

Geographically close but morally a world away is the bohemian world of the Tenderloin, a square mile of midtown Manhattan devoted to theater, big gambling houses and honky-tonk ranging from plush brothels to noisy dance halls where vice thrives under the protection of a corrupt police force. Stage-struck chorus girls amuse themselves there with high-spirited bachelors who have flocked to the city seeking their fortunes, but the young beauties save their most seductive charms for the uptown millionaires like Whitney and White, who frequent the Tenderloin for a lively good time—and perhaps something more. Adventurous pleasure seekers, they are at ease in the bohemian haunts of the Tenderloin, where the pleasures are illicit but seldom dangerous. For them, Tenderloin vice has a tawdry glamor that offers pleasures more like entertainment—albeit of the forbidden variety—than sin. Its delights are perceived as distinct from those of the degrading and dangerous vice dens of the slums—the dark underside of the city that festers, neglected and largely unacknowledged by the swanning socialites at Whitney's ball.

At the Fifth Avenue mansion, the champagne is flowing and the revels well under way when the appearance of a tall figure with bristling red hair and a great moustache causes a frisson of excitement to ripple through the room. As the news that Stanford White has arrived travels at lightning speed, heads turn to focus on New York's most celebrated architect, tastemaker, and man-about town.

White is a close friend of his host, who also happens to be his most lucrative client. It is White who has pillaged Europe to furnish Whitney's palace with carvings, paneling, staircases, tapestries and entire gilded and coffered ceilings stripped from the Continent's ancient castles and shipped off to Fifth

Avenue. And it is White whose luminous buildings many credit with rescuing the city from its drab brownstone past—a dull uniformity that Edith Wharton once decried for its lack of "towers, porticoes, fountains or perspectives": for its sheer "ugliness."

When they are out on the town White and Whitney are often joined by banker Charles Barney, whose marriage to Whitney's sister has allowed him to penetrate the highest circles of New York finance and to deploy his considerable financial skills as president of high society's bank, the Knickerbocker Trust Company. All three men have Gilded Age tastes, but while Whitney has the fortune to fund his extravagance and Barney is a wizard at making money multiply, White, who often expresses his conviction that an architect should live better than his clients, has put himself deeply in debt in the effort. White's work for the grandees of the Gilded Age is handsomely paid, but money slips through his fingers. In 1884, he had married Bessie Smith, a member of a prominent Long Island family who later inherited a substantial fortune. She has been generous in sharing her inheritance with her husband, though she remains a country girl with little interest in New York society and the lavish life of its millionaires.

White, who is keenly interested in just that, is convinced, like so many of the era's aspiring titans, that the best way to become a millionaire is to make a killing on the stock market, and he has been increasing his speculative activity since the early 1890s, largely with borrowed money, often with loans arranged by Barney, his banker, client, and longtime friend. Predictably, his losses have outpaced his gains. By 1901 he is deeply in debt, a crushing burden that has had no visible effect on his exuberant social and amorous life or his obsessive acquisitiveness. To the revelers at the Whitney ball, there is no sign of his rising panic; he appears, as always, the irrepressible, charismatic man of the hour.

To a reporter watching the party from outside, the view through an enormous bay window reveals a sliver of the vast ballroom. Brilliantly illuminated, the lavish showcase for the spoils of White's European raids seems to him to glow "like a great ball of fire." White's voracious appetite for Old World treasures is well known among the men and women circling the ballroom, and most are doubtless aware of his equally passionate pursuit of sensual pleasures, notably those involving beautiful young women. Unlike Whitney, however, White stays clear of married women, preferring the younger, more available showgirls and dancers.

While it is not uncommon for married men of White's caste to spend clandestine evenings with young, unattached women, White pushes the limits, providing not just a more exuberant aesthetic for the new century but carrying the banner for a sybaritic brand of sexual freedom to extremes. He entertains often and extravagantly, keeps a series of secret trysting studios, showers gifts on his amorous interests and within a few months will enter into the most ardent—and costly—affair of his life with the captivating sixteen-year-old chorus girl Evelyn Nesbit. For White, the gilt on the surface is a thin veneer covering a life of dangerous excess. Just as the world he and his high-living clients inhabit is the upper crust that distracts from the urban misery below.

While the grandees are exploiting the imbalances, hypocrisies, and corruption of the city for their private advantage, others have taken up the cause of reform. Chief among them is William Travers Jerome, the fiercely ambitious Court of Special Sessions judge who will soon run a spectacular campaign for District Attorney of New York County. Jerome has been making a name for himself as an incorruptible crusader, capable of cleaning up what people are calling Sin City. After getting his career off to a slow start, he has blazed into glory, seizing unprecedented judicial authority to conduct hair-raising raids on gambling joints and arraigning culprits on the spot before they can bribe their way out of trouble. The raids, during which he joins his ax-wielding men, have sealed his reputation as a rough and ready man of action and created a new star in the political firmament. In his remarkable campaign for DA in the fall, he will vow to not only rid the city of its vice dens and the corrupt police force that feeds off them but also follow the trail of corruption wherever it leads. Even if it takes him to higher-ups in corporations like the Metropolitan Street Railway Company and stops at William Whitney's door.

Newspaper reporters have been at his heels ever since the first raid. Writers are hailing him as an American "of the new time," "a new type of man in practical politics," and he is eager to assume the mantle. He eschews the funereal wardrobes and florid oratory of Old School politicians and has an impressive command of profanity when provoked. He likes his whiskey, good conversation and an occasional card game, and he prefers cigarettes (still called "pimp weeds" by the disapproving) over cigars. He has an easy manner but is keenly aware of his own brilliance and incorruptibility and frustrated by his delayed ascent to a position of political prominence when less qualified men have vaulted ahead. Tolerant of harmless personal indulgence, he is quick to condemn the sins of the self-serving powerful. His willingness to make enemies of them is a point of pride, and he aims his attacks not only at the NYPD and Wall Street but at the clubmen who are his peers, the lawyers and judges who are his colleagues, and—especially risky—at the tabloid press.

During his first term as DA Jerome is a heroic figure—St. George of Manhattan, slayer of crooked Tammany dragons and defender of the oppressed—but in his second term he will come under increasing criticism for his failure to deliver on his campaign promises, putting his reputation and his political career in jeopardy. Then, just as the forces against him are coalescing, he is presented with a unique opportunity to restore his reputation by performing brilliantly as the prosecutor in a trial that promises to capture the whole world's attention. At the center of the case is the bizarre and deadly sex triangle involving Stanford White, his former lover Evelyn Nesbit, and Evelyn's husband, the unstable millionaire Harry K. Thaw. With all the elements of a sensational drama—sex, money, murder, and madness—the case promises to captivate the whole world, and Jerome sees his chance to prove that in a contest between money and justice he can lead justice to victory.

In the end, what the trial will prove is that money worship and greed in Gilded Age New York have created a society with no moral compass, where everything has its price, and where the rich have all the power—and all the fun. *People v. Harry K. Thaw* will reveal a deeply divided city where the building resentment against high society hedonists like Whitney and White, who are able to gorge every appetite and reap every reward of their celebrity status without consequences, is encouraged by the lurid coverage of their depravity in the sensational press.

This is a story of a time, not unlike our own, when New Yorkers were swept up in a contagious lust for riches, when the *New York Herald* could declare, "In this city money marches before everything else." It was a time when four hundred of the wealthiest New Yorkers could continue their revels into the next morning in a scene that reminded a *Times* reporter of "some court ball in a European palace." For Whitney's elite guests it was a crowning moment, their dreams of matching Old World extravagance undeniably achieved. Unaware or indifferent to the people's rising resentment, they danced through the night, mindlessly putting the city on course for escalating class conflict.

1901

1

"THE JUDGE WITH THE AX"

"Tut, tut!" said Jerome with a grin,
These games are disguised very thin;
When you hear a cop snore
By a strange-looking door
It's a cinch there is gambling within.
—WALLACE IRWIN

At the height of the business day on Monday, February 18, 1901, no one at the Parade Turf Club is expecting any trouble. Members who have paid one dollar for a passkey and privileges in what is actually one of lower Manhattan's most popular gambling houses are blissfully unaware of the forces about to converge on 20 Dey Street, where the "club" occupies two floors above Vath's saloon. Not the most swank of the illicit gambling dens thriving under the protection of a corrupt constabulary—Vanderbilts and like-minded members of the "gambling gentry" are partial to Richard Canfield's antiques-filled uptown establishment—but it is extraordinarily profitable.

The Turf Club's seedy, smoke-filled rooms are buzzing as nearly a hundred men hover around the roulette wheels, the faro bank and the crap tables, ignorant of the raiding party organized by Justice William Travers Jerome, which is already heading their way. Jerome, angry and frustrated by Tammany's corrupt control over the police force, whose burly chief, William ("Big Bill") Devery, routinely tips off targets of imminent raids, has thrown off his judicial robes at the Court of Special Sessions and leapt from the bench to take action.

By early afternoon a carriage has arrived to take him downtown to the Cortlandt Street ferry, where six trustworthy police sergeants and two assistant district attorneys are waiting to join him on the top-secret raid. As the driver guides the horses through the chaotic streets of lower Manhattan—then the most densely populated area on earth—Jerome lights up a cigarette. Every precaution has been taken to prevent word of his plan from reaching Devery and the debased police department, but by taking the fight to the enemy, attacking suddenly with a force of ax-wielding men, he is breaking new ground, and his nerves are on edge. As the carriage sways and jogs, he sits upright, his wiry frame, tall and trim, tensed for battle.

For the last half dozen years he has been stuck on what he dismisses resentfully as a "little squirt of a court," condemned to sentencing longshoremen for brawling and meting out justice day after day to the multitudes of such petty offenders. Highly ambitious, fearless and frustrated, he is too much the fighter for a post requiring patience and an imperturbable disposition, and too politically ambitious to remain stalled in a dark corner of the political arena. He has had to put his ambitions for higher office aside for too long while others, far less qualified in his eyes, have vaulted ahead of him. Now, action at last!

Arrived at the foot of Cortlandt Street, Jerome searches the crowded chaos of the waterfront for the men assigned to wait for him there. Frigid weather has left huge chunks of floating ice to compete with the tumultuous waterborne traffic of tugboats, sloops, railroad ferries, and steamers pushing their way to the piers. Today is warmer, with a slight drizzle, and the gulls are adding their shrieks to the cacophony of the bustling harbor, where rumbling vans and carts are the bass notes underlying a dissonant chorus of longshoremen's shouts, bellowing foghorns, and piercing blasts from the tugs and ferries.

He finds the eight men and they head for their destination in two carriages. Meanwhile, Jerome's ally, District Attorney Eugene Philbin, after first stopping at the Dey Street corner to make sure the carriages are not far behind, enters the Church Street police station, throws his ID card on the desk, and orders a platoon of policemen at once. The men in blue, swiftly assembled, are moving en masse toward 20 Dey Street when the two carriages pull up at the saloon and the raiding party enters.

"Gentlemen, what will you have?" the barkeeper asks.

"I think we'll have that door first," replies Jerome.

Ignoring the barkeeper's protests, Jerome and his men rush for a door behind the bar and are climbing a stairway just as the platoon led by Captain Westervelt arrives, filling the street and the room with policemen and sowing panic.

Confronted by a closed door at the top of the stairs, Jerome shouts, "Open in the name of the law!"

There is a storm of protest from the men on the other side, along with threats of reprisals from powerful political connections. Scurrying sounds are followed by stillness. Then the door flies open, revealing an empty room, another stairway, and another door at the top. Rushing to reach the door, the raiding party hears a loud slam and sounds of heavy locks sliding into place.

"Get a sledgehammer!" someone shouts, and after a half dozen good blows the door opens in time for the men to witness a wild scramble for trapdoors in the roof. But there is no escape. Sergeants Clark and McCafferty have scaled the building and are waiting for them.

When the men realize they are trapped and the commotion dies down, Jerome takes a tour of the rooms. In a lounge he is surprised to find eight members of the police force in mufti, who stoutly maintain they are working "under cover." They have been placed there for the past thirty-five days, they inform him, to collect evidence of gambling—of which they have found not a trace.

The hundred or so gamblers rounded up in another room are also in for a surprise. Justice Jerome, whose personal participation in a gambling raid is unprecedented for a magistrate, is about to defy convention even more radically. Declaring the room a courtroom and himself a presiding judge, he takes a position behind a poker table while each of the men is served a blank subpoena stating, "In the name of the people of the State of New York—To John Doe, the name John Doe being fictitious, but the person served herewith, whose name is unknown, is the party intended . . ."

As the documents are being distributed to the dejected captives, a well-dressed and distinguished-looking man detaches himself from the others and approaches the judge to claim the privileges of his station, relying on Jerome's honor as a fellow clubman and a member of his own caste to "do the right thing."

"Mr. Jerome," he whispers discreetly, "I can't afford to be caught here. You must help me get out."

But he has misjudged his man.

"Court's in session," snaps Jerome. "You can take your choice and take it quickly: go to jail for contempt of court, or hold up your hand and be sworn."

Faced with the choice of using his real name or spending the night in the House of Detention, the unwilling prisoner, whom Jerome and the others have immediately recognized, gives his name: he is Maurice Holahan, president of the Board of Public Works. Afterward, when Holahan protests to the press that he was at the gambling house not to gamble but in search of his "wayward son," a snide reporter comments that Holahan's excuse is causing "the town to shake with irreverent laughter." (Worse, the alibi so angers his son that he will take his revenge by spilling family secrets, alleging that Holahan has had crooked dealings with contractors doing business with his department.)

The other prisoner witnesses, offered the opportunity to leave the Dey Street Court and be spared identification in the press in exchange for a promise to give testimony to the court in private, take the deal. It is late when the proceedings end, but the alleged proprietors of the Parade Turf Club have been arraigned and there is the promise of testimony from reputable men, confirming—contrary to the ludicrous denials of the "undercover" cops—that they have been playing the horses and otherwise indulging their taste for illegal betting at the Parade Turf Club for years. Jerome is pleased with the day's work. He has a useful list of illicit gamblers for his files and he has their grudging pledge to testify.

In the heyday of yellow journalism, in a city of "voracious newspaper readers," the high drama of the Dey Street raid is not lost on reporters always on the lookout for a sensational story, a new hero, or a scandal to tie to the filthy rich and serve up "piping hot." For readers bored with the daily dispatches from a distant war in the Philippines and baffled by the incomprehensible machinations of titans like J. P. Morgan as they move to take control of the nation's industries, the many-columned accounts of Jerome's derring-do are a welcome diversion.

Another boon for the press in the weeks following the Dey Street drama is the long-running, highly entertaining duel it sets off between the swashbuckling anti-corruption crusader—"the judge with the ax"—and "Big Bill" Devery, the Tammany machine's buffoonish bagman, illicit gambling's protector and beneficiary. At under six feet, with a fifty-inch waist and a size 17 shoe, Devery has the silly pomposity of a character in a comic opera. Before finding his niche as a Tammany stooge, he had been a bartender and a boxer. In 1897, having risen to the position of police captain, he had been convicted of extortion, then had rejoiced as his conviction was overturned—a victory generally credited to police solidarity, his enormous popularity, and a certain animal cunning beneath the buffoonery. Reinstated to the force and appointed chief of police in 1898, he had resumed his deplorable behavior as reformers watched in helpless rage. Occasionally absenting himself from police headquarters for days at a time on legendary boozing binges, he was likely to be recognized, drunk and full of high spirits, touring the city in a hack, tossing handfuls of silver coins to crowds on the sidewalk and watching the scramble to retrieve them.

Never one to settle for the straightforward locution, Devery is a fount of hilariously highfalutin pronouncements and cheerful endorsements of graft—all highly prized by reporters. Among a slew of widely quoted Devery-isms is his rant deriding Jerome and his men as "little tin soldiers runnin' around this town with pop-guns on their shoulders, shootin' them off in the streets and degradin' the community. It's an outrage. Jerome ain't goin' to run this town if I have anythin' to do with it." Another favorite is the warning the Chief was overheard delivering to his men, should they ever be "caught with the goods."

"Say nothin'," he told them—sage advice that inspired a popular ditty in the Devery vernacular:

> *Hear, see and say nothin';*
> *Eat, drink and pay nothin'.*

For the young journalist Lincoln Steffens, just launching the career that will bring him fame as a muckraker, Devery is a gift. "As Chief of Police, he is a disgrace," Steffens acknowledges, "but as a character he is a work of art."

For his part, Jerome has rarely missed a chance to charge Devery not only with heading a corrupt police force but also with overseeing Tammany's vast graft operation in the vice districts, deploying his men-in-blue to collect protection money from illicit gaming rooms and from the madams, pimps, and procurers—the full panoply of parasites feeding off the thousands of prostitutes working the streets and brothels. Day after day, the Jerome-Devery duel has played out in the press as a quasi-comic melodrama pitting good versus evil—"Saint George of Manhattan," who has made it his mission to slay Tammany's pet dragon before moving on to his boss, the machine's grand pasha, Richard ("Boss") Croker.

Vice, like almost everything else in the city, has been allowed to operate only with Croker's permission and under Tammany's costly protection. Croker's kingly powers have been such that no city contract, no nomination—from alderman to mayor—has been allowed to go forward without tribute. No bridge, street, or sewer can be repaired, no brick laid or streetlamp replaced. The son of Irish immigrants who settled in a shantytown that later became part of Central Park, Croker rose to power with street smarts, iron discipline, and a certain perverse but sincere belief in his mission. "Graft at the top," he once explained, "helped the few," while "graft at the bottom helped everybody."

Under Croker's leadership, Tammany's Democratic machine provides food, shelter, jobs, coal in winter and turkeys at Thanksgiving for the immigrant poor in exchange for votes and kickbacks—a winning strategy in a city that offers no public services. Graft collected from the city's vice dens is just one source of the profits that sustain Croker's vast empire of illicit operations, but it is the most visible. In Jerome's plan, netting smallfry in his raids is merely a first step as he works his way up from the machine's small-time but hugely profitable ventures in gambling to finally bring down the whole Tammany operation and expose its highly placed corporate sponsors. For the moment, though, there is satisfaction in knowing that the raids are giving Croker and his cohorts the cold sweats.

Night after night, Jerome has continued to storm his targets, risking his life alongside his men, always trailed by reporters and photographers, whose reward for their high-risk participation has been a steady stream of sensational copy. Robert Dunn, then a reporter for the *Commercial Advertiser*, later recalled that he seldom came so close to death as when he accompanied Jerome on his raiding parties. On one occasion, during a raid on a joint disguised behind the silken drapes of a milliner's shop, lookouts took several "potshots" at Jerome, narrowly missing him and the young Mr. Dunn. Customary procedure was to "rush the joint," which usually involved hacking down doors and engaging in a free fight that sometimes climaxed with gunfire. Then, in minutes, it would all be over. A truck would arrive at the door to load on the roulette wheels and other paraphernalia as "the pistol smoke cleared from the rear fire escape."

To Croker's frustration, Jerome's celebrity has increased with each report of another hair-raising raid. Passionate reformists rejoice in his give-'em-hell attitude, his willingness to push the limits of his judicial authority, abandon accepted protocol, and offend the powerful. For the oppressed in the tenements, resentful of the rich while they live in wretched conditions under Tammany rule, he is a hero, hailed for his fearless attacks on the status quo and praised for finally trying to hold the elites to account. Less enthusiastic are many of Jerome's social peers, especially those in William Whitney's circle of uptown clubmen and captains of industry who are not apt to dwell on the plight of the poor or the evils of gambling. Content with—and deeply invested in—the status quo, they view Jerome and his inconvenient crusade with alarm. Jerome, whose scorn for the "hard-hearted" privileged is well known, remains unconcerned. If they are grumbling over their whiskeys in the cushioned luxury of the Metropolitan Club, disparaging his "reckless methods" and unreliability as a defender of their interests, so much the better.

That he may be alienating some among them who actually share his goals for the city and could be helpful in achieving them does not concern him. Only much later will he come to understand that Tammany's enmity poses less of a threat to him and his crusade than the distrust of the rich and powerful of his own class.

2

PASSION SPARKED

My first experience of Mr. White was that he was very unprepossessing,
very kindly, and that he was safe.
—Evelyn Nesbit

On a sweltering day in August Stanford White is expecting guests at his 24th Street hideaway. Headed his way in a hansom cab are two young dancers from *Florodora*, a bit of musical froth that is having a spectacularly successful run at the Casino Theatre on Broadway. Edna Goodrich, the older of the two, "a big girl, plump and voluptuous," is a showgirl with whom the 47-year-old White has had a long acquaintance. Her companion, and the real reason for the little lunch party to which White has also invited his friend Reginald Ronalds, is Evelyn Nesbit, the beauty who will become the greatest passion of his life.

Slim, dark-haired, and just sixteen, Evelyn has been dancing with the famous "*Florodora* Girls" for barely a month, but she is already getting noticed. After arriving in New York from Pittsburgh to join her mother, who had come earlier to look for work, she had easily found work herself as an artist's model and achieved almost instant celebrity for her exotic beauty. Modeling led to work on the stage, and she has been cast as a "Charming Spanish Maiden" in the *Florodora* chorus line. Though minimally talented, her striking stage presence has brought more fame, along with a boost in her income that has enabled her to support her widowed mother and younger brother, Howard.

Night after night, seats at the Casino Theatre are filled with lustful young men and millionaire connoisseurs of feminine beauty who keep reserved seats in the theater they refer to as "the temple of pulchritude." They have come to see for themselves this girl whose lovely face, suggestive of both sensuality and virginal innocence, has appeared countless times in newspapers and magazines.

Like them, White, an avid theatergoer whenever his workload as the city's busiest architect and the rituals of his social position allow, has seen the photos and read the paeans to her seductive allure. One magazine devoted to theater news has described her as "a slight, almost fragile girl, with a magnificent head of hair, fresh eyes, and a smile that is girlish winsomeness itself"—a characterization that comes uncannily close to White's own ideal of feminine beauty. Youth, slenderness, innocence, and vulnerability never fail to charm White, whose preference has always been for young beauties like Evelyn, poised between girlhood and womanhood and seemingly in need of his guidance and protection. He has seen several performances of *Florodora*, and now, finally, having recruited Edna Goodrich as his intermediary, he is about to entertain Evelyn in a setting he has arranged just for her pleasure. Practiced and patient in the art of seduction, he has planned carefully, and although no one who knows him doubts that the pleasure he takes in helping the young women he fancies is genuine, or believes that his generosity in entertaining them and showering them with gifts is no more than a ruse, neither are even his greatest admirers apt to believe that his motives are pure.

As the cab bumps along on its way downtown, Evelyn is euphoric, keyed up, and fidgety at the prospect of expanding her horizons beyond the bleak boardinghouses of her impoverished past, the chilly artists' studios, the bare-bones rehearsal rooms, and the narrow world of middle-class propriety that her mother aspires to. Financially and socially insecure, Mrs. Nesbit is obsessive about maintaining appearances but weak whenever abandoning her scruples promises to ease the family's finances. It has taken days to persuade her that Evelyn's invitation is indeed to a "society luncheon party" and that the society involved is "the real thing," not the kind likely to arouse the suspicions of Anthony Comstock and his Society for the Suppression of Vice.

Mrs. Nesbit's fears are not unfounded. Comstock, the city's self-appointed anti-vice lord, whose obsession with sex is both priggish and prurient, has lately been focusing his zealous crusade for moral purity on the theater district, denouncing it as an "open sore" spreading filth in the streets. His legions of snoops have been prowling the district to find and "save" stagestruck, underage girls whose dreams of glamor and riches, Comstock predicts, will inevitably break their hearts and send them "brothel-bound." Loathed by civil libertarians and lauded by church-backed groups, Comstock had formed his anti-vice society in 1873 and was later made a special agent of the United States Postal Service, giving him police powers for enforcing public morals, including the right to carry a weapon. He sees himself as the supreme protector of innocent girls and young women, but his approach to "saving" them from the streets or the stage is as ineffective as it is terrifying. And while he is scathing in his attacks against those who would lead them astray, he also rails daily against the "New Woman" and her efforts to save herself by breaking the bonds imposed by a male-dominated society that would have her remain perpetually girlish, pure, and compliant. In his zeal, Comstock has one of them arrested for smoking a cigarette on Fifth Avenue.

When finally Mrs. Nesbit does acquiesce to Evelyn's luncheon plans, she insists that her daughter dress like a schoolgirl, conveniently disregarding Evelyn's nightly Broadway performances before an audience of ogling men. Evelyn, exasperated, is obliged to comply, permitting her mother to cling to the notion that no harm could possibly come to a fresh-faced girl in a dress with a skirt cut short at the knee and a huge white sailor's collar.

Evelyn's friend Edna, jostling alongside her in the cab, is, by contrast, the image of fashionable sophistication, outfitted in a floor-length lavender dress, her hair upswept in a stylish pompadour.

"Sweet costume," she remarks, eyeing her companion's childish outfit, but Evelyn, who has seen her praises sung in the press and recognized the desire in the eyes of her fans, is not, after all, unaware of her beauty and the power it exerts over men. More vexing than Edna's condescension is her refusal to reveal where they are headed. Evelyn imagines that she may finally be about to set foot in the Waldorf or another of the posh hotels she has been aching to see, but her hopes are dashed when the cab draws up to a shabby building on West 24th Street off Broadway and stops in front of "a dingy little door."

Dismay turns to delight when the door, through some electrical magic, opens automatically at their approach, admitting the girls, who climb a flight of stairs to the landing, where White is waiting for them. Once inside White's hidden sanctuary, they find themselves in an intimate version of the splendid salons he has fashioned for the Fifth Avenue mansions and country estates of his wealthy clients. Evelyn will remember the room as "the most gorgeous" she has ever seen, exquisitely oriental with its sumptuous divans piled with "great billowing cushions." There are "tiny little tables" artfully placed in a decor conceived entirely in red. Crimson curtains shut out the daylight, and indirect lighting—a cutting-edge innovation—casts a warm, rosy glow. Among the tapestries and paintings, a luminous nude catches Evelyn's eye.

White, who has lavished his prodigious talent on every detail of the room, has achieved the environment of sensuous intimacy he had in mind. There are no window views to distract the girls from their gorgeous surroundings, no opportunities for the curious to peer inside. As a married man, White needs to keep his serial philandering from public view, though in entertaining young women he is doing just what many of his wealthy contemporaries are doing with the tacit agreement of an indulgent upper-crust culture. But if the peccadillos of the privileged merit little more than a wink and a nod among friends, enemies with access to the press are another matter. Like other errant husbands, White's first line of defense against exposure has been to secure a place on the list of "immunes" kept by the flamboyant publisher of the popular scandal sheet *Town Topics*, Colonel William D'Alton Mann. Mann, a Civil War hero and cheerful blackmailer, has acquired enormous power over society with his dossiers on its scandal-prone members. Like other paid-up "immunes" on the Colonel's list, White can expect his dalliances to escape the notice of Mann's army of spies deployed to beat the bushes for scandal wherever the wealthy can be expected to get into trouble.

White has also put Abraham ("Little Abe") Hummel, New York's most unscrupulous attorney, on retainer. A favorite with the criminal underworld, the dwarfish but dapper Hummel (drawn by one caricaturist as Humpty Dumpty) is also a genius at saving the skins of swells caught in compromising positions, at an exorbitant price. Hummel's specialty is breach-of-promise blackmail. In exchange for a ritual burning of the love letters of besotted family men who have made foolish promises after a night of delirious love-making, a fat "legal fee" is extracted from the "client" to be shared with the heartbroken maiden who has provided the letters. More serious from the point of view of reformers, who have him in their sights, are Little Abe's dealings with the underworld, which are widely suspected of going beyond the defense of its crimes to participating in their commission.

Despite his meticulous planning, White's imposing size and galvanic personality do not work in his favor at first. Evelyn will recall that her first impression was that White was "not a bit handsome." To put her at ease, White has invited his friend Reginald Ronalds to make a party of four. White adopts a fatherly manner, indulging Evelyn with her first taste of champagne but limiting her to only one glass. He is rewarded when she begins to enjoy herself, pleased and flattered by the frank admiration of the two men—even more intoxicating than the wine. Appealing to the child that Evelyn has not quite outgrown, White surprises her with his playful exuberance, his powerful laugh delivered as he throws his head back and lets loose. He does nothing to disguise his infatuation.

After lunch and the departure of Reginald Ronalds, White takes the girls upstairs to yet another fantasy room, where Evelyn's wonder at the extraordinary red velvet swing suspended from the high ceiling is just what he had hoped for. He urges her to climb on, and as she grips the red ropes entwined with smilax, he pushes her higher and higher until her foot pierces a giant Japanese paper parasol hung from the ceiling and they both laugh so hard she complains that her sides ache.

A second lunch at the 24th Street hideaway leaves Evelyn with an even more favorable impression of White, who treats her in "a very fatherly manner." After that he bombards her daily with gifts and flowers and has cabs waiting at the theater to bring her to his Madison Square Garden Tower studio whenever he hosts one of his fabled parties that mix artists and social-ites. On another front, he launches a charm offensive to win over Evelyn's mother. He invites her to meet him at the impressive McKim, Mead & White offices, where, surrounded by reminders of his professional success and social status, he makes his case. Presenting himself as Evelyn's well-to-do and trust-worthy patron, he offers to pay for whatever she needs. With money per-petually in short supply, the promise of a rich and kindly benefactor is too tempting and Mrs. Nesbit gives her consent, little realizing how consequential a decision it is.

When in late September Mrs. Nesbit lets it be known that she yearns to return to Pittsburgh for a few days, White urges her to go and assures her that he will look after Evelyn while she is away. A few days after her mother's departure, he gives Evelyn the tour of the offices of McKim, Mead & White. Stopping to introduce her to his partner Charles McKim, he explains, "This little girl's mother has gone to Pittsburgh and left her in my care."

"My God!" is McKim's stunned response.

That night, White sends a Union Club cab to fetch Evelyn at the theater and bring her to 24th Street. Arriving to find no party, she can't hide her disappointment, but White soon has her laughing as he tells tales about some of his more outlandish clients. In return, she gives him the latest backstage gossip. As they talk, he is pleased to see her yielding to the effects of the cham-pagne, to his gallantry, and to the beauty of her surroundings—"the cozy room with its shaded lights, its thick carpet, its divans, its rare objects of art."

After supper, as she is preparing to leave, White coaxes her to stay, prom-ising to show her rooms she has never seen. He leads her up a tiny hidden staircase to a small room, its walls and ceiling sheathed in mirrors. Indirect lighting casts a soft glow, and the mirrors create multiple reflections, which have a disorienting effect. White leaves her seated on an immense couch covered in moss green velvet and returns a few minutes later with a beautiful yellow satin Japanese kimono for her to try on. He sits down beside her and fills her glass from a small bottle of champagne before leading her back to yet another room she has not seen before—a tiny rear bedroom dominated by a large four-poster bed with a mirrored canopy. Miniature electric bulbs are tucked around the interior of the canopy and a cozy log fire flickers in the fireplace.

Buttons that control the lighting over the bed produce different colors, and White encourages Evelyn to play with them. An amber glow in the mirrored canopy bathes her in gold. Another button produces a soft rose effect and another a soft blue. Later she will recall finishing her champagne at White's urging though it was making her groggy. Evelyn's account of the evening's events will vary depending on the time and the occasion, but her story of being overcome by drugged champagne proves persuasive. In it, she remembers nothing after she blacks out until she wakes and screams with horror to find herself undressed, lying next to a naked White, with telltale signs of blood on the sheets. In her recollection, White, jolted from sleep by her screams, attempts to soothe her, "petting and kissing" but trembling himself. In the light of day, his carefully orchestrated seduction looks like what it is—the rape of a sixteen-year-old girl, whose shock and revulsion are unmistakable. White, the seasoned seducer, is clearly shaken. His conquest this time, barely past childhood, is unacceptably young in the eyes of the law and in civilized society—it goes beyond even what his circle of loose-living elites would be willing to tolerate. And because Evelyn, so obviously horrified, is also the object of his undiminished infatuation, he trembles at the thought that he has not only just put his reputation at risk but he has also risked losing her. As they dress, he cautions her to tell no one, not even her mother, and then takes her home. When White arrives the next afternoon to check in on Evelyn, he finds her in a trancelike state, sitting in a chair, where she has spent a sleepless night absorbing the shock of her sexual trauma. He tries to soothe her, kneeling at her side and kissing the edge of her dress. He praises her beauty, and resuming his role as guide to a world that he insists has much to offer a girl like her, he assures her that everybody does "these things." She is so pretty, so slim, he pleads, he can't help himself. He tells her that he can do many things for her if she will only keep the truth from her mother and let him help her and her family. His fervor is flattering, his promises tempting, and gradually his pleas to his "Kittens" have the desired effect. What he says may not be right, nor even the truth, but his worldliness, his wealth, and position overwhelm her capacity to resist.

At sixteen, though still impressionable, Evelyn has a long history of dealing with loss—of her father, of her home, and of all the treasures of her childhood. She was just eleven years old when her father's sudden death had left the family penniless and Evelyn bereft of the parent who had been closest to her, the father who had recognized her lively intelligence, had picked out books for her personal library and promised to send her to Vassar. Winfield Nesbit had been her "sun and moon," she later recalled, and she "his little shooting star." Without him, the family had struggled to survive, eating one meal a day as often as not and relying on charity. One after another her mother's attempts to provide for her children had failed, and it had fallen on Evelyn to be the strong one, to put away dreams of Vassar and harden her resolve to do whatever was necessary to overcome her panicky fears of poverty and abandonment and keep the family afloat.

Now, having lost the last vestige of her childhood innocence, she has survival skills to fall back on. She opts to accept White's worldview, his generosity to her and her needy family, and a role as his lover in a city whose elite worships at the altar of McKim, Mead & White. When she agrees to see him again, it is the start of an affair whose intensity and duration will astonish White's fellow philanderers and dishearten his rivals for Evelyn—the second-tier swells and stage-door-johnnies who can never hope to compete with the celebrated and charismatic Stanford White.

One exception is a tall, bug-eyed fan whose almost nightly presence at the Casino Theatre has caused little notice. A relative newcomer to the city, his arrival in early 1901 had been heralded by a brief notice in *Town Topics*.

Writing in his column coyly signed "The Saunterer," Colonel Mann had noted that Mr. Harry K. Thaw of Pittsburgh, very rich and very showy, has been "knocking at society's portals," has "procured a card for Mrs. Astor's ball," and "has arrived." With the confidence of a man whose vast fortune has always bought him whatever he craves, Harry K. Thaw is hatching a plan to acquire the "Charming Spanish Maiden" for himself.

3

A DIFFICULT LAUNCH

It is heaven's truth when I tell you that I didn't smile for six months.
—WILLIAM TRAVERS JEROME

By the summer of 1901, at the age of forty-two, William Travers Jerome, having overcome more obstacles than a man of his class might normally confront, believes his time on the political fringes is about to end. His daring raids have earned him a reputation as a swashbuckling crusader against vice, crime, and corrupt politicians, and his political future looks bright.

In an interview published a few years later in the *Chicago Tribune*, Jerome spoke candidly to writer James Morrow of the difficulties he had faced to get to that moment, beginning with his early youth, when poor health and a dysfunctional family had made his childhood a misery.

"I had one attack after another of membranous croup," Jerome told Morrow. "My winters were seasons of terror and suffering. I lost much time from school, and tutors had to come to the house. Besides, my eyes were astigmatic and I was twenty-seven years old before I knew it."

The implication was clear: someone at home should have recognized the problem and done something about it, but his mismatched parents had other priorities. Catherine, his overprotective and moralizing mother, was intent on keeping her Travers, as he was called in the family, in her suffocating embrace.

His father, Lawrence Jerome, always more interested in fast horses, beautiful women, and swift yachts than in his four sons, was content to abandon Travers's upbringing to his wife's iron solicitude.

The Jerome brothers—his father, Lawrence, and uncle Leonard—were then among the most popular men on Wall Street, high livers who spent their time winning and losing fortunes, forging opportunistic alliances with Tammany, chasing women and hobnobbing with the very gamblers and pols that Travers would one day set out to destroy. They had married sisters, but while Leonard chose the lively and complaisant Clara (and fathered Jennie, who married Lord Randolph Churchill and gave Travers his famous cousin Winston), Lawrence had inexplicably yoked himself to the straitlaced, puritanical Catherine. Her ridiculous yearning for respectability, her shock at any hint of bawdiness or irreverence had exasperated her children, who referred to her as "the Plague." She kept a joyless home and, like his three older brothers, Lovell, Roswell, and Lawrence, Travers could not wait to escape. Lovell, born ten years before him, left for West Point and had a successful military career, but the middle sons, Roswell and Lawrence, so disgraced themselves that Travers began to suspect some hereditary family flaw—a propensity for reckless high living and moral laxity—and he would never stop worrying about his own vulnerability. Roswell, who studied law, drank himself to death at the age of twenty-three, while Lawrence, always wild and ungovernable, ran off with the family cook, never to be seen by anyone in the family again. Disinherited "on account of his unfilial conduct," he lost the only reason he might have returned. Little wonder that Travers, despite a temperament more akin to his father's broad-mindedness than his mother's narrow-minded rectitude, was appalled by such destructive self-indulgence and determined to defend himself against it.

Throughout his boyhood, Jerome told Morrow, he had chafed at his mother's oppressive coddling, which his poor health had only encouraged. She had forbidden all vigorous activity, judging him too frail, and kept him home from school at the slightest pretext. Isolated and unhappy, he had suffered knowing that his peers were leaving him behind. Catherine, fearing the influence of her loose-living husband on Travers—not to mention the example of her other two wayward sons—had been relentless in her efforts to mold him according to her own strict code of behavior, upheld by the twin pillars of propriety and decorum. Her distaste for her husband's libertine friends—racecourse habitués, yachtsmen and womanizers who found manly fellowship in the Union Club—had been no secret in the family. As a woman of puritan ideals, she had thoroughly disapproved of her husband's way of life and had once famously observed, "The Jeromes seem to have so much sense of honor and hardly any sense of sin."

Most upsetting to Catherine was her husband's association with the wild young publisher of the *New York Herald*, James Gordon Bennett, who, though much younger, had attached himself to the jolly circle surrounding Larry and Lenny. Charmed by their high spirits and dash, Bennett, who disdained the grim greediness of titans like his archenemy, the abominable Jay Gould, had been especially taken with the brothers' free-spending ways.

Jerome recalled that the admiration had been mutual, remembering that his father had delighted in his friendship with Bennett, whose occasional visits to the Jerome household had provided some rare relief from the pall cast by Catherine. Even when Bennett's riotous personal life had necessitated his exile to Paris, he had frequently turned up back in New York for business, always managing to fit in some hedonistic carousing with Larry. This had so infuriated Catherine at one point that she had banned Bennett from the Jerome house, a blow to her children but no problem for Bennett, who had invented ingenious ways to circumvent it. On one notable occasion he had summoned Larry by telegram to a hospital where he claimed he was breathing his last. The "hospital" had turned out to be a brothel, and when the "patient" threw off his bandages and the "nurses" revealed what was under their uniforms, the fun had begun.

Jerome confided to Morrow that when he finally left home to enroll at Amherst at the age of nineteen—older than most of his classmates—he had felt enormous pressure to make up for lost time. He had signed up for a heavy schedule of studies, and when he'd been asked to take over as assistant instructor in chemistry in his second year, he had assumed the extra burden. Determined not to take the same reckless path as his brothers, he was all work and no play, which was just as well, since play of the undergraduate partying variety was beyond his budget. By this time, his father's luck on the Street had run out and the family's high-flying days were over. Born too late to benefit from those days, Jerome harbored some resentment at missing out on the privileges his older brothers had so spectacularly squandered.

By his junior year, the ruinous pace he had been keeping in his studies—made even more difficult by his still uncorrected blurred vision—caught up with him and he had collapsed under the strain.

"What other fellows could do at college without much effort wore me down and tore my nerves," he said, arriving at a crucial moment in the account of his early years. With his health completely broken, he had to leave Amherst and the expectation had been that he would return home to his mother's care. Instead he had made a decision with enormous consequences for the rest of his life. Rather than return home, he had surprised everyone with his decision to work as a laborer on an upstate farm. There, free of the psychic burden of Catherine's overbearing presence, he had subjected himself to a regime so effective in developing his physical and mental toughness that he could boast to Morrow of being almost immune to illness ever since, though "I eat too much, I suppose, and take as little sleep as possible."

He spoke candidly with Morrow about his resentment against his mother for imposing her pinched moral code when he was her captive, but he had not been able to entirely discount her influence on his own uncompromising standards for civic probity. The strength of his convictions and the swiftness of his political judgments as his career had progressed inevitably drew some critical fire and even upset some of his staunchest supporters. Arthur Train, his youthful friend and colleague (later a successful author of legal thrillers) once admitted to being horrified by Jerome's unprovoked attacks on potential allies, which seemed to Train "to court political extermination." Another young novelist, reformist, and close observer of the political scene, Alfred Hodder, was more forgiving when he wrote that in Jerome, "there burns beneath a cavalier exterior the wrath of a Hebrew prophet." The cavalier exterior, a repudiation of his mother's preoccupation with propriety, was, as Catherine had feared, his father's legacy. But, as Jerome would not deny, he had also found much to emulate in his father's example, including a lifelong aversion to puritanism, an irreverent wit, and a gift for enjoying life, often with friends who shared a taste for tobacco and alcohol.

As a descendant of a long line of puritans on one side and playboys on the other, Jerome had been prepared, after taking control of his health and his future, to draw from both. Fiercely ambitious, physically fit, and finally free, he had enrolled in Columbia Law School and been admitted to the bar in 1884.

"Then," said Jerome, looking back on the obstacles he had faced at the start of his legal career, "I became a clerk in the office of Stanley, Clark and Smith, lawyers with a large practice, but my family had gone to smash in Wall Street and when that happens everything goes, so I had no means of getting clients for the firm I was with."

Seeing no future at the firm, Jerome had hung out his shingle.

"Those were dreary and desolate years—four of them. I lived at home. I couldn't have lived elsewhere and paid a dollar a week for my board. But I put in my time."

He had studied the Harvard law course "alone and to the end," read all the law he could find, and searched out its history. But "life dragged," he told Morrow. He was "madly in love," engaged to be married, but too poor to support a wife and "most miserable."

In 1888, his father, showing more sympathy for his grown son's misery than he had displayed for the sickly child, stepped in to help. Lawrence, "The Prince of Metropolitan Wags," the man who was everyone's friend, had called in a favor from Tammany Chieftain Richard Croker, who had once implored Lawrence to intercede with his friend James Gordon Bennett on his behalf. Bennett's *Herald*, ever allied with the interests of the society rich, had been hurling insults at the declassé Croker, a barrage that was causing Mrs. Croker much mental anguish.

True to his reputation for finding the good in almost everyone, Lawrence Jerome, "the man without an enemy," had found something to like in the thuggish Tammany chieftain, his polar opposite.

"My father was interested in the frank and manly character of the man and after hearing his story, agreed to see Mr. Bennett. The *Herald* stopped its attacks." Calm was restored to the Boss's household, and a grateful Croker was ready to look kindly on a request from Larry to find a place for his son in the district attorney's office.

"I have arranged it" came Croker's swift reply.

So in 1888 Jerome had taken up his duties as an assistant district attorney, a brilliant anomaly among the dull, mostly indolent and corrupt hangers-on and family members on Tammany's payroll.

"It was a hard place for a young fellow," Jerome recalled, "the jaws of hell" in the best of times and at its worst then, when "matters were awful." Thrust among men charged with prosecuting crimes that were being committed by people under the protection of their Tammany bosses (to whom they kicked back 10 percent of their salaries), he could only wonder at the static, smoke-filled atmosphere of an office that should have been a hive of activity. Arthur Train would later describe the district attorney's office Jerome entered as "somewhat resembling a home for aged, infirm and jobless men," who looked, in their tall silk hats, frock coats, and high stiff collars, "as though rigor mortis was setting in."

A chance to practice his legal skills and to get a close look at the way Tammany operated had been enough at first to compensate for the hellish environment and his discomfort in knowing that, though honest himself, he had made a deal with the Devil in acquiescing to the corruption of the office that was meant to fight lawlessness.

"I toiled like a galley slave preparing briefs and getting not only the facts but the law. My work impressed the assistants and by-and-by one of them said, 'That fellow can try cases.'"

He was sent into the courtroom, and of his thirty-six months on the job, twenty-eight were spent dutifully arguing cases, suppressing his outrage and keeping his own counsel. With his salary of $3,000 a year he had enough to get married at last, though not to the socially prominent young woman who had broken their engagement when her patience ran out. To the pain of a lost love was added the sense that time pressed, that his contemporaries were getting on with it, not just in their careers but in their domestic lives.

Acting "on the rebound," as his friends had viewed his baffling courtship of Lavinia Taylor Howe, he had seemed to them bizarrely intent on following the same path his father had taken in marrying a woman with whom he had nothing in common and who lacked any capacity to enjoy life. Tight-lipped on the subject of his marriage, Jerome offered his interviewer no explanation of his decision to marry the dowdy Lavinia, who had never shown any interest in politics, cultural life, or anything other than her membership in the Colonial Dames and, eventually, her son. What she had been able to offer was a chance for Jerome to put his heartbreak behind him, to return at the end of his turbulent days to the wifely comfort of a quiet, undemanding presence, and—perhaps most important—to establish the kind of respectable domestic arrangement the public expected of any man with political aspirations. In any case, there had been no time to waste. Almost five years older than Jerome, Lavinia was teetering on the brink of spinsterhood, while at twenty-nine Jerome had lost one chance at marriage and had no wish to wait any longer. On a spring day in 1888, marriage bells had finally rung for Jerome, who, with the birth of his son William Travers Jerome Jr., had a family at last

4

ON TOP OF THE WORLD

I found myself almost as I had been before that night, with interests as keen, with as poignant a sense of humor as ever, though a change had come to me and though my angle of vision had altered..
—Evelyn Nesbit

Though she will later describe her "deflowering" in terms designed to emphasize her defiled innocence, Evelyn nevertheless adjusted to her role as the object of the celebrated architect's obsessive attentions in the ensuing months. She is, as she later acknowledged, falling "head over heels in love with him." White, swamped as always with work, manages nevertheless to see his "Kittens" just about every day, for the rest of the year, though never in public. Quick to deliver on his promise to act as Evelyn's guide and protector, he arranges to move the Nesbits into the Wellington, a fashionable new hotel at Seventh Avenue and 56th Street, and takes charge of the apartment's decoration. The walls of Evelyn's room are covered with white satin, and her canopied bed is crowned with white ostrich plumes. A crimson carpet, a white bearskin, and white swan-shaped planters complete the look. White pays the bills, gives the Nesbits a weekly allowance of $25, and hires a piano teacher for Evelyn, who has a white piano to practice on. White also pays the tuition for her brother Howard at the Chester Military Academy, pays a dentist to correct a slight imperfection in Evelyn's teeth, and provides a constant flow of expensive gifts. A draftsman at McKim, Mead & White later recalled Evelyn's frequent appearances at the firm, "dripping with furs."

Best of all for Evelyn, who has been yearning to break loose from her mother's tight rein and experience the glamor and excitement of the city, are the luncheons and late-evening suppers at White's exquisite studio in the famous Madison Square Garden Tower. Crowned by sculptor Augustus Saint-Gaudens's statue of a lithe, bare-breasted Diana the Huntress, the Tower dominates New York's 19th-century skyline, and Madison Square Garden itself is among White's most celebrated creations, a pleasure palace for the city's most stupendous events. For Evelyn, the intimate eighth-floor retreat where White has assembled some of his smaller treasures is a magical place, furnished with the "gorgeous divans" he favors, along with "exquisitely carved antique chairs." Bear, tiger, and leopard skins are draped over the divans and cover the floors. An aquarium is stocked with Japanese fish, and artificial orange trees bathe the room in a rosy glow cast by cleverly electrified "oranges." Best of all is the spectacular view from the windows that look down on the Roof Garden Theater, with its potted palms and thousands of twinkling lights, and over the rooftop to the great sparkling city beyond.

Invitations to these fabled parties in White's Tower studio, which sometimes last all night, are highly prized by the cream of New York's social, artistic, and theatrical milieus, and White is never less than an exuberant and attentive host. One guest described her enchantment on stepping out of the elevator into a room where a "crescent table was covered with old golden damask and spread with orchids, lights twinkled in surrounding bay trees, a mandolin band shed music like a sprinkling fountain and about the table were women as lovely and varied in type as he ever assembled."

Here Evelyn meets celebrated artists, theater people, the wealthy and powerful, "suns in their chosen spheres or on the way up over the horizon of fame," as one columnist rhapsodized. Among them are Gus Saint-Gaudens, Stanny's old friend whose nude huntress atop the Tower scandalizes Comstockian sensibilities; Jimmie Breese, White's well-heeled fellow carouser and famous man-about-town; author Mark Twain; actress Ethel Barrymore; and, on one consequential occasion, Ethel's gauntly handsome and rakish brother, Jack, who is far more dazzled by Evelyn than by all the suns in their celestial spheres. Sparks will fly between the beauty and the future matinee idol, who will solicit her phone number and wait for his chance.

Politicians, usually too circumspect or too obnoxious to add to the revels, are seldom invited. Nor would most career politicians think it wise to risk cavorting in the company of so many bohemians. Former US vice president Levi P. Morton, extolled by his friends for his "lovable personality," is one exception. He is conservative in all the right ways—the Senate over which he had presided was known as a "millionaires' club," its members unabashed spokesmen for industry. But Morton is out of office now, and as a wealthy and influential banker with a well-connected, very social wife, he moves comfortably in White's orbit, where indifference to politics is the norm.

Not since the 1896 presidential election, when the Great Commoner William Jennings Bryan ran against Republican William McKinley, has White shown much interest in a political contest. At the time, Bryan's populist focus on the inequities of wealth distribution in the United States had briefly given White pause, and he had joined the throngs at Madison Square Garden—albeit in a box at a safe remove from "the awful crowd"—to hear the great orator denounce the "evil money power." In the end, mindful that egalitarianism hardly aligned with the elitism that sustained his extravagance, White had reverted to his nominal Republican allegiance. His election-night party at the Tower was an all-out celebration of McKinley's victory and its promise that his capitalist clientele would continue to build mansions and furnish them with appropriate opulence.

Unlike most of his clients, White was not born into wealth, but his upbringing, culturally rich and socially secure, prepared him well for his role as friend and aesthetic adviser to some of the richest among them—men who found politicians mainly useful to the extent that they protected their financial interests. White's father, Richard Grant White, was a gifted man of letters with a long and proud American lineage and a circle of acquaintances that encompassed many prominent literary figures. A recognized authority on Shakespeare, an accomplished cellist and a composer, he was, nevertheless, a disappointed man who complained constantly that he was ill paid for his labors, and who bewailed America's lack of refinement and a cultivated upper class. His carping earned him few friends and apparently some enemies; at one point in the 1860s word leaked that he had been blackballed at the magnificent Century Association, where he might have found the cultivated clique he considered worthy company. Through its portals passed nearly all the distinguished writers and artists of the day, and he might have been consoled to know that his son would one day design its handsome new clubhouse at 7 West 43rd Street and be one of its most popular members.

From the time of his earliest youth the mischievous little redhead with the precocious artistic talent and winsome ways had inspired hopes in his father that Stanny would have a smoother path through the social minefields and achieve the riches that he could not in his own life. In a letter to his wife written during his travels on the lecture circuit, Richard White had lamented his perpetual penury, remarking bitterly that it seemed his fate was "to get through life by the skin of my teeth."

Though Stanny was closest to his quiet, clever, self-effacing mother, Alexina, who lovingly referred to him in one of her poems as her "wee busy mannie," in many ways—including a sense that he was meant to be rich—he was strongly influenced by his accomplished but deeply flawed father. Richard White's attitude toward women also passed from father to son. "Unusually susceptible to beauty in women," in his biographer's delicate phrase, Richard Grant White was a self-professed admirer of "womanly weakness and trust" and a collector of books of erotica. Growing up, White had surely been aware of his father's philandering and his inability to make a comfortable income— let alone realize his dreams of riches—despite a prolific journalistic output, public lecturing, and, eventually, a steady job as a customs official. He may not have been aware of rumors that his father had a longtime mistress, with children, which, if true, must certainly have been a drain on the family finances.

Perhaps because of related expenses, there had been no money for a university education for Stanny and, in any case, he was set on a career as an artist. He had shown an exceptional talent for drawing and painting from the time he was able to pick up a pencil or brush, and his ambition was to become a painter. In 1870, his father arranged for him to meet with John LaFarge, a family friend, with the idea that the celebrated artist would have some useful advice for his son. But LaFarge, himself perpetually short of money, had instead urged Stanny to forget about painting and try architecture, less subject to fashion and far more remunerative. There were no architectural schools in America and only a few trained architects, but the best among them, H. H. Richardson, the Falstaffian progenitor of the American Romanesque style, had recently opened an office in Boston and might need an apprentice who could draw. LaFarge offered to write a letter of introduction to "the Great Mogul"—a reference to Richardson's girth as well as his prominence—and in 1870, at age seventeen, Stanny headed for Boston.

His supervisor at the firm was chief draftsman Charles Follen McKim, who would become his lifelong friend and professional colleague. A child of Boston's evangelical aristocracy, Charles was the son of the ardent abolitionist James Miller McKim, well known in his day for smuggling runaway slaves to safety. McKim was six years older than White and one of the first Americans to study at the Ecole des Beaux-Arts in Paris. Another lifelong friend, also brought into the Richardson circle by John LaFarge, was sculptor Augustus Saint-Gaudens. Gus and Stanny had first met in New York in a memorable encounter when, climbing the stairway in the German Savings Bank Building, White heard a strong tenor voice bellowing out the Andante of Beethoven's Seventh Symphony. Curious, he investigated and found Saint-Gaudens at work in his studio. The two men immediately hit it off, recognizing in each other the same high spirits, humor, and passion for art, music, and architecture. Saint-Gaudens was recruited in 1876 to take charge of the wall murals of Boston's Trinity Church, Richardson's major project at the time. With only five months before the scheduled consecration of the new church building in February 1877, he, White, and LaFarge worked frantically to complete the interior on time.

McKim, originally in charge of the project, had left to start his own firm in 1872, turning his responsibilities over to White, who spent the next six years traveling around the Northeast attending to the firm's projects. His schedule was hectic, his responsibilities enormous, but he was mastering the fundamentals of his craft and learning how to please members of the nascent American aristocracy of wealth whose demand for private palaces and magnificent public buildings promised prosperity for an architect like himself—talented, experienced, and socially engaged. With the post–Civil War economy expanding dramatically and New York well on its way as the nation's financial capital, the city was awash in money. Newly minted million-aires, eager to shed the pinched esthetic of Old Knickerbocker New York, wanted to live as elegantly as the European blue bloods whose clubs and mansions they had admired in their travels.

In one of his many madcap messages to his mother, White complained that the cold and the heavy demands of the work had him feeling as though he had been "standing on my head all the week." Miraculously, he reassured her, he was still in his "right mind, though how Richardson can be, I can't tell, for setting aside all the brandies, gins, wines and cigars, it seems to me he chiefly subsists on boiled tripe, which he still insists on calling the 'entrails of a cow.' How's that?"

In February 1878, White informed Richardson that he planned to leave his position for an extended visit to Europe, something he had long wanted to do. To Saint-Gaudens, who had relocated to Paris in 1877 with his new bride, he wrote that he had booked passage to Europe and that McKim was coming along. Gus, missing "the adventurous swing of life" he had enjoyed as a student, was persuaded to join them, and "the three redheads" set off in high spirits to behold the glories of Old World architecture and taste the pleasures of European nightlife.

For White it was a formative trip, so crammed with wonders, as he wrote his "Dear Mama," that "your whole thought is how you can hop around and see what there is to see compress what should be a week's work into two or three days pack our bag and catch the midday train…" It was not just the architecture and the old towns that were enough "to set you wild," there were paintings beautiful enough to "make the nails grow out of the end of your fingers with pleasure." In the huge amphitheater at Nimes—"the most perfect in the world after Verona"—the trio took top-row seats and imagined themselves ancient Romans. Then, as White reported in a letter home, while McKim and Saint-Gaudens watched with astonishment, "I went down and rushed madly into the arena, struck an attitude, and commenced declaiming. They heard me perfectly. I stabbed five or six gladiators and rushed out with the guardian in hot pursuit."

The weeks were a whirlwind of hyperactivity and shared hilarity, at the end of which White was happy to settle in for a stay in Paris with Saint-Gaudens and his wife, Augusta.

"I hug St. Gaudens like a bear every time I see him," he wrote his mother, "and would his wife, if she was pretty—but she ain't—so I don't."

Paris was, however, teeming with "pooty girls" and brimming with other delights. "Not in this world," he wrote, "is it possible to find another place where your wants, intellectual and physical, are so catered to; nor another place, such being the case, where you accomplish so little." He did manage to spend some time in Gus's "ballroom studio" on the West Bank working with the sculptor on the monument to Union Admiral David ("Damn the Torpedoes") Farragut that Saint-Gaudens had been chosen to create for Madison Square in New York. Hearing of the commission, White had written to Gus from New York asking if he might help with the pedestal, adding, "Then I should go down to Fame, even if it is bad, reviled for making a poor base for a good statue."

Shortly before he boarded the *Olympus* to return to New York in 1879, White received a proposal from Charles McKim and William Rutherford Mead to join their firm. White's "great talent" as a young man working for Richardson had impressed Mead, a Vermonter, who later recalled that "in these years, he was our close neighbor and became our very intimate friend." Seven years older than White, Mead had perfected his craft studying in Florence before signing on with McKim as an assistant in 1872. In 1877 he had joined McKim & White on a sketching expedition to New England—an important source of Colonial Revival ideas.

It was the defection of a third member of that expedition, William Blake Bigelow, an early partner of McKim and Mead, that created the opening for

White. A complication had arisen in the partnership, then named McKim, Mead and Bigelow, when Bigelow's sister, Annie, whom McKim had married in 1874, left him in 1877, taking their two-year-old daughter with her. Her departure, marked by dark accusations and resentments, left McKim devastated and put Bigelow in such an uncomfortable position at the firm that he chose to withdraw from his partnership. White, seeing McKim—always susceptible to depression—so completely debilitated by the failure of his marriage had practically dragged his friend aboard the *Periere* to join him on the European tour, which had proved restorative. Returning to New York ahead of White, McKim was able to resume his work at the firm.

There was a place for White with Richardson when he returned, but White chose to take the offer from his friends McKim and Mead. The pay was not high but he could count on a companionable working environment where his lack of any formal education and his limited potential for bringing in clients would be overlooked by people who knew what he had to offer. As McKim once observed, he could "draw like a house afire." He could work at breakneck speed, and with his exuberant, imaginative design sense, he had strengths to complement those of his partners: McKim, the urbane, sophisticated genius who suffused his buildings with an "air of distinguished breeding"; Mead, the engineer/artist who always knew what designs would actually work. As one observer put it, referring to the firm's logo, "Vogue la Galere" (Let the ship sail on), White was the sail, McKim the hull, and Mead the rudder.

Three days after White arrived in New York harbor on September 5, 1879, he wrote to Gus that he had "gone into partnership with McKim and Mead." Two days after that White entered the firm's offices on the top floor of 57 Broadway at the corner of Tin Pot Alley and almost immediately found himself working with McKim on a commission from the notorious editor-publisher of the New York *Herald*, James Gordon Bennett, bane of polite society and playboy protégé of the rambunctious Jerome brothers. Bennett had become persona non grata at the Reading Room, an exclusive Newport club, after he had encouraged one of his polo-playing pals to ride a horse up the front steps of the club. The episode had ended Bennett's reign as one of the club's most popular members and inspired his plan to spite Old Guard Newport and give the resort a lively alternative to the stodgy Reading Room by building his own club. In choosing Charles McKim to carry out his plan, he gave the young firm of McKim, Mead & White an opportunity to design one of the Gilded Age's most dazzling resort clubs. The Newport Casino, McKim's first major commission, featured a gold-trimmed theater designed by White and was a resounding success with Newport society. It established the reputation of the young firm and showed White to be perfectly attuned to the demands of enlightened plutocrats craving elegant places for play and pleasure.

Still in his twenties, White was now a successful architect and a popular man-about-town, as comfortable with the nabobs of smart society as with a bohemian circle of artists who preferred the company of models and chorus girls to that of dowagers and debutantes. He was living with his family at 118 East 10th Street but seldom came home. One night he was hurrying off in swallowtail and knee breeches to a society event, the next he was headed for the libidinous downtown wilds, leaving his father to lament that he was absent at breakfast, rarely present at dinner, and then after dinner "he don't stop patome more than ten to fifteen minutes but is off to the Benedick."

The Benedick, an apartment building at 80 Washington Square East designed especially for bachelors by McKim, Mead & Bigelow shortly before White replaced Bigelow at the firm, was the focus of Stanny's bohemian social life. Named for the character in *Much Ado About Nothing* who spends most of the play railing against marriage, the Benedick attracted unattached men with an interest in the arts and a passion for beauty, which in Stanny's free-thinking set included beautiful women and, among a subset of homosexuals, beautiful young men. There were long nights of art talk and musical evenings called "smoking concerts," and when, eventually and inevitably, women were invited to attend, there was sex.

In 1882, at the age of thirty, White initiated an arduous courtship of Bessie Smith. Bessie's father, J. Lawrence Smith, was a prosperous judge whose family had settled Smithtown, Long Island, and her mother, Sarah Nicoll

Smith, was the favorite niece of dry goods magnate A. T. Stewart's childless widow, Cornelia Clinch Stewart (reputedly the richest woman in the United States). Bessie was one of five sisters and, at eighteen, in no hurry to distance herself from her siblings, the father she worshiped, and the countryside where she was happiest. Striking rather than beautiful, the youthful Bessie had a slim, athletic figure that appealed to White, who, aware that no money would be coming his way from his own family, probably also recognized a financial advantage in marriage to Bessie. Marrying well had proved a wise move for others—his friend Gus Saint-Gaudens among them—and White was no doubt aware that Bessie's mother was well connected and due to inherit a fortune that would eventually pass down to her daughters. Also in Bessie's favor was her upbringing in a household dominated by the forceful Judge Smith, which was likely to have prepared her for a world in which males have prerogatives, sexual or otherwise. The courtship, as White's brother-in-law Prescott Hall Butler once remarked, was a "protracted siege," apparently not hastened by any impatient ardor on either side. It lasted for two years before the wedding finally took place in February 1884. At White's bachelor party, attended by some fifty of his friends, most from the New York art community, poet Richard Watson Gilder recited a verse he had composed for the occasion, which captured the character of his friend in a few words:

> *"I'm a young man*
> *From Man-hat-tan!*
> *I'm the tail of the kite*
> *of McKim, Mead, and White,*
> *My hair stands up straight,*
> *I am five minutes late,*
> *And as usual with me,*
> *In a terrible hurree!"*

The evening ended riotously when a pair of tabletop dancers became entangled in the vines used to decorate the room and, in their drunken efforts to extricate themselves, managed to entangle almost everyone else. A note White wrote to his mother on the evening of his marriage revealed another side of her ebullient son who took such pleasure in raucous nights with "the boys." In it he told her how much she meant to him. He assured her that he would always be there for her and stressed that she "must always think of me, dear mama, now and ever, as your loving son."

A honeymoon trip to Europe was "a very gay time." White delighted in showing his bride the sights, and Bessie, who had never traveled beyond New York, was happy to have such a knowledgeable and fun-loving guide, confiding in a letter home that she was enjoying herself "heartily." White spent lavishly, reveling in the flamboyant purchase and the grand gesture that were becoming more and more his way. Bessie accepted the extravagance but seemed to understand what it might portend.

"Stanford's main idea is never to do anything halfway or to economize in small things," she wrote her sister from Venice. Every day they enjoyed "the best of the gondolas"; every night was an occasion to put on her "best black silk" and dine in high style.

As they were preparing to sail home, Stanny added a postscript to a letter to his mother claiming to have "forgotten" the most important news: "Here is Bess telling me that I have forgotten the most important piece of news, to wit, that you must invest in a pair of spectacles and some gray hairs forthwith our arrival—for I cannot get the idea out of her head that she means to present you with a grandchild before the year is out."

In December 1884, a son was born and named after his grandfather, Richard Grant White. It was a joyful event during a brief period of genuine happiness in the marriage. Then the death of White's father in April 1885 was followed just four months later by the tragic death of the couple's infant son during an epidemic of cholera. The loss of their first child was a terrible blow, painful for both parents but perhaps more devastating for Bessie, whose deepest consolation came with the birth of her second son, Lawrence Grant White in September 1887. By this time, she was spending more and more time on Long Island at Box Hill, the "summer" house they had purchased in

St. James. The house, set in the countryside that she loved, and adjacent to the homes of two of her sisters, offered a haven from the New York social whirl Stanny reveled in and which she found distasteful.

In 1890, Bessie inherited a half million dollars in money and property, her portion of the fortune left to her mother by Mrs. Smith's multimillionaire aunt, Cornelia Clinch Stewart. It was a help in the struggle to keep up with White's extravagance but not necessarily good for their marriage. Though the relationship never ceased being a fond one, and Bessie was generous in sharing her fortune, it was nevertheless hers. When she was no longer dependent on her husband for support and protection, she ceased to be the kind of vulnerable young woman that Stanny, like his father, was most drawn to. She was no longer "his." When she began putting on weight, she became even less attractive in his eyes, and within a few years of their wedding he was leading a double life, though always faithful to his weekend visits with Bessie and Larry. Her stays in their city home on 21st Street were less and less frequent as the period of romantic happiness that had followed their wedding yielded to an affectionate but rather empty marriage.

5

GOO-GOOS AND GRAFTERS

*The vast system of blackmail in this city is known by everyone
but the District Attorneys, who have never done anything to root it out.*
—WILLIAM TRAVERS JEROME

The nearly two years that Jerome spent as a junior cog in the Tammany machine were, as he told James Morrow of the *Chicago Tribune*, nearly as miserable as his cloistered childhood. He had been repelled by the high tolerance for graft and corruption in New York City, where the police, the politicians, and the underworld all worked together to steal from the public, but he had held his tongue. His livelihood depended on his ability—and willingness—to defend Tammany's corrupt interests, and, with a wife and son to support, he had allowed his fear of failing them to override his conscience.

Then, in 1890, the conflict between his paycheck and his personal integrity had come to a head. The stress of acting against his principles was becoming intolerable, and, seeing hope for change in a growing reform movement, he had decided to risk the consequences and defy his bosses. He had been assigned to prosecute an assault case brought against a Tammany district leader, James Barker, whom the *Times* described as "a big, burly ruffian." Barker had viciously attacked a much smaller man in a saloon, knocking him to the barroom floor and pounding him to the point where the poor man had to be hospitalized for eight months and would never fully recover. Instead of twisting the law to protect Barker, Jerome had conducted the case fairly and seen the thuggish Barker convicted. He was fired from the DA's office, as he knew he would be, but his betrayal of the machine had brought him to the attention of reformist groups, and certain that the tide was turning against Tammany, he had joined them in throwing his support behind the anti-Tammany ticket in the 1890 elections.

"I even convinced Mrs. Jerome that we were bound to win, that there was to be an upheaval and that virtue was to be enthroned where sin was wont to congregate," he recalled. Then Tammany had won the election, throwing him into "the most hopeless gloom of my young life." With $300 in the bank, a wife, a baby, no job and some angry enemies in power, there was nothing to do but hang out his shingle again and wait for clients to come "straggling in."

It was another setback, but there was some consolation in having salvaged his integrity and been noticed for it. His defiance of Tammany had excited the newspapers, which had heaped praise on the political hero who had risked his job to do the honorable thing. A proud Uncle Leonard, in a letter to his wife, had written excitedly that "Travers has just made a great hit by the conduct of a case and an hour's speech in court as Assistant District Attorney. He fought a great Tammany leader on a brutal assault and got him convicted…" Jerome's proud mother had perhaps allowed herself to take some credit for Travers's brave stance against evil, while any misgivings his father may have had concerning his son's attack on Tammany and his firing from the job he had interceded to get him were likely offset by the press raves glorifying a Jerome.

While the newspapers soon lost interest in him, his willingness to take on Tammany had recommended him to some newly active champions of good government, sardonically dismissed as "Goo-goos" by the New York *Sun*, but dead serious and on the march. In the early '90s, while he was struggling to make his now-private law practice pay, he had begun to work with them on the side.

It was a time, Jerome reminded Morrow, when there was widespread disgust with the city's reputation as a prime destination for vice, a place where every imaginable form of human depravity could be indulged, and the good government forces were determined to make a clean sweep. Their sights were set on the fabled Tenderloin, the gaudy section of midtown Manhattan crammed with theaters, saloons, dance halls, and harlots. Among the estimated twenty-five thousand prostitutes plying their trade in the city, thousands were concentrated in the brothels of the Tenderloin and the Bowery. These establishments ranged from two-dollar whorehouses to palatial establishments where full evening dress and a certain perverse decorum prevailed—all of them flourishing virtually under license from the New York Police Department. On the noisy late-night streets of the Tenderloin's square mile dedicated to erotic pleasures, uptown sybarites jostled for space with streetwalkers, criminals, and perverts from every segment of society—the haut monde, the demimonde, the underworld. Only the roughest hoodlums were not tempted, generally preferring the cheaper, seamier downtown vice dens.

A few preachers had been railing against rampant vice for years, but despite periodic bursts of reform activity, nothing had decisively cracked the complacency of New York's Sunday Christians until one day in February 1892, when, from the pulpit of his majestic Madison Square Presbyterian Church, the Reverend Dr. Charles H. Parkhurst had delivered a blistering sermon that jolted his well-heeled congregants out of their Sabbath torpor. Parkhurst, a slight man with a mane of white hair, had shocked and shamed them with a thundering attack on "the damnable pack of administrative bloodhounds that are fattening themselves on the ethical flesh and blood of our citizenship..." By which of course he meant Tammany. His stunned congregants were even more astonished when the frail-looking Parkhurst followed up with late-night evidence-gathering forays into the dark heart of the vice districts, uncovering more than enough to ignite public outrage. Under pressure, New York State had launched an investigation of the New York City Police Department, naming state senator Clarence Lexow as chair.

The Goo-goos had seen to it that Jerome was named assistant to the Lexow Committee counsel, John Goff. A tiny, self-educated lawyer with a prophet's beard, Goff had piercing blue eyes and "the cold vision of a python" in the words of one of his victims. He was a terrifying figure, having found a way to compensate for his limited legal bona fides with a ruthless style of cross examination bordering on savagery. An Irish terrorist in his youth, Goff had developed an ulcer later in life, a condition that reduced his food intake to next to nothing and increased his irascibility.

In need of a job and undaunted by the prospect of working with Goff, Jerome had welcomed the opportunity to work behind the scenes, directing the efforts of the Committee's investigators and giving its members the benefit of his hard-earned familiarity with the underworld-police-Tammany connection. And by observing Goff's merciless grilling of every Tenderloin figure the Committee could round up—his relentless marshaling of evidence, his method of ensnaring witnesses in their own lies—the future DA had picked up some valuable tricks for success in the courtroom.

No sooner had the Committee's investigators hit the streets than Tenderloin vice lords and madams had begun packing their bags and skipping town. (Manhattan brothel owners fled in such numbers that on reaching Chicago they formed their own expatriate community.) Not about to be left behind, Boss Croker had hastily booked passage for himself on the ship *Umbria* and hightailed it to safety on his English estate. Those who failed to act with dispatch were rounded up and made to sizzle on "Goff's Griddle." Some seventy-four sessions later, 678 witnesses had testified to so many instances of Tammany-sanctioned illicit activity, police shakedowns, and graft that no one could deny that New York had become a sewer of vice and official corruption. With the 1894 municipal elections on the horizon, reformers were feeling the wind at their backs, and once again the newspapers were taking notice of Jerome. Lincoln Steffens, on the police beat at the time and a close observer of the investigation, gave Jerome much of the credit for the Committee's success, describing him as a figure of "great dash, vigor and courage."

Even before completing his work for the Committee, Jerome was participating in plotting a campaign capable of crushing the Tammany machine and bringing integrity back to municipal government. He would rush off to join in the conspiratorial strategy sessions held in the elegant brick and marble clubhouse of the University Club—a not-altogether-unfamiliar setting for Jerome, whose uncle Leonard had built it as a home for his family in flush times some thirty years earlier. In 1894, the club was a hotbed of reform, and Jerome was in the thick of it. His coconspirators were mostly the young sons of New York's high-minded upper-crust elites, who were horrified by the growing influence of the Tammany political machine—"those people" who were degrading their city. Many who joined him in the anti-Tammany strategy sessions were recent graduates of Ivy League universities and law schools, and though they were no doubt richer than Jerome, his family bona fides were genuine and entitled him to the same social privileges they enjoyed. Like them, he was eminently "clubbable," and, like them, he preferred the University Club for its unstuffy atmosphere, which made it a natural choice as a place to meet and engage in the kind of "bull sessions" he most enjoyed. When he was exchanging ideas with them for a winning anti-Tammany campaign, he was as energized and exhilarated by their can-do optimism as they were by his passion and tactical brilliance.

After coming alarmingly close to sacrificing his integrity for a comfortable life with a regular paycheck, he was greatly relieved to have thrown off the Tammany yoke. If, as he had always suspected, there was a tendency toward moral laxity and loose living in his family, he had beaten it back. He had done the right thing and faced the financial consequences, and he was free to follow his conscience—and perhaps show some belated respect for his mother's stern code of ethics.

By the time the plotters had settled on wealthy Republican businessman William Strong to be their candidate on a Fusion ticket joining Republicans with anti-Tammany Democrats, the election was just weeks away. With no time to lose, Jerome had agreed to act as Strong's campaign manager and taken up the task like a man possessed. Finally given a position worthy of his ambition, talent, and drive, he had given the assignment his all, whirling around town in a hack, speaking half a dozen times nightly under torchlight to crowds who filled the streets and roared their approval of the message and the charismatic messenger. He had the Jerome dash—the optimism and charm passed down from Larry and Lenny—along with the passion and an integrity he had long suppressed, and which New Yorkers, shocked by the state of their city and fed up with windbags and liars, were primed to embrace.

He had been thrilled, wherever he stopped, by throngs who cheered his attacks on the "Tammany Tiger," his blunt denunciations of the smug upper classes, and his defense of the suffering underclasses. At the end of each speech he left the crowds howling, "Down with Tammany!" and "Let the Tiger's pelt be taken!" He was hailed in the newspapers as an electrifying speaker; his "form was erect, his carriage confident and unaffectedly graceful," wrote one reporter, who added that he seemed "thoroughly at ease, enthralling his listeners after three minutes and leaving them shouting for more at the end."

On election day, confirming the worst fears of Croker and his cronies, thousands had lined up at the polls to vote for reform candidate William Strong over Tammany's "amiable stooge" Hugh Grant. That evening, hoarse but exultant, Jerome had read out the bulletins announcing Tammany's rout to loud cheers from the crowd. After weeks of frenetic activity, he had allowed himself to bask in the glory of the moment, absorbing the adulation of so many reform-minded citizens who credited his tireless campaigning for their victory. "The Tammany Tiger Has Been Flayed Alive," the *Times* had proclaimed in a jubilant headline.

Secure in the knowledge that he had proved himself with his spectacular winning campaign, Jerome had waited expectantly for a plum, a political appointment that would permit him to make up for the years lost to obscurity. He was thirty-five and a rising star. Everything was still possible, but he desperately needed to spread his message. He needed a position of prominence, a high-visibility platform to show the world what he was capable of. Instead, he had suffered the familiar pangs of deep disappointment and frustration when the triumphant administration he had campaigned so strenuously and successfully to elect rewarded him with a career-stalling appointment to a minor court and a chance to watch the neo-Puritans in City Hall and the Police Department overplay their hand.

He had miscalculated, believing that his strength lay with the voters who would have sent their hero straight to the White House given the chance, and he had failed to take into account the power of the professional politicians who considered him a dangerous maverick—incorruptible, dedicated, and unmanageable. No one should have been surprised that an administration led by Republican businessman William Strong, who took a puritanical approach to reform, would find a place to hide the masses' unpredictable idol.

Sworn in on July 1, 1895, condemned to handling the appeals from police courts and misdemeanor cases that came through the Court of Special Sessions, Jerome had watched from the sidelines as Theodore Roosevelt, Mayor Strong's choice to head the new city Police Board, set about enforcing every one of the city's blue laws, chasing down Sunday beer drinkers and casual card players and alienating ordinary New Yorkers who liked their beer, sex, and cards.

As an unapologetic participant in the amenities of club life—the convivial drinking and low-stakes card games—Jerome had been particularly pained by the puritanical zeal of the excitable Roosevelt. Among the most offensive of Roosevelt's relentlessly enforced laws was the one prohibiting public watering holes from serving beer on Sunday—grossly unfair in Jerome's view, since it deprived working men of their Sunday pint while the elite drank freely in their private clubs. Asked at one time for his opinion on the crusade against the sale of liquor on Sunday, he had answered with subtle mockery aimed at Rooseveltian fanaticism, calling the ban "the result of good intentions gone astray."

Though he and Roosevelt had much in common—upper-class backgrounds, triumph over youthful frailty by sheer force of will, intelligence, audacity, inexhaustible energy and high political goals—a strong sense of rivalry was inevitable. From their first encounters in the New York reform movement, Jerome had disliked Roosevelt, considering him a laurel-grabbing latecomer to reform while other, worthier reformists (like himself), with impressive records of fighting corruption, were relegated to obscurity. Never did he doubt that he was as physically attractive, politically bold, shrewd, and charismatic as Roosevelt, which had only heightened his resentment at having to waste his time on a "squirt court" while Roosevelt was making news and vaulting ahead on a path that promised to take him to the top.

For a while, Strong's clean government campaign had proved popular. The streets were clean and New York was decently governed. Before long, however, even some who had called most loudly for the tiger's pelt were looking back wistfully on the days before they were overrun by the neo-Puritans in City Hall who disapproved of almost everything that gave them pleasure. Jerome's dismay at Roosevelt's letter-of-the-law enforcement might have been tinged with jealousy, but he was far from a lone dissenter. When Roosevelt and his men began hounding pinochle players in the back rooms of saloons, snatching even the small joys from daily life, the bulk of the working class had had enough, and the violent public resentment had given Jerome the satisfaction of hearing his own disapproval expressed in far more vitriolic terms. The once popular Roosevelt, in very bad odor with the Republican bosses and Mayor Strong, was accused of being the "biggest fool who ever lived" and of wrecking the Republican Party. A bomb threat had proved a hoax, but the *World* warned ominously that "the next bomb will be deposited in the ballot box in November…"

When his support for William McKinley, who took office as president in 1897, earned Roosevelt an appointment as Assistant Secretary of the Navy—albeit a promotion engineered by his party to be rid of him—there had been a great sigh of relief among Sunday drinkers and city Republicans. A confident Croker, feeling it safe to come home, had recrossed the Atlantic, a voyage hailed by cartoonists as "The Return from Elba."

As their candidate for mayor in the 1897 election, Tammany had settled on an obscure and compliant judge, Robert Van Wyck, to run against the Goo-goos' choice, the stolid and "damnably dull" president of Columbia University, Seth Low. No one was surprised—least of all Jerome, who disliked the humorless Low—when Van Wyck won handily. Some may have been taken aback, however, when many of the same people who had poured into the streets just three years earlier to celebrate Strong's victory for the reformists exploded in wild jubilation over Low's defeat. Exuberant crowds snake-danced through the streets shouting, "To hell with reform!" and organized vice, along with Sunday beer, had returned overnight.

Back on top at Tammany headquarters, Croker had wasted no time in installing "Big Bill" Devery as police chief, and within a few weeks the *New York Times* was reporting that a Tammany "commission" consisting of two state senators, one city official, and the czar of the city's poolroom syndicate was collecting $3,095,000 each month in graft. While sensualists like Stanford White and his friends among the bohemian elite had welcomed the Tenderloin revival, considering its joys a necessary safety valve for release from the hypocritical prudery of New York society, others continued to see it as a blight on the city and rededicated themselves anew to sweeping it clean.

When Roosevelt was elected governor in 1898, having resigned his post with the navy to serve in the Spanish-American War and returned as a war hero, he was as eager as ever to see New York City rid of its vice dens and fleshpots. He had convened yet another state committee to conduct yet another investigation into city corruption, a probe reminiscent of the Lexow Committee's investigation only five years earlier. The report of the Mazet Committee, released in December 1899, confirmed what the previous one had revealed and what most people already knew: that vice was organized and controlled by the police and politicians. But the report's most shocking revelations involved an unscrupulous financier, Charlie Morse, who, in cahoots with Mayor Van Wyck, Croker, and others, had schemed to monopolize the natural ice market and then raised the price of ice to unaffordable levels. Without ice, milk spoils, children suffer, and sometimes even die. The newspapers had seized on the ice scandal, reporting alarming numbers of infant deaths and awakening New Yorkers to the sad reality that corruption can have fatal consequences and that Sunday beer had come at a high price.

For reporters, the outrageous but uncomplicated story of financial chicanery had proved irresistible. Its mechanisms were easily understood, and, better still, at the center of the scandal was a cheerfully heartless villain whose country cunning contrasted rather comically with the sophisticated maneuvers

of Wall Street titans. Morse's insistence that nothing he did was any different
from what occurred daily in the financial community was greeted with particular glee in the newsroom of Joseph Pulitzer's pseudo-moralistic *World,* a
Democratic organ proud of its crusade in defense of the "little man" against
evil Wall Street. At the same time, it was the *World,* along with William Randolph Hearst's *Journal,* that was giving the world the term *yellow journalism*
to describe the kind of newspaper specializing in salacious, sensationalized
stories of dubious veracity that a huge segment of New York's population
looked to for its news.

Morse, the cocky little scoundrel who had cooked up the ice scheme, had
arrived in New York in 1880 from Bath, Maine, where his family prospered
with tugboats, shipbuilding, and a brisk trade in ice. As a baby, Charlie had
been stricken with infantile paralysis, and though he recovered, the family had
continued to pamper him throughout his youth, leaving him with the impression that he could do no wrong. His intention in coming to New York was to
look after the family's interests and join the ranks of the trust lords, a plan he
had launched by buying up ice companies, selling inflated stock, and acquiring
a monopoly on the sale of ice throughout the city with the help of his good
friends Croker, Van Wyck, and their henchmen. He was soon notorious on
Wall Street, a hugely successful misfit later described by a contemporary as
"physically ugly, amoral," rich beyond reason, rapacious, and shady. Jerome,
like everyone who had read the Mazet report and been appalled by the extent
of his fraudulent schemes, despised Morse as corruption personified.

The report's shocking revelations had failed to galvanize any effective
action until history repeated itself and a clergyman's searing denunciation of
public apathy accomplished what nothing else could. In an open letter written
by Episcopal bishop Henry Codman Potter to Mayor Van Wyck in November
1900, the celebrity pastor to the social set expressed his disgust that in New
York "vice is not only tolerated but shielded and encouraged by those whose
sworn duty it is to discourage it." Describing conditions in the tenements as
"a living hell," Bishop Potter, like the Reverend Parkhurst before him, had
shamed his uptown parishioners and roused some of New York's "best men"

to action. Calling themselves the Committee of Fifteen, they had turned to Jerome to play a role similar to his previous work for the Lexow Committee, taking charge of evidence-gathering investigations into the sordid vice dens of the Tenderloin. Well funded by the wealthy patricians who had been stung by the bishop's scolding, the Committee employed detectives to roam the vice districts and file reports of illicit police-protected activity.

This time around Jerome was not limited to a role as enabler. The investigators' secret reports, turned over to him, had provided the evidence he needed to conduct his raids without fear of police tip-offs and to break free of his sentence to serve on a court he considered beneath his qualifications.

There is a point in the *Chicago Tribune* interview when Jerome relates his response to colleagues who asked why he had chosen to ignore precedent and personally conduct his sensational raids. "I always held that a magistrate ought to have inquisitorial as well as judicial power," he said. "I told them I thought we should take the worst thing at hand, which was gambling, attack it, and then let our policy shape itself. New York was as wide open as any tough town in the far west and the police were in partnership with the gamblers."

By the summer of 1901, he had tested his theory and was pleased with the results. He had taken an unprecedented leap from the bench to the streets, conducted hair-raising raids against gambling joints, and held court on the spot. He had closed down scores of gambling dens and brothels, depriving Tammany of a prime source of graft and putting Boss Croker and his henchmen on the defensive. He had emerged from the shadows. He was making headlines again, and his future looked bright.

6

SOARING CELEBRITY, SOARING DEBTS

Stanford White was everyone's favorite bon vivant and American boulevardier.
—JOHN RUSSELL

I n the decades following his marriage and the birth of his son Larry, commissions for private mansions and public buildings for the upper classes have poured into the firm, and White's reputation has soared. By 1901 he has given the city many of its most beautiful residences, as well as such radiant landmarks as the festive Madison Square Garden, the classically inspired triumphal arch at Washington Square, and the Metropolitan Club with its imposing aura of wealth and social status. Lionized as the architect who has brought beauty and gaiety to a lackluster cityscape, he is also admired for creating sumptuous interiors using an exuberant mix of exquisite Old World furnishings, rich fabrics, and exotic props. Always as excited by the possibilities for artistry on the inside of buildings as on the exterior, he is giving the firm's clientele the spectacular interiors that perfectly reflect their wealth, power, and unflinching opulence.

He is at the height of his celebrity just as his affair with seventeen-year-old Evelyn Nesbit is at its most intense. He is spending recklessly on extravagant gifts and support for her family and using his influence to promote her career. Dynamic and indefatigable, he is juggling the demands of his erotic life with those of his profession, choreographing elaborate trysts with Evelyn almost every evening, accepting more commissions than he can reasonably handle, and spending more than he earns as his debts mount.

Of the firm's many wealthy clients, it is William Whitney who possesses the greatest fortune and the most ravenous appetite for luxury and magnificence—tastes he naturally looks to his friend and fellow carouser Stanny to satisfy. With Whitney, owner of at least ten townhouses and country estates, the work has been near constant, and the rewards—including the 10 percent commission White takes on what will amount to a million dollars' worth of furnishings purchased for Whitney from White's network of high-end dealers—are considerable. Even before the completion of Whitney's Fifth Avenue mansion, the princely palace previewed at his niece Helen Barney's spectacular debut ball was being hailed by the *New York Times* as a house "without rival in this country," raising White's status another notch.

Among his many residential projects, another that is giving him pleasure is a double townhouse for his friend and sometime broker Henry Poor. Publisher of the very profitable *Railroad Manual*—essential reading for any investor—Poor gives White carte blanche and is pure delight as a client. Very rich, highly cultured, and nothing if not game, Poor, who effortlessly reads a dozen languages and collects rare books, is a longtime member of White's circle of intimate friends who pursue young beauties after hours. Seeing themselves as modern men, challenging a stultifying culture that celebrates drabness and perpetuates a sour Victorian view of sensuality, they are respected members of society by day and uninhibited pleasure seekers by night. On evenings when they are not obliged to participate in the social rituals expected of men of their rank, they can be found carousing with the denizens of New York's demimonde.

The residence White creates for Poor overlooking Gramercy Park, directly opposite his own 21st Street home, is shaping up as one of the architect's most impressive and White's network of European agents has been alerted to send their most beautiful and rare antiques for its interior. White is also creating a squash court and a stable for Poor a block away and the two men decide to put a "secret" room in the stable, another of the dozen or so hideaways that White will use for his trysts over the years. It will not be as exotically decorated as his Tower Studio or as exquisitely arranged for seduction as the multilevel loft on 24th Street, but it will be more convenient, in better taste, and safer than rented spaces like the room in the Benedick that was shared by White, Saint-Gaudens, his brother Louis and others for gatherings of the suggestively named Sewer Club. When work on the magnificent townhouse is finally finished—after two years and expenses that soar skyward from the initial $130,000—a delighted Poor writes to his friend, assuring him that "any excess of cost over the original estimates amounts to nothing in view of the result obtained, and to say that I am satisfied with it puts it mildly!"

Another project for a friend is more problematic. Back in the early 1880s White had designed one of his first urban townhouses for Charles Barney, Will Whitney's brother-in-law and then a rising star in the banking world. At the time, it being the fashion to give each room a different theme—an Arabic room, a Renaissance room, a Medieval room, etc.—White had embraced the concept with such exuberance that one critic berated the results as a "mad orgy of bad architecture." White survived the blow to his professional pride, Barney was apparently pleased with his house, the two discovered a common passion for art, and the friendship flourished as one rose to become president of the Knickerbocker Trust Company and the other ascended to celebrity status. Now, when the debt collectors are at White's door, Barney can usually be counted on for a loan, and though he is more circumspect than the all-out carousers White likes to assemble for his nighttime revels, he is sometimes among them. Recently, Barney had decided that the house White had created for him on 55th Street was no longer adequate given his rise in stature, and had sold it to *New York World* publisher Joseph Pulitzer. After purchasing a more suitable residence on Park Avenue, he had hired White to take charge of a complete renovation.

This time, however, the work is not going well. Over-scheduled as usual, White has spread himself too thin and progress is slow. As the renovation drags on, Barney's ill-advised association with the unsavory Charlie Morse, who had initially approached him for financial advice and ultimately embroiled him in his schemes, is also causing Barney enormous headaches. Though the slippery Morse has emerged from the ice scandal with his fortune intact and enhanced, public outrage has been festering ever since against him and his Tammany cronies who had dared to steal from the poor. Court hearings and bad publicity are making life unpleasant for Charlie, while Barney, high-strung and obsessively concerned with his public profile, lives in fear that the dark cloud over Morse will descend on him. In November 1901, as work on the town house drags on, Barney suffers another setback when his country home in Southampton, Long Island, burns to the ground with everything in it. In a letter to White, Lily Barney writes of her husband's "tendency to mel-ancholia" and implores the architect to speed up the work on their house so that they can move in. "Charley is horribly depressed," she writes. "He seems to have 'let go' entirely and I dread to think of what the future may hold for him if I cannot get him out in his own home soon."

The two men have known each other now for more than a decade and the friendship is strong enough to survive these tensions. As president of the Knickerbocker since 1897, Barney is well on his way to taking the bank's deposits from $10 million to $61 million, establishing himself as a star among bankers and his bank as the trusted steward of society wealth. Having decided that it is time for new headquarters that will reflect the bank's current prominence (and his own), Barney has asked White for a design. Somehow, White is finding time to work on plans for a new Knicker-bocker Trust building to be erected on the northwest corner of 34th Street and Fifth Avenue, a prime city location. What is taking shape on his drawing board is a spectacular Corinthian-columned temple of Vermont marble out-side, Norwegian marble inside, with a central banking room nearly three stories high. Perhaps buoyed by visions of fashionable patrons entering the hushed interior of White's gorgeous temple to Mammon and serenely entrusting their money to the Knickerbocker, Barney will battle back from his depressed state to perform heroically as White's financial adviser and principal support, but his "melancholia" at this time is a grim foreshadowing of what is to come.

As White is falling further and further behind on other projects, he is struggling to complete a Venetian-style palace on East 73rd Street for publisher Joseph Pulitzer, whose former residence, purchased from Barney, was destroyed in another spectacular fire in 1900. It is a lucrative commission, too lucrative to pass up, though White is well aware that pleasing Pulitzer is nearly impossible. There had been endless problems earlier when the publisher had hired him to renovate Barney's former house on 55th Street. Extremely nervous and excitable, the nearly blind Pulitzer is phobic about noise, adamantly against anything French, and opinionated on just about everything. But the White-Pulitzer relationship, which one mutual acquaintance characterized as an "armed truce," had hit bottom back in 1895 when the two men had clashed not over a design decision but over a humiliation suffered by White in the pages of the *World*.

On that occasion, White, his old friend and carousing companion Jimmie Breese, and Henry Poor had hosted a stag dinner in Breese's photography studio, which had been lavishly decorated by White. Served by scantily clad young women, some fifty or so men had ingested Rabelaisian quantities of food and drink—a thirteen-course meal, gallons of wine, and 144 bottles of champagne. When it came time for dessert, a huge pie had appeared out of which popped a flock of birds and a nearly nude underage girl. Though every effort had been made to keep the revels secret, word of the scandalous "Pie Girl Dinner" had leaked and White had been obliged to go hat in hand to his friends in the press and implore them not to publish the story. While others had complied, Pulitzer had not. The *World* had blasted "the bacchanalian revels in New York's fashionable studios" and excoriated men who would corrupt young girls for their pleasure.

Friends like Charles Barney are aware that White has little "money sense" and do their best to help him avoid financial disaster, though Barney himself—known as Wall Street's "top speculator"—shares the gambling instinct that inspires both men to go for the "big killing," the windfall that will catapult them into the ranks of the titans. Encouraged by a barely regulated stock market and the vast new wealth arising from the nation's extraordinary postwar economic expansion, White and Barney are hardly alone in the speculative frenzy that has investors courting catastrophe in the delusional belief that fortunes can be made out of debt and thin air. White in particular has been gambling heavily on oil, mining, and railroad stocks, usually with borrowed money, and by 1901, his market losses have far exceeded his gains.

Railroads and their proliferation across the country have been tempting speculators for years, though Henry Poor's *Railroad Manual* had correctly reported back in 1884, with only minimal hyperbole, "that the entire capital stock of the railroads . . . represented water." White is hard hit by the collapse of his stock in the Northern Pacific Railroad in the spring of 1901, a monumental market disruption that causes many other stocks to plummet. In two days, May 8 to 9, White loses more than $350,000, is buried in debt to his brokers and bankers, and laments that he has been "wiped off the face of the earth." He covers his debts to Poor and Breese with valuable art objects from his huge storehouse of acquired treasures, but his financial situation is dire. To a friend he writes, "The truth is you can't run architecture and stock-jobbing at the same time."

Stressed and overworked, White holds depression at bay with a frenetic social life that keeps him perpetually in motion. From the ballrooms and banquets of smart society to the bohemian haunts he frequents with his livelier friends, and the rented "studios" where he conducts his amorous adventures, he is as ubiquitous as he is popular, bustling around town "radiating energy like a broadcasting station," as one of his peers put it. Despite his crushing debts, he entertains as lavishly as ever, continues to spend enormous sums on paintings, Oriental rugs, tapestries and precious objects while carrying on the most intense—and costly—affair of his life. He is burning the candle at both ends, and the flames are fast approaching the center.

1

A HERO ON THE HUSTINGS

If the people want blackmailers and other criminals vigorously prosecuted without fear or favor, they will elect Judge Jerome.
—The *New York Herald*

In the dog days of August 1901, Boss Croker is growing gloomy. The "Grand Sachem of Tammany Hall," absolute ruler of the corrupt Democratic machine, sees trouble ahead in the fall elections. Recalling the 1894 election debacle, he is instructing his men to throttle down on gambling and prostitution until after the election. Reform is again in the air and anti-Crokerism's most fearsome champion is Justice of the Court of Special Sessions William Travers Jerome.

In September, the nation is traumatized by the assassination of President McKinley, his slow death, and the ascension of Roosevelt to the presidency. With those dramatic events behind them and the municipal elections imminent, reporters are happy to focus again on the antics of Police Chief Devery and the heroics of Judge Jerome. Lincoln Steffens, now city editor of the *Commercial Advertiser*, seizes every opportunity to strike at Tammany, making a specialty of lambasting Devery as entirely unfit to head the police force. Yet, unlike Croker, Devery remains supremely confident that voters will reject another experiment in "panty-waist rule" and endorse his claim to be uniquely qualified for his position (which has enriched him by an estimated quarter of a million dollars). Looking beyond the strut and the bluster to explain Devery's unwavering optimism, writer Alfred Hodder, observing the political circus, ultimately concludes that Devery, though certainly ridiculous, is, "in his own world, formidable." His hold on the seven-thousand-man force has always been "masterly" and, at his command, they walk "in the eye of the lord."

Croker's mood grows even darker when the Citizens Union, a Goo-goo party formed to nominate reform-minded candidates, pressures managers of the Republican Party to accept Jerome's nomination to run for district attorney on a combined ticket, which they refer to as the "Fusion." Though they consider Jerome "unsafe" and predict he will be "a drag on the ticket," they are obliged to admit that the one thing he brings is a genius for getting himself talked about. In that, he does not disappoint. After his nomination, reporters follow him wherever he goes, quoting from his fiery speeches and hailing him as a new kind of politician for the 20th century.

Jerome's decision to install his campaign headquarters—two uncarpeted rooms above a saloon—on the Lower East Side, far from New York's fashionable precincts, also raises eyebrows and reinforces fears that he will be an unreliable defender of Republican interests; that he will disrupt the status quo that Republicans, as members of the party of business, believe must be maintained if commerce is to continue to flourish free of profit-draining regulations, labor unrest and attacks on the privileges of wealth, of which they are the main beneficiaries.

"What is the use of opening headquarters in the brownstone district?" asks Jerome in response. "The voters there are for the Fusion ticket whether we tell the truth or no . . . the side to win votes from is the *other* side."

Shattering traditions and conventions at every turn, Jerome conducts a campaign like no other. Racing around the city in an automobile, he makes eighty-six speeches in six weeks, sometimes delivering eight or ten a day, creating drama and excitement wherever he goes. Organizers, wary of his unpredictability but forced to acknowledge his power over a crowd, have to scrap a plan to keep him from speaking on the same platform with the other Fusion candidates. As a result, they are forced to watch restless audiences wait impatiently—and sometimes loudly—for Jerome to take the podium.

Speakers who precede him frequently find themselves struggling to make themselves heard over shouts for Jerome. When their hero does rise to speak, someone (a plant?) invariably yells, "Who's going to eat the Tiger?"

"Jerome!" roars the crowd.

Offering himself as the defender of the oppressed, Jerome rages against Tammany crooks and their criminal cohorts, drawing cheers and gaining notice in the national and even the international press. Ever since he had overcome his physical frailty on an upstate farm, unaided and alone, he has believed himself capable of achieving whatever he sets out to do and that he is meant for big things. A fighter, temperamentally more suited to the attack of campaigning than to quiet, lawyerly maneuvering, he sees in the monstrous Tammany machine the greatest threat to his times and the city, a powerful force against which he can prove himself by boldly attacking, slaying the monster and saving his city. People everywhere are gripped by the unfolding morality play.

No one is exempt from his attacks, which can sometimes leave his supporters aghast. Arthur Train, observing Jerome as he is beginning to taste power after years of frustration, sees a man who is a fighter but also "sentimental and emotional," often "carried away by his own enthusiasms and resentments." Sure of his own abilities, Jerome has chafed at being relegated to "an inconspicuous minor judgeship," which, in Train's view, has made him "authoritative, somewhat domineering, even slightly arrogant."

Jerome's fusillade aimed at Tammany is no surprise, but even his supporters are stunned by his blunt assertion that "the men who are dominant in Tammany Hall are not politicians, they are grafters . . . working for their own pockets all the time…" Party bosses across the board are denounced—by name. Republican boss Thomas Collier Platt, longtime absolute monarch of the state Republican machine and legislature, who had reluctantly agreed to throw his support behind Jerome, is promptly insulted and alienated, even charged with conspiring with William Whitney to defeat Jerome at the polls. Before an upper-class audience, Jerome derides his social peers as "heartless" and dismisses them as "of no use to this city." He treats their wives even more harshly, calling them "perfect children about what is happening in this city" and instructing them not to meddle in the tenements but to content themselves with raising money, the only possible way they can be useful.

Some of the loudest cheers are raised when Jerome vows to hunt down corporate wrongdoers even if their tracks lead straight to the offices of the Metropolitan Street Railway Company. "No one knows better than I do," he insists, "that when I am attacking the Metropolitan Street Railway Company I am arraying myself against the most dangerous, most vindictive and the most powerful influences at work in this community." No one in his audience doubts that his main target is the Metropolitan's ringleader, William Whitney, who, in league with the cutthroat financier Thomas Fortune Ryan and others, has grabbed nearly full control over the municipal transit system. Even Jerome's least sophisticated listeners harbor deep resentment against the Metropolitan and Whitney in particular, whose Fifth Avenue palace, a White masterwork, is a galling reminder of the vast wealth he has garnered from the company's virtual monopoly of the city's trolleys and streetcar lines without improving in any way the decrepit, overcrowded system they are obliged to endure.

Among some with a more intimate knowledge of Wall Street's wiles, it is understood that Whitney is among Boss Croker's chief financial supporters (perhaps even the Boss's boss) and that the franchises needed to monopolize public transit were bestowed on him by a grateful Sachem. They are incensed that he has betrayed the public trust and failed to act on promises to modernize the system. They also strongly suspect that he has been defrauding thousands of small investors by issuing nearly worthless watered stock in the company.

By the end of October, Jerome is confident enough of victory to relax a little and inject some levity into his speeches. When "Big Tim" Sullivan, one of Tammany's powerful leaders with sovereignty over the teeming Lower East Side, charges that "Jerome lives on highballs and cigarettes," Jerome takes the occasion to attack Sunday saloon closings and cheerfully admits to having indulged on the Sabbath himself. "I have never found that my own thirst stopped at twelve o'clock on Saturday night and began again at five o'clock on Monday morning," he declares. "I have always found that I was just about as thirsty on Sunday as on any other day…"

With his easygoing attitude toward human frailty when it is harmless to others, his bluntness of speech, his engaging sense of humor and conviviality, Jerome has enormous appeal for youthful idealists impatient with the remnants of 19th-century rectitude and offended by the hypocrisy it entails. Among the many who join Jerome's campaign, thrilled to support a politician so free of fusty bombast and so fiercely devoted to truth-telling, is the budding novelist Upton Sinclair, just out of college. In his autobiography Sinclair will recall the excitement surrounding Jerome's 1901 campaign and how he "took fire" from Jerome's oratory. He does not share Arthur Train's dismay at Jerome's propensity to turn an opportunity to advance his prospects into an occasion to "make a savage attack on some prominent official or influential citizen in such a way as apparently to court political extermination."

There is an awkward scene at Jerome's final rally when, intoxicated by the enthusiasm of the crowd, he grabs his wife, "kissing her tenderly again and again" in a sentimental display that seems to traumatize her and puts a decisive end to any further involvement in her husband's hated political career. In fact the two are utterly incompatible and Jerome's home life has long been intolerable. Just as his father did, he has married a woman with whom he has nothing in common, one who hates politics and politicians and finds society distasteful. As a result, Jerome is rarely at home and spends most of his time in his office or at his clubs. When he is at his Lakeville, Connecticut property, he spends his time in the workshop he has built on the grounds as a refuge from his wife and a place to indulge his love of working with metal.

At 10:00 P.M. on election night, when it is clear that Jerome has been elected DA, that Seth Low has won the mayoralty, and Tammany has been swept from City Hall in a rout, there is pandemonium. The same crowd that had snake-danced in the streets to celebrate reform's defeat a few years earlier, shouting, "To Hell with reform!" is back to cheer the other side. Thousands of citizens gather around Madison and Herald Squares to roar their approval.

Van Wyck, trounced in his bid for a seat on the State Supreme Court, is so hated for his role in the ice scandal that thousands of ballots have to be discarded because of scurrilous comments written around his name.

News of his victory reaches Jerome at his country home in Lakeville. The following day a reporter for the *Times*, one of many who have trailed Jerome from the city, describes how hundreds of villagers, hastily joined for a torchlight parade, had marched to the Lakeville house bearing celebratory signs, some hailing "Our Billy," one with a more complicated message: "New York, 3:35 P.M.—Dr. Jerome operates successfully on the Tiger and then leaves town." Swarming over the lawn to the edge of the "spacious veranda," they had shouted for Jerome, their clamor subsiding only when he mounted a porch pillar to give a rousing speech that left no one in doubt that DA Jerome would be no less feisty than candidate Jerome.

"In the fight just closed, we were opposed by the great Metropolitan Street Railway Company, the center of one of the most iniquitous influences in the nation...," he had declared, going on to deliver a fearless challenge to thieves in high places: "When you have told the truth and kept self-respect, you can fearlessly meet the issue. It will not fail."

Newspapers everywhere report total victory for the forces of reform. Croker is pilloried and leaves, once again, for England; Dick Canfield closes his elegant gaming palace and slips off to Europe. Devery and other police are forced to resign. The defeat of Tammany's troops is linked to Jerome's galvanizing campaign and to the shocking discovery of Tammany's involvement in the ice scandal, which had exposed their sham generosity in delivering turkeys and coal to the poor with one hand while stealing milk from babies with the other. Charlie Morse, who had cashed in his chips in a timely fashion, is reviled for his part in the ice scandal and bombarded with lawsuits, but he is $12 million richer.

The day after the election the *New York Times* editorial page calls Jerome's campaign "one of the most inspiring things that New Yorkers can remember." The *Evening Sun* credits the victory to "the virile personality and vigorous speeches of William Travers Jerome" and adds that "the spirit and lofty resolution which Mr. Jerome has infused into the canvass have swept over the greater city like a prairie fire, kindling a sentiment for reform which has struck panic into the ranks of organized corruption..." The *Times* (London) praises Jerome's "fearless and stirring denunciations," and Berlin's *National Zeitung* comments that "political morality has gained a brilliant and, we hope, decisive victory." At a huge victory rally, Mark Twain tells the exuberant crowd, "Tammany is dead and there is wailing in the land. We shall miss so many familiar faces. Van Wyck, the gentle peddler of lifesaving ice at 60 cents per hundred, is gone."

The campaign has earned Jerome legions of supporters who view him as the most glamorous and inspiring public official ever to have graced the hustings. He has also made some powerful enemies.

"MAD HARRY"

"I am Harry K. Thaw of Pittsburgh."

At the height of the 1901 theater season, *Florodora* is the most popular show on Broadway and Evelyn Nesbit is its biggest draw.

From early evening the scintillating night world between 14th and 23rd Street, blazing now with dazzling electric light, is alive with people heading for the stylish restaurants, theaters and brothels illuminated by incandescent lamps that turn the sky into a purple haze. Like moths to a flame, top-hatted eligibles, married magnates on the prowl, and newly minted middle-class hedonists flock to the Great White Way. Their luxurious carriages fill the streets, their well-tended horses add a rhythmic clop-clop to the hum of gaiety and excitement. A visiting journalist, awed by the resplendence of the New York night, writes of "huge electric trolleys sailing in an endless stream, profusely jeweled with electricity" and elevated trains "like luminous winged serpents, skimming through the air."

At the Casino Theater, as Evelyn dresses for her performance as a "Charming Spanish Maiden" with the "*Florodora* Girls," a mostly male audience is filling the seats inside the spectacularly exotic Moorish-Revival theater. Originally intended as a concert hall, it has become the city's most popular showcase for light opera, frothy revues and burlesque. Described half-jokingly as "a respectable seraglio" conjured with faux Moorish flourishes and props, it is a place where a millionaire in search of a beautiful paramour might easily acquire a young showgirl beguiled by money.

The show's featured Floradora Sextette is famous for its dancing, prancing, risqué allure (and for its heartbreakers and home wreckers) but Evelyn is pleasantly aware that the flood of flowers, lovesick letters and marriage proposals arriving each day at the theater is now mostly addressed to her. Encouraged by White, bolstered by her celebrity as a model and now as a performer, she is aware that 20th-century men have wearied of the fleshy voluptuousness typical of the old music hall sex idols and prefer a more modern look, one that she embodies with her slim figure and exotic allure.

What Evelyn is not aware of is that one of her most persistent anonymous correspondents is watching her most nights from the shadows of a darkened theater box. His letters, in which she has noted an unusually refined use of language, have lately escalated to include invitations to join him for lunch and $50 bills wrapped around American Beauty roses. She has politely declined the lunch invitations, explaining that she doesn't make a practice of meeting with strange men or accepting their money. When at last he identifies himself as Mr. Munroe, Evelyn's curiosity is piqued, but there are scores of similarly besotted men desperate to claim her affection, and none can offer her more glamor and excitement than Stanny.

In fact, Mr. Munroe, who is well aware of his rival and determined to remove Evelyn from his influence, is in reality Harry K. Thaw, the rich but reprobate heir to a multimillion-dollar Pittsburgh fortune traceable to his father's timely acquisition of Pennsylvania Railroad bonds. Back home, Harry's reputation as the black sheep of the family dynasty has never been in question. As a child, he was prone to bouts of insomnia, incoherent babbling, and temper tantrums that made it difficult to retain household help. Harry's father, recognizing that his bug-eyed, baby-talking, addled son was not normal and would squander his inheritance, had written strict limits on Harry's income into his will—limits that Harry's doting mother, Mary Copley Thaw, had nullified as soon as her husband was safely underground, raising her son's annual allowance from

$2,400 to a more comfortable $80,000. Even that has never covered the considerable expenditures necessitated by Harry's perverse tastes. Barely out of adolescence, he was amusing himself betting on cockfights, brawling in bars and experimenting with whips, drugs and irregular sex. When reparations were called for, Harry could always count on the family-proud matriarch to pay off his victims, silence the press, and preserve the family honor.

Iron-willed, self-righteous, and utterly devoted to her three interests in life—Harry, the family honor and the Presbyterian Church—Mother Thaw has long ruled over a certain segment of Christian society as the dowager empress of Pittsburgh. Known for her good works on behalf of the church and for her minor philanthropy, she is often approached by the needy for help. Some receive it and some do not, as a mortified Mrs. Nesbit discovered. Once, at a low point in the aftermath of her husband's sudden death, when the family was in dire straits, Evelyn's mother had swallowed her pride to walk the few blocks that separated the Pittsburgh boardinghouse where she and her children were living from Lyndhurst, the Thaw family mansion. A hideous pile, gloomy and menacing, the mansion would play a different role in Evelyn's life in just a few years, but, on this occasion, she was unaware of her mother's desperate decision to approach the magisterial Widow Thaw for a handout, and of its humiliating outcome. After steeling herself and ringing the bell, Mrs. Nesbit was shocked when she was rudely turned away by a gray-gloved servant, an experience she never forgave or forgot.

When Harry had set his sights on entering New York society, mother and son had been crazily confident that New Yorkers would find Harry irresistible. After all, hadn't *Town Topics* spread the news that Mrs. Astor, undisputed queen of New York society, had seen fit to admit him to one of her famous balls? Buying his way into society's top tier promised to be as easy in New York as it had been to crack international society during his recent travels abroad.

For the past five years Harry had been tearing through Europe, ostensibly pursuing the education interrupted after his expulsion from Harvard for "immoral practices." Instead, he had taken the opportunity to insinuate himself into the world of the wandering rich—the high-living American expatriates and Old World blue bloods whose lives looked to Harry like a perpetual moveable feast. Members of the European smart set, unaware of the bizarre behavior that had people back home calling him "Mad Harry" behind his back, had seen only a rich young American who dressed impeccably and spent lavishly.

"I am Harry K. Thaw of Pittsburgh," he would announce to each new acquaintance, as though Pittsburgh were the Celestial Kingdom and he the heir to the throne.

With eligible bachelors always in high demand, they had included him in their endless dinners, their elaborate excursions and manor-house weekends. He had reciprocated by hosting lavish dinners for them in the best European hotels, later filling his diary with details of his pointless extravagance and the names of his social conquests—the Philadelphia Phippses, the Duc and Duchesse d'Uzes ("so cheerful,"), and the lovely Lady Mary Montague. After a tête-à-tête with Lady Randolph Churchill, who is the daughter of Jerome's uncle Leonard and has become her father's match in amorous conquests, he wrote that, despite being in mourning, she had been "charming."

At one dinner in Paris, his guests had included social celebrities like Mrs. Potter Palmer of Chicago, the uber-aristocrat Vicomte Charles de la Rochefoucauld, and the fabulously rich Lord Lonsdale, notorious for devoting his wealth to a life of ostentatious pleasure. John Philip Sousa's band had played for the party, offering rousing renditions of "The William Tell Overture" and Liszt's Second Rhapsody, which, wrote Thaw, "lifted the roof off, as it were." There were also rumors of less decorous revels, perhaps the most sensational a "Beauty Dinner," also in Paris, for a bevy of "the more exclusive demimondaines of the city." Each guest had reportedly found a thousands dollars' worth of jewelry wrapped in her napkin, a party favor from the host, the only man present.

At first Harry's social aspirations in New York seem destined to triumph over the rumors from across the Atlantic. He boasts of attending dinners "with all the better people" and seems to be riding high. It is generally accepted that the rich are fair game for gossip and that much of it is nothing but vented resentment or, worse, attempted blackmail. Tales of Harry's questionable escapades are not taken too seriously until he subverts his own cause by treating them as amusing table conversation. Guests are aghast at one gathering when he regales them with a cheery account of the day he crashed his car into a shop window to punish an impudent salesperson. The damages were paid, so what was the problem?

Tales of even more troubling behavior begin to gain credibility. Hushed up but leaked is an incident when Harry viciously flogged a young hotel employee, then literally rubbed salt in his wounds. Another story making the rounds involves his fondness for a West Side brothel where the madam obligingly provides girls for Harry to whip. His perversities are no secret in the carnal bazaars of the Tenderloin, where the reigning madams have been quick to peg Harry as one of those "Pittsburgh Queers."

Society's portals soon begin to slam shut. He is turned down by the Metropolitan, Century, Knickerbocker and Players Club. His attempt to ride a horse into the Union Club after being turned down for membership is a scandal so public as to test even the resourceful Mary Copley Thaw's abilities to erase it from history. The Whist Club is one of the only men's clubs where Harry is allowed entrance.

Far from blaming his own behavior for his humiliations, Harry, who has taken to heart his mother's unwavering belief in the entitlements owed to members of the Thaw clan, easily deludes himself. He is convinced that he is being blackballed and maligned by certain influential "old money" members whose transgressions are overlooked while his are exaggerated. And the one he holds most responsible is Stanford White, whose celebrity and success in living the fast life in New York he most envies and resents. White, who parties with showgirls, hobnobs with high society and refuses himself nothing he fancies, seems to have everything Harry craves and has been raised to expect as the idol of Mother Thaw's heart.

The germ of Harry's obsessive hatred of White had predated his obsession with Evelyn, planted one evening not long after his arrival in New York when he made the mistake of snubbing someone he shouldn't have. He had persuaded Frances Belmont, a member of the Floradora Sextette, to round up some of her female theater friends for a party, promising to invite some well-heeled men. Then, on the night before the planned festivities, Thaw had failed to return Frances's greeting at Sherry's restaurant, not wishing to acknowledge his acquaintance with a demimondaine while in the company of society friends. Furious at the snub, Frances had organized her revenge. Instead of attending Thaw's party, she had shepherded her friends to White's Tower Studio for an evening of spiteful merriment, leaving Thaw in the lurch. An item in *Town Topics*—"*Florodora* beauties sing for their supper in White's Studio while Thaw orchestra fiddles to an empty room at Sherry's"—had broadcast his humiliation, enraging Thaw, who blamed White for sabotaging his party. After that, Thaw would hold the man he referred to as "the beast" responsible for just about everything that would go wrong in his life. It would become a lifelong fixation.

Meanwhile, his plan to steal Evelyn from White is entering a new phase. On a day in late December 1901, when the city is sparkling in full holiday regalia, Evelyn agrees to accompany a friend who has been after her to have tea at Rector's. Since the restaurant, a favorite haunt of the theatrical crowd and the so-called midnight supper society, is apt to be empty at teatime, Evelyn has been reluctant and, indeed, the place is almost deserted when the two women arrive. No sooner are they seated than, to Evelyn's surprise, a tall, well-dressed man with an odd, mirthless grin approaches their table and asks to join them. She is even more surprised to learn that he is the man who has been bombarding her with letters and flowers for almost a year, the phantom Mr. Munroe who is, in fact, the notorious playboy from Pittsburgh, Harry K. Thaw.

This first encounter is not pleasant. Thaw's eccentric manner, rapid speech and oyster eyes unnerve Evelyn. Annoyed at her friend's subterfuge in arranging the meeting, she rises to leave but Thaw refuses to take her offered hand. He demands to know why her mother permits her to see Stanford White, "the beast" who blackballed him at the Knickerbocker Club. Repelled, she leaves the meeting convinced that the backstage gossip of Thaw's unsavory habits is probably true. Years later, describing her unease when confronted for the first time by Thaw, she will remember sensing "some indefinable quality about his whole personality that frightened and repulsed me."

When she tells Stanny about her encounter with Mr. Munroe, alias Harry K. Thaw, he reacts with alarm. Harry Thaw is well known along both Fifth Avenue and Broadway, he warns, and she should keep away from him. "He's a bounder, and worse!"

Evelyn is happy to comply and Thaw recedes, temporarily, back into the shadows, though the notes and gifts never cease. Other men, too, continue to shower her with flowers and jewelry, but all are turned down. "I loved Stanford White," she later recalled. "I wanted only to be with him." In the first flush of their affair, they are seldom apart, thrilled with each other and with the sparkling city festooned for the holidays.

Stanny will naturally be spending Christmas day with his family but on Christmas Eve, which also happens to be Evelyn's birthday, the lovers celebrate together in his Tower Studio, a fairyland made even more festive by a profusion of hothouse flowers. Filling the rose-tinted room with their heady scent are American Beauty roses, long-stemmed calla lilies, gardenias, orchids, hydrangeas and, saluting the season, potted holly bushes. On each blossom White has sprinkled a dusting of confectioner's sugar to simulate snow, creating the surreal impression of a winter wonderland in a perfumed tropical paradise. Seating Evelyn on one of the "gorgeous divans" that had caught her eye on her first visit to the Tower, he tells her to close her eyes, then draws from behind his back an oversized red velvet stocking. Too excited to play the adult, she grabs it and empties its contents: a large pearl on a platinum chain, a set of white fox furs, a ruby and diamond ring, and two diamond solitaire rings. A week later, on New Year's Eve, Evelyn is delighted to be among the dazzling guests at White's annual year-end party at the Tower and to know that the host, so universally adored, adores *her*.

1902

9

INTO THE FRAY

[DA Jerome] was the perfect chief, wholly democratic and
with no air of superiority, who counseled with his young men and stood behind
them in all their mistakes, taking the blame himself.
—Staff member Augustin Derby

On January 1, 1902, Jerome moves into the district attorney's office in the Criminal Courts Building on Centre Street, judged "one of the gloomiest structures in the world" by Arthur Train, who has joined Jerome's staff as an assistant DA. An anachronism at its completion in 1894, it was lambasted by the *Architectural Record* as "ugly and vulgar," an exercise in "architectural bombast" and "upon the whole, quite the most discreditable edifice the city has ever erected."

The first thing Jerome does is to sweep the office clean of its years of accumulated dust, clutter, and stale odors, and make of it the big, airy command center he needs to direct the largest criminal law practice in the world with roughly 13,000 cases a year, some thirty lawyers and an executive staff of one hundred. The transformed office, as described in the *Meriden Morning Record*, is "simplicity itself." The *Record*'s James Bentley goes on to provide a "complete inventory" of its contents: "a flowered green carpet, a commodious desk in the middle of the floor, a large safe, a bottle of filtered water in a corner, a newspaper rack, and on the walls the photographs of half a dozen of his predecessors."

From Tammany's hacks Jerome has inherited a morass of neglected cases and work left undone by a staff of indolent Tammany in-laws and cousins. Having anticipated the worst, Jerome has used the weeks between his election and his swearing-in to prepare. Among his first hires—this one at his own expense—is a spy to infiltrate the gambling dens and gather evidence against them. The man, recommended as a New Yorker who "knows his way around," is one of the city's vast army of professional spies who thrive by doing the investigative work the police have refused to do, or actively thwarted. Jerome mentions the name of his spy to no one, and never personally meets with him.

He also has contacted many of the young acolytes who had supported his campaign for DA or served with him on reformist committees as eager volunteers—many straight out of law school. From their ranks he has assembled a cadre of fiercely loyal, fire-eating assistants who worship him, to replace Tammany's lethargic seat-warmers. Encouraged by Jerome, who enjoys nothing more than joking, drinking and debating with them in boisterous bull sessions, the band of bright young men quickly banishes all traces of the former regime's crumbling bureaucracy. Gone is the atmosphere of futility and lassitude, replaced by a new sense of purpose and collegiality.

There are more than a few future luminaries of the New York bar among the newly minted assistants but perhaps the most brilliant is Isidor Jacob Kresel, who speaks Yiddish, Russian, German, Polish, French, and Italian and is soon known as Jerome's designated "digger-in-chief." One of his admirers later described how, confronted with "twelve bushels of confusing documents," Kresel would "tunnel into corporate mysteries for all the world like a miner with a lamp in his hat and come out with an action ready for trial—conviction guaranteed." The scientific method he introduces, examining records of every kind—bank accounts, income tax returns, brokerage accounts, leases, mortgages, and more—revolutionizes investigative procedures. Among Kresel's first such exhaustive probes is an examination of Charlie Morse's records, which, alas, yield no actionable evidence.

A Jew who was raised on the Lower East Side by his widowed mother, Kresel has no social status whatsoever and is physically so unprepossessing that an office joke claims he can "run under a table wearing a high hat." He is an exception among colleagues who, like Arthur Train, are mostly impeccably Anglo-Saxon and socially prominent. Train, a well-bred Bostonian, is the one closest to Jerome, though his Brahmin diffidence sometimes makes him uncomfortable with Jerome's New York exuberance. Not yet the well-known writer he will become, Train is fascinated by the complexity of his friend's character, full of admiration for his integrity but perhaps more conscious of Jerome's flaws than his colleagues are.

Alfred Hodder, in his book about Jerome's 1901 campaign, reveals a similar fascination with Jerome's impolitic attacks on power, but takes a more admiring view of his fighting spirit. "A Fight for the City" is Hodder's tribute to his subject's courage as a truth-teller, a man of the new age "trained to science rather than to eloquence, preoccupied with facts rather than words..."

At a banquet on January 12, intended to bring everyone together after the hard-fought campaign, Jerome wastes no time in shattering the mood, sparing no one, not even his own backers. He vows not to get "too friendly" with the reform administration. "I might have to indict some of them," he tells his stunned audience.

One of Jerome's early acts as DA is to open a branch office at 8 Rutgers Street in the teeming Lower East Side. He announces that it will be open every night, and that no matter how late the hour, any person seeking justice need only ring the bell. It takes some time for the poor with complaints to overcome their suspicions, but after the first few arrive with grievances and actually have them looked into, as many as forty a night ring the bell. The force on "ghetto duty," as Jerome's irreverent assistants call it, is doubled, then tripled. One complainant, recalled by Hodder, is a seamstress earning fifty cents a day who finds Jerome himself on duty when she rings the bell. She pleads with him to rescue her fifteen-year-old daughter from a house of prostitution and when he refuses the ten-dollar bill she offers in payment, she flees in despair, convinced that his refusal means he won't act. Before the night is over, however, detectives are able to locate the missing girl, and mother and daughter are tearfully reunited.

The all-night office is a novel approach for a district attorney, far in excess of his actual duty. Even more surprising is Jerome's decision to provide a residence for himself and his family in the same tenement. The Jeromes are well off and the neighborhood is not one to attract anyone who can live elsewhere. Surely it comes as no surprise to Jerome that his wife prefers the more congenial surroundings of their city home or the rural pleasures of their country place at Lakeville. There could have been no expectation that she would subject herself and their son to life in a tenement home in the center of her husband's hated political activities. Her anticipated refusal to join him there has the benefit of freeing him from his increasingly intolerable domestic situation. Though he will miss the regular contact with his son, William Jr., of whom he is as fond as any father could be, at least he will be spared having to witness his wife's constant coddling of the boy, all too reminiscent of the suffocating treatment his mother inflicted on him. To his horror, his wife has nicknamed their son "Chinky-Dinky," a name that, unfortunately, sticks.

Perhaps he could have put up with Lavinia's strong distaste for society and politics, her deplorable housekeeping, and joyless temperament, but the presence of her two brothers as permanent guests in their home is a strain requiring more forbearance than Jerome has in reserve. The brothers, Gus and Nick Howe, had lived with their mother until she died, leaving them helpless and needy. Charming but hapless, neither has ever been able or willing to make a living. Nick was educated as an architect but the Lakeville house, his only attempt to work at his profession, is considered an architectural catastrophe by Jerome, who prefers to occupy his workshop on the grounds when he is in Lakeville. Gus is without any practical resources at all and both brothers, cared for by their mother for most of their lives, now rely on their sister to take up the task, and on her absentee husband to pay the bills.

Within a few months Jerome and his crew of dedicated assistants are able to make spectacular progress in ridding the city of its gambling houses and vice dens. The two thirds of the population who live in the tenements worship him but he is losing ground among the remaining third with his attacks on enemies and allies alike. He blasts the venal press, the corrupt judiciary, "the criminal rich," and the complacent elite. The newspapers, which loved him in his guise as anticorruption crusader conducting spectacular raids on gambling dens, are more critical now that he is in office. Detractors in the Republican press, stung by his lack of respect and eager to hold him to his campaign promises, are needling him to do something about Dick Canfield's elegant uptown gambling establishment, supposedly shut on the eve of Jerome's swearing-in but which many believe is continuing to operate in secret. Even some of the reform-minded newspapers are on the case, scandalized by the profligacy of Canfield's clientele. (There are rumors that Reginald Claypoole Vanderbilt once dropped $70,000 in one evening at Canfield's.) The doors at 5 East 44th Street have slammed shut but no one can believe that Canfield has not found a way to keep his high-rollers happy, conducting business as usual somewhere inside the immense establishment that the *Times* has described as "the most magnificent gambling house in the United States."

Jerome's failure to deliver swiftly on his campaign promise to pursue higher-ups in the corporate world is also causing him problems among disillusioned union activists. At a labor meeting in September 1902 he is denounced as "a tool of capitalism" after counseling patience to union members enraged by organized capitalism's treatment of striking coal miners in Pennsylvania. Tempers also flare when "Big Bill" Devery's name is mentioned at the meeting, prompting boos and foot-stomping. But cheers erupt when someone in the hall shouts out that Devery "may murder the King's English" but it is William Travers Jerome who "has stabbed the working man in the back." Sir Galahad's armor sustains a fresh crack.

10

PASSIONATE PLAYMATES

As the weeks passed, I couldn't help but marvel
at the strange effect I had upon him . . .
—EVELYN NESBIT

Just weeks into her affair with Stanny, Evelyn had begun to notice a shift in their relationship. What had begun as the capitulation of a confused and sexually inexperienced sixteen-year-old to the ardor of one of the most powerful men in New York has a new dynamic. Stanny remains her benefactor, helping with her career, supporting her family, and filling her life with fun and fantasy. But lately she has come to realize that he does not hold all the power, and that when they are together, she is the master of his emotions.

"Whether at his office or in the intimacy of his rooms, always when he first put his arms around me—or only touched me—he would start trembling. I was the type he adored and fell slave to," she reflected years later.

In this, the period of their most passionate intimacy, White is as much playmate as mentor, and Evelyn's uninhibited sensuality is beginning to rival his own. Though resentful at times of having to hide her role in White's life— they can never be seen together in public, he can never pick her up at the theater or dine with her in a restaurant—she is not immune to the thrill of the forbidden. Stanny's view that "darker chocolate is much richer and sweeter than the milk variety" has made an impression.

They meet as frequently as possible, sometimes at the Tower Studio, sometimes on 24th Street, where White loves to push Evelyn "stark naked on the
red swing." One day she arrives to find him in particularly high spirits, wearing
a toga. He perches her on his shoulders after she has thrown off her clothes,
and they march around the splendid red room, singing at the top of their
lungs, drinking champagne, devouring grapes and laughing until they collapse. There seems to be little distinction in White's mind between the pleasures of play and those of the flesh. For him, neither is a moral matter, and
Evelyn finds his delight in both irresistible. After a party at the Tower, Evelyn
often lingers for more drinks with Stanny. Sometimes there is a drunken trip
to the top of the tower to admire the city spread out before them. At other
times White goes to work at his drawing table while Evelyn curls up nearby for
the night, her absence from the Wellington apparently unremarked by Mrs.
Nesbit, who has all but delivered her daughter to White.

When the popular *Florodora* ends its run in January, producer George
Lederer swoops in with a starring role for Evelyn in a musical he has named
The Wild Rose because, he says, she reminds him of a wild gypsy rose. He pays
for her singing lessons and is so obviously besotted that his wife names Evelyn
when she sues for divorce. Like so many others, Lederer proposes marriage
and is turned down. She is in love with Stanny, or at least in love with the life
she has with him. As his lover, she is discovering the joys of the bohemian life
with all its uninhibited pleasures. At his parties, she basks in the reflected glow
of his celebrity and in the notion that, unbeknownst to the world, he belongs
to her, though at times his attentions to other women shake her confidence
and allow jealousy to creep in.

It is at one of those parties, early in the summer of 1902, that Evelyn
is introduced to a man who is no celebrity but who has the extraordinary
advantage of youth and spectacular good looks in a gathering where most
of the men are at least twice his age. At twenty-two, John Barrymore, known
as Jack, is gauntly handsome and darkly seductive. The younger brother of
celebrated actors Ethel and Lionel Barrymore, Jack is determined to stay
out of the family business and off the stage. Working as a sketch artist for the

Morning Telegraph and leading the dissolute life for which Park Row journalists are notorious, he is a heavy drinker, perpetually rumpled ,and indifferent to comfort. His meager income from a job at the margins of respectability is enough to pay his bar tab, while his chiseled profile guarantees plenty of female companionship. Even Stanny's "Kittens" cannot keep her eyes off him as supper is being served, nor can he resist throwing admiring glances her way.

As he makes the rounds of his guests, White may be unaware of the sparks flying between his protégée and her newest admirer, or he may be unwilling to acknowledge them. To Evelyn's chagrin, he has always seemed impervious to jealousy. At a moment during the party when White is called to the phone, Barrymore sees his opportunity and, leaning in closely, he whispers to Evelyn, "Quick! Your address and telephone number." With characteristic carelessness, he writes the number on his frayed shirt cuff, and that night he sends her a bouquet of violets with a sentimental card.

The Wild Rose is an immediate hit when it opens at New York's Knickerbocker Theater, and images and articles focusing on Evelyn and her success on Broadway are everywhere, increasing the number of White's rivals. Yet he maintains his apparent lack of concern. The rich old capitalists with their gifts of diamonds and their marriage proposals do not worry him. He knows Evelyn to be too intelligent, too impressed by "the artist's immense and complex soul," as she once put it, to settle for an ugly, boring old man with only money to offer. But eligible young men do worry him.

As the summer wears on and their passion loses a bit of its initial heat, Evelyn is increasingly annoyed by White's continued friendships with other women, and particularly by his practice of sending extravagant bouquets for their birthdays. He is amused by her pique but is not so amused when she accepts dinner invitations with one or another of her young admirers. Jealousy is the new strain in their relationship, though White is careful to hide his from Evelyn. Suspecting that her contact with the young men known around town as the Racquet Club Boys might be particularly irksome to White, Evelyn encourages their attentions and lets it be known how "young and gay and full of fun" they are. Several are in love with her, including Bobby Collier, son of the publisher of *Collier's Weekly*, of whom she is particularly fond.

One night, in a private room at Rector's, the Racquet Club Boys throw a party at which she is the only guest. They crown her as their princess, and in a game they devise for the occasion, they block her vision as, one after another, they feed her oysters while describing their love for her. In turn, she must guess who is feeding her. When they vie for the privilege of escorting her home, she chooses the love-smitten Bobby Collier. Collier proposes, and, convinced that she has real talent for drawing, he offers to send her to art school in Paris. When she gently refuses, he tells her that the offer stands and that whenever she wants to go to Europe he will send her. As an effort to make Stanny jealous, the ploy apparently fails and the birthday bouquets continue. It will take a more serious dalliance to get a rise out of Stanny, with risks that Evelyn is perhaps too ready to take.

11

"THE KING OF GAMBLERS"

It was a night of tremendous excitement in the Bohemian life of the city, and the police themselves have seldom seen anything like it.
—The *New York Times*

Richard Canfield, the "King of Gamblers," is a short, pudgy man with the fat, florid face of a heavy drinker, and the cold eyes of a ruthless enforcer. The sworn enemy of William Travers Jerome, whom he detests, he had shuttered his magnificent gambling emporium at 5 West 44th Street the night before Jerome took office and spread the word that he was leaving town.

The press, doubtful that Canfield's clientele—some of the richest and most influential men in the country—has been abandoned, isn't buying it. Sniffing suspicious activity behind the closed doors, the newspapers have been relentlessly needling Jerome to deliver on his campaign promises and shut down Canfield's spectacularly profitable criminal enterprise. The New York *World*, a Democratic paper proud of its crusading spirit, joins the attack, publishing a photograph of Jerome catnapping at his desk. Here is the evidence, crows the *World*, that Jerome sleeps while criminals roam free.

Nothing would please Jerome more than the chance to put a permanent padlock on Canfield's door and end the constant editorial nagging, but, to his enormous frustration, the legislative tools to authorize a move against private property used for gambling are nearly nonexistent. Without a mole capable of passing himself off as a high-roller and collecting evidence on the inside, Jerome sees no opening into staging a coup. Ironically, his late uncle, the high-flying Leonard Jerome, whose politico-financial alliances had included Commodore Vanderbilt and Tammany's Boss Tweed, had been one of Canfield's favorite drinking companions, always welcome at the elegant brownstone conveniently located next door to Delmonico's, high society's favorite restaurant.

Until his death in 1891, Leonard Jerome had passed unchallenged countless times through the heavy bronze doors and proceeded directly to Dick Canfied's top-floor private apartment, bypassing the lush gaming rooms and the extravagantly decorated parlor with its white mahogany paneling, antique furnishings, Chinese porcelains, and paintings by Canfield's close friend, James McNeill Whistler. There the bibulous but cultivated Canfield and the connoisseur of food, wine, fast horses, and lovely women would often drink into the night, reflecting upon life's great questions and the pleasures of a life surrounded by beauty and steeped in culture. On one such evening Canfield had confessed to his friend that his taste for literature had been acquired during a six-month jail term, the result of a raid on his first gambling house in Providence, Rhode Island. After his release from prison he had risen rapidly to his status as gambling-world royalty, operating unhampered by scruples as he freely admits. To reporters he boasts that he has "no more morals than a cat."

In late November, after almost a year in office without anything to show for his efforts to move against Canfield, "the best known gambling resort proprietor in this country," as the press is fond of reminding readers, Jerome finally gets the break he has been waiting for. He receives information from a man who claims to have obtained entry to Canfield's. The informer says he lost money at the tables and when he volunteers to sign an affidavit to that effect, Jerome immediately accepts. Armed with the affidavit, he obtains a warrant to enter Canfield's and search the premises. Had he been under less pressure, Jerome might have found it strange that this heaven-sent source, a $25-a-week detective named Joseph Jacobs, had pulled off an evening with the high-stakes players at Canfield's. But he is already tasting sweet victory over his tormentors in the press and throws himself into preparations for a raid so secret that even the local precinct police captain is unaware of his intentions.

On the evening of December 1, Jerome is among the festive guests gathered in the ballroom at Delmonico's, which is hosting the annual dinner of the St. Andrew's Society. Seated next to him is Deputy Police Commissioner Piper, and both are awaiting a signal that the raiding party has arrived at Canfield's. At a little before 11:00, as they chat distractedly and check their watches, a ramshackle wagon is making its way up Fifth Avenue. When it stops at the corner of Fifth Avenue and 44th Street, prompting sneers from coachmen in the showy carriages lined up in front of Delmonico's next door, Jerome and Piper get the word and rush out into the cold, starry night.

"Alright," Jerome orders, "let's go!"

At the signal, a score of detectives, investigators and assistant district attorneys pour out of the wagon and head for Number 5 East 44th Street, followed by a scrum of reporters and photographers. Though others, including policemen of the local precinct, have been left in the dark, the press apparently has not.

A reporter for the *Times* watches with wonder as one of the men positions a ladder against a high window, having wisely decided against attempting to breach the huge bronze doors. Using an ax, he smashes the window "into a thousand pieces," causing "wild excitement" among the coachmen, who are no longer sneering. The commotion brings Delmonico's patrons streaming out into the street in evening dress "to witness some of the excitement" and they are soon joined by a huge crowd of gawkers.

Relishing the moment, DA Jerome climbs the ladder with his assistants and enters the gorgeous parlor through the shattered window, but though the room is brilliantly illuminated, there is not a soul to be seen. With the press following close behind, Jerome and his crew climb the baronial staircase to be greeted at the top by Canfield, his manager David Bucklin, and his lawyer John Delahunty in full evening dress. Suave and unruffled, Canfield welcomes the party but laments the trouble they have given themselves when he would have been happy to admit them "at the reception door." Assuring them that "there is nothing here that is needing your attention," he graciously offers them "the freedom of the house."

Jerome explores every closet and drawer on the second and third floors finding nothing of interest, but a locked closet on the fourth floor arouses suspicion and he demands that Canfield unlock it. When there is no response to his order, Jerome repeats it. At this point Canfield drops his mask of amiability and hotly refuses.

"It's an outrage upon a man's private property," he protests, and Jerome knows he is on to something. His men smash the door, and there it is: gambling paraphernalia of every sort, including three roulette wheels, five poker tables, and hundreds of chips. Jerome orders three more wagons to carry away the confiscated equipment while Canfield, who has regained his composure, calmly identifies the contents of the closet as "merely some property from my country place in Rhode Island," adding, "it doesn't belong here at all."

David Bucklin, very loyal and very unlucky, is arrested after being identified by Joseph Jacobs as the dealer who had taken his money. When confronted by Canfield, however, Jacobs stoutly insists that he cannot identify him as having been a dealer "at any of the times I have played in this house."

The December 2 edition of the *Times* covers the raid in detail, devoting much of the article to breathless descriptions of the magnificently decorated rooms heretofore seen only by a very few of the very rich and a subject of intense curiosity among the excluded public. The article also states with some certainty that the raid had been anticipated, an obvious conclusion given the presence of Canfield's lawyer and the absence of anyone else except for the unfortunate Bucklin. So, once again, the elaborate precautions taken to assure secrecy had been futile. Someone had tipped off the King. But who?

Jerome has little interest in pursuing the question now that he has his cache of confiscated equipment and Reggie Vanderbilt's IOUs in the amount of $300,000, which turned up in Canfield's safe. He is confident that he can make a case against Canfield by summoning witnesses known to have gambled at his place, and he is encouraged by a wave of praise from the press. A *Times* editorial congratulates him on his coup and declares that "powerful gamblers" will no longer be immune from prosecution "as long as D.A. Jerome is in office." An exuberant Jerome is effusive in his praise for Jacobs, "a wild and woolly Westerner with no social connections [who] did the job," and contempt for Canfield, who, like all gamblers, is willing "to take every cent a man has got, no matter what his station."

Reporters, back at Jerome's heels, are delighted in the days following the raid by the verbal sparring between the urbane Canfield and the cerebral DA, who quote poetry at each other. Jerome announces that private hearings will be held before a judge, at which such Wall Street grandees as Harry Payne Whitney and Mortimer Schiff will be invited to recall details of their alleged sessions at Canfield's. When an outraged Canfield files complaints against Jerome and other leaders of the raid, charging them with illegal entry, Jerome derides the move as the "intolerable cheek" of a felon and quotes Tennyson's line on "men of long enduring hopes" caring little for the actions of "little would-be popes." Canfield counters with an equally erudite defense of his complaint, citing a citizen's rights regarding the sanctity of his home and quoting John Greenleaf Whittier to the effect that he would shun no "pang beneath the sun" where "human rights are staked and won." When Jerome summons Canfield's alleged Wall Street patrons and they refuse to answer his questions, it is the beginning of a legal contest that the undaunted DA is sure he can win. And when a friend of Canfield's claims that Jerome's star witness, Joseph Jacobs, has never set foot in the famous house next to Delmonico's, Jerome lashes out and denounces Canfield's friend as a liar, a crook and a hothead—a hotheaded response in itself, and one he will have reason to regret.

12

ERRANT EVELYN

. . . the Bohemian Barrymore paid swift and
tempestuous court to the Broadway Beauty.
—TOWN TOPICS

White's hectic schedule seems to leave less and less time for Evelyn and she is becoming uneasy. Frustrated by his continued gallantry toward other women, puzzled by his loyalty to his wife, and disappointed when he seems to take her own flirtations in stride, she hopes, and sometimes still believes, that she is the one he prizes above all. But there are moments when she suspects she is just one among many and fears for her future.

Union Club cabs, once dispatched regularly by White to pick her up at the theater and bring her to him, arrive less frequently now and it is sometimes a long wait between trysts. She takes some comfort from the flowers and gifts he still sends every day, unaware that they are extravagances he can ill afford. After the huge market losses of 1901, White is so deeply in debt that he has had to borrow heavily from friends, take on more work than he can handle, and is gambling on increasingly desperate financial maneuvers, hoping to keep his creditors at bay. Yet he continues to live like a millionaire—on credit—and only his partners at the firm and the intimate friends who lend him money are aware of how close he is to financial ruin.

While he presents a convincing facade to clients and acquaintances, the stress of his precarious finances and his struggle to juggle family, work, a frenzied social life and a demanding affair are affecting his health and his morale. Back in February, Charles McKim had expressed alarm to see his partner so "terribly nervous and run down." A doctor had agreed with McKim, and, on his orders, White had taken a trip to Florida and the Bahamas, returning refreshed. Come summer, White is eager to escape again, this time to Quebec, where the Restigouche Salmon Club, a rough-it-in-comfort retreat for millionaire sportsmen, is the one place on earth where he is able to truly relax. As his partner William Mead once observed, the annual fishing trips have always been something White "looked forward to and out of which he took the greatest pleasure of his life."

Traveling leisurely upriver aboard one of the club's rustic but luxuriously outfitted houseboats, far from the chaos of his life in New York, White can put his problems aside. He and the other well-heeled fishermen enjoy every amenity as farm horses tow them through shallow water, pausing along the way to allow them to fish where guides know they will succeed. In the evening, thirsty after a day of fighting the salmon, White joins the others for drinks in the lounge while a cook prepares their evening meal. An open-air larder, stocked with caged chickens, tethered lambs, and sometimes even a cow for fresh milk, provides everything necessary to satisfy lusty appetites whetted by alcohol and the great outdoors. Cabins one member pronounces "more comfortable than home" are an invitation to untroubled sleep.

While he is engaged in his favorite pastime, White is blissfully unaware that Evelyn is embarking on a passionate affair with the rakish Jack Barrymore. No more than twenty-four hours after White's departure for Restigouche, Jack had consulted the shirt cuff where he had scrawled Evelyn's number and called to ask her to join him at Rector's after the theater. By then he had seen Evelyn in *The Wild Rose* more than a dozen times and had been dreaming of her ever since their Tower encounter. He had been stunned then by her beauty and encouraged by the hint of recklessness he thought he saw in her eyes. She in turn had been struck by his "Byronesque" beauty and careless

charm. Intrigued, and perhaps hoping to crack White's apparent complacency, she had accepted his invitation.

That night at Rector's, thoughts of making White jealous quickly recede
as Evelyn finds herself irresistibly drawn to the charismatic Jack and thrilled
to be romantically courted. He wastes no time in sweeping her off her feet
with his wit and romantic ardor. For the two weeks that White is away, he
arrives at the stage door every night with a bouquet of violets and their evenings are spent sharing stories and jokes over supper at one or another of the
city's fashionable restaurants. More expensive than violets, painting the town
with his "Evie" is causing Jack's tabs to soar, which is alarming proprietors
at all the best places. One evening, when the owner of the Algonquin raises
the issue with Jack, he is treated to a preview of Barrymore's innate talent
for histrionics. Flushed with feigned indignation, Jack leaps to his feet and,
assuming the role of an arrogant aristocrat outraged by an "inferior's" effron-
tery, throws down his napkin and roars, "By God, we'll go to a restaurant that
doesn't insult its guests!"

For Evelyn, it is a giddy pleasure to be out on the town with Jack. Caught
up in the romance of the moment, she cares little for how their revels are
funded or that they are on public display, laughing and nuzzling like any other
couple in love, an indulgence never permitted with Stanny. To the normal
caution of a married man entangled in an affair is added, in White's case,
an obsessive fear of public exposure dating back to those deeply distressing
weeks in the aftermath of the *World*'s scathing expose of his Pie Girl stagfest.
He cannot afford to risk putting his delicately balanced and scrupulously protected public profile once more at risk.

By contrast, Evelyn and Jack make no effort to hide their whirlwind
romance from the press and gossip columnists can't get enough of "Evie and
Jack." The *Herald* reports on blissful afternoons when they "drive or walk
through the Park." The *Morning Telegraph* hails Evelyn as a "wild Pittsburgh
rose" who has moved her swain "to dreadful poetic heights." Still another
columnist compares the lovesick couple to "two happy children" with eyes
only for each other. Evelyn hardly minds when she is teased by her backstage

friends, who are particularly amused by reports that at Rector's the ardent Jack had ordered a glass of milk, floated two rose petals on the surface, and passionately declared, "Those are your lips."

White, having returned briefly to New York in July, leaves again for Resti-gouche on August 1, first instructing his florist to deliver white roses to Evelyn each morning during his absence and red roses at night. He is either unaware of Evelyn's affair with Barrymore or unconcerned, perhaps even relieved to think that she has become less emotionally dependent on him and will be content to trade her role as lover for that of an affectionate friend. It would certainly be less of a commitment for him, financially.

Eventually, even Mrs. Nesbit, who disapproves of gossip columns and pro-fesses never to read them, gets wind of her daughter's romantic idyll. Terri-fied by what it might mean for her daughter's future financial security, not to mention her own, she makes a scene, berating Jack as "a slick, penniless, hard-drinking ne'er do well" and demands that Evelyn stop seeing him. Evelyn, perhaps suspecting that her mother is more interested in White's generous subsidies than in her daughter's happiness, is defiant, declaring that "if Jack wants to see me, to marry me even, then I want to be with him!"

Then, as Evelyn will tell the story in her 1934 memoir, she and Jack make a careless mistake and their romantic idyll comes to an end. After making a meal of breadsticks and cheese and drinking "gallons of red wine" at a cheap restaurant where the bill will not be a problem, the two become hopelessly drunk. Rather than face Mrs. Nesbit in their drunken state, Jack wraps Evelyn in a cape he tells her was once worn on the stage by his father, Maurice Bar-rymore, as Romeo, and they sleep it off in Jack's bedroom. Waking at 11:00 the next morning, Evelyn is panicked, dreading her mother's reaction. She has always been careful to return home before dawn and now she correctly predicts that the first person her furious mother will call is White, who is back in New York. And now, at last, White is jolted out of his complacency. Among other worries, he is desperately afraid that if Mrs. Nesbit pursues Barrymore for seducing Evelyn and makes a scandal, his own role in her young life will come to light.

Using all of his solicitous charm to calm her down, White assures Mrs. Nesbit that he will handle the crisis. Evelyn is grilled about just how far she has gone in her fling and, not surprisingly, is doubted when she insists that she has not slept with Jack. White takes her off to his physician, Dr. Nathaniel Potter, for a gynecological examination and she spends a miserable day being probed and questioned in his examining room. In the end, Dr. Potter has no choice but to confirm that she is no longer a virgin and probably confirms that she is pregnant. But, if so, the question of who is responsible remains.

Is Barrymore the father? Or is it Stanny? Evelyn, overpowered, and with no one but the reviled Barrymore to support her should she put up a fight to make her own choices, remains loyal to White throughout the ordeal. To White's immense relief, she reveals nothing of the truth of their affair, which he is desperate to keep hidden.

When he finally rescues her from the examining room, White drives her to his Tower studio and sends for Barrymore, intending to demand that he stay away from Evelyn. The confrontation takes a startling turn when Barrymore announces that he has already taken Evelyn to a doctor and that she is indeed pregnant. Having naturally concluded that Evelyn's pregnancy had been discovered and was the reason he had been summoned, Barrymore declares his honorable intentions.

"Will you marry me, Evie?" he asks.

When Evelyn appears ready to accept, White storms and rages in a fashion that can only delight Evelyn, who has tried countless times to elicit just such a reaction with no success. She turns down Jack's proposal, explaining later that she was still fixated on the possibility of a future with Stanny, still obsessed with "a fanciful notion that a man who loved a girl ought willingly to give up all others." But while she resigns herself to giving up Jack, the baby is another matter.

When hints of the drama involving the celebrity architect, the beauty, and the Barrymore scion filter out, the rumor mill goes into overdrive. Some are sure there will be an abortion. White is well connected with Dr. T. Gaillard Thomas, a client of McKim, Mead and White and the city's leading abortion specialist for New York's upper classes. The soul of discretion when the privacy of his socialite patients is at stake, Dr. Thomas could be counted on to do the deed and keep it a secret. Others take a more romantic view and believe that Evelyn will insist on keeping her love child, a scenario scoffed at by realists who point out that in a few months her pregnancy will be obvious, and then what?

Whether it is to hide her from view as her pregnancy progresses or to aid her recovery after an abortion, White arranges for Evelyn to enroll in a New Jersey boarding school in October. Getting her out of the city will also serve his purposes by removing Evelyn from Barrymore's orbit and it might even give him some respite from the worrisome rumors. While a brokenhearted Barrymore tries to drown his sorrows in drink, Harry K. Thaw, who has been waiting in the wings and is not so easily discouraged, sees an opening. He will begin by ingratiating himself with Evelyn's mother, counting on overcoming her loyalty to White by dropping a few hints of the "beast's" unwholesome taste for other young girls while pressing the case that Harry K. Thaw of Pittsburgh is the answer to a mother's prayers for a millionaire son-in-law.

1903

13

CHARLIE'S FOLLY

Who could accomplish that in which the law was powerless?—Hummel.
—ARTHUR TRAIN

Canfield is jubilant. A judge has ruled that the gambling gentry are under no legal obligation to answer Jerome's questions. Triumphant, he sails for England to sit for a portrait by his friend Whistler, who obliges with a brilliant portrayal of the pudgy ex-con, irreverently titled *His Reverence*. Jerome, commenting from across the Atlantic, is unimpressed. That Canfield has traveled "so far and at so great expense to have his portrait painted" is a shame, he asserts. Had he stayed home, "he might have had his picture taken at the expense of the public."

A mug shot, a trip up the river, and a striped suit are what Jerome has in mind for Canfield and as soon as "His Reverence" sets foot back on native soil Jerome has him arrested as a common gambler. The charge doesn't stick but Jerome, determined to fight on, takes the war to another front: if, for lack of a relevant law, a felon goes free, then there must be a new law to plug the loophole. He persuades state senator Victor Dowling to introduce a bill in Albany amending the criminal code to force the recalcitrant gamblers to talk. Predictably, the bill is fiercely opposed by its targets and their powerful friends, who count Canfield's among the entitlements of their rank and now must consider the possibility that they are felons.

Jerome is loudly denounced by Canfield's powerful habitues but he is vigorously defended by Dowling, who points out that no one attacked Jerome for his anti-gambling crusade until he "declined to consider 5 West 44th Street as an art museum" and raided the place. Then, suddenly, he "became obnoxious to the high society connections now opposing this bill." The debate rages on for weeks, and even after the bill eventually passes it is subject to months of delay while challenges wend their way through the courts.

While he awaits the outcome, Jerome turns his attention, once again, to master swindler Charlie Morse. Already reviled for his scheme to take in staggering profits by raising the price of ice to unaffordable heights, leaving thousands to endure a torrid summer of rotting food, tepid beer, and spoiled milk, Morse has been fighting off multiple lawsuits and terrible press, aided by the ubiquitous Abe Hummel.

At the same time, paradoxically richer and cockier than ever, Charlie is attempting to spend his way into the ranks of the Fifth Avenue swells. With an absurdly high opinion of himself, dating back to his coddled Maine childhood, he is reinventing himself to fit his new role, abandoning his rough Yankee ways and adopting a more uppity style. By living as large as his neighbors, he is confident that he can overcome their disdain, even as he continues to maneuver in the shadowy corners of the financial market where the unethical is not always criminal. Which is, he contends, no different from what the clubby Wall Streeters do. Jerome, who has been watching Morse buy up undercapitalized coastal steamboat lines, has no doubt that Charlie is up to his old tricks—issuing inflated stock and employing the same fraudulent methods to build a monopoly that he had used as the "Ice King." So he waits and watches, focusing on Morse's shady business practices when, in fact, it is Charlie's personal life that bears watching.

Back in June 1901, Jerome had been as amused as everyone else when Morse and his former landlady, Clemence Dodge, had celebrated their nuptials as elaborately as though he were the trust lord he aspired to be and she a dewy-eyed debutante. In fact, Charlie was a widower whose three children were being cared for by his sister in Maine, and Clemence, a divorcée, had ended her marriage to Charles Dodge three years earlier. No matter, in full bridal regalia she had swept down the aisle at the fashionable Fifth Avenue Presbyterian Church to join her proud groom, whose best man was Mayor Van Wyck.

Charlie had moved his bride into a handsome Fifth Avenue townhouse, for which he had paid a hefty $185,000, and the couple had begun acquiring the appropriate seigneurial trappings. When they entertained, their good friends William Gelshenen and his wife, Katherine, were usually on hand, and often Van Wyck, a lifelong bachelor known for his antics, would be there to enliven the party. Gelshenen, a banker and master of financial finagling, had taught Charlie a few of his tricks when Charlie was forming his ice company and in the years since they had become close friends and business collaborators.

Now, after less than two years of marriage and high-style living, Charlie suddenly realizes that his marriage was a huge mistake; Clemence is not, after all, the love of his life. With William Gelshenen's sudden death in March 1903, the flicker of amorous interest Charlie had felt in Katherine's presence had burst into flame. He is madly, passionately in love with Katherine and determined to marry her, despite his own marital status and her insistence as a strong Catholic that he must first obtain an annulment of his marriage to Clemence.

To perform this miracle, Charlie needs New York's wiliest lawyer, and, once again, Abe Hummel is his man. With scores of grateful bookmakers, counterfeiters, forgers, pickpockets, thieves, madams, and prostitutes to vouch for his genius in keeping them free, Hummel is the obvious choice to untie the marital knot and liberate Charlie. With a $15,000 retainer for inspiration, delivered by Morse's salty Down East uncle, Captain Jim Morse, Hummel comes up with an inspired idea to be funded by Charlie. They will offer Clemence's ex-husband, Charles Dodge, a degenerate drifter, a $5,000 bribe to perjure himself by swearing that back in 1898 he had never been served with divorce papers ending his marriage to Clemence. If the divorce is indeed invalid, then Clemence was already a married woman on the day she and Charlie were so conspicuously wed, and Charlie, single again, is free to marry the object of his newfound passion.

Morse and Hummel are well aware that the scheme could have legal repercussions and that DA Jerome—the one they must look out for—has long had them in his sights. Nothing would please Jerome more than to nail them both in one stroke, and while bribery and suborning perjury—civil offenses—could likely be settled with fines, conspiracy is a criminal charge that could put them both behind bars. Should Morse be revealed as the one funding what amounts to a loony conspiracy to circumvent the law in the name of love, their game would be up.

Jerome's spies have been watching Morse for any missteps and when Dodge takes the $5,000 bait and signs an affidavit swearing the divorce papers were never served on him, they give a grateful Jerome what he has been waiting for. He is being talked about for governor and if he can prosecute Dodge for perjury and move up the prosecutorial chain to snare Hummel for suborning perjury and Hummel's client, Morse, for conspiring to deceive the court, his political prospects will be greatly enhanced. City newsrooms are receiving tips—probably traceable to Jerome himself—that the DA might be onto something big, and reporters can hardly wait. They would be even more eager could they foresee the rich comedic material coming their way in a farcical soap opera that the press will refer to as "the Dodge-Morse Tangle" and play for laughs for nearly two years.

14

HEADING FOR TROUBLE

Mr. Thaw seemed absorbed in my welfare so far as my health
and happiness were concerned.
—EVELYN NESBIT

To her own surprise, Evelyn is not as miserable as she had feared once she settles in at the Pamlico School for Girls. Forced exile from "the light and glitter of Broadway" to New Jersey and the "peaceful dullness of a convent school" had seemed a "dismal prospect." She was to be one of just fifteen students in the school run by Mathilda DeMille (mother of the future film producer Cecil B. DeMille), whose mission was to make the school "just like home" for her girls. Evelyn, who was still just eighteen, and whose experience of home has not always been pleasant, was not enticed.

Then, on a crisp day in late October, as she had approached the large yellow building in the Ramapo Hills, where the trees were aflame with vibrant fall color, her resistance had weakened. Classes in music, literature, psychology and philosophy reawaken the love of learning that her father had recognized and encouraged, and when it leaks—despite White's precautions—that she has come to them from a career on the stage, she becomes "something of a heroine" to her classmates. Amused and pleased by their thrilled reaction at having "a real live actress transplanted into their midst," Evelyn helps them stage little plays and teaches them that tooth powder can substitute for face powder and rouge can be manufactured from various substances readily available even where makeup is strictly forbidden. She shares a room with a girl nicknamed Prunes in a small cottage across the road from the main building, dutifully dons the requisite schoolgirl uniform each morning and reports to her diary, with some amusement, that at night she sleeps in one of the room's "two virtuous white beds." Illustrating her entry with a sketch of a nun, she writes, "I suppose I will be a noble character before I get out of here."

In fact, by her own account, the months spent at the Pamlico School are among the happiest of her life. "What a sublimely happy time I spent at the school," she wrote years later. "Here indeed was my lost girlhood regained. I couldn't absorb enough…"

If a contraband magazine with her photo or some careless comment by a visitor had not revealed her identity, certainly the periodic appearance of reporters and photographers hoping for a picture of their favorite soubrette in her school uniform would have done so sooner or later. The press has not lost interest in the angel-faced beauty whose romantic entanglements and seductive poses have sold so many papers. One story in the *Philadelphia Enquirer* under the headline AMERICA'S PRETTIEST GIRL MODEL HAS EXCHANGED THE ROSE AND THE GAUZE DRAPERIES FOR THE STUDENT'S CAP AND GOWN asks, "What will be the future of this young woman whose face is the most perfect ever seen?" No stealth photographer surfaces with a picture of Evelyn that might suggest motherhood as the answer. Nor does any word of suspicious physical changes affecting the Pamlico School's most glamorous student filter out from her classmates. White's precautions aimed at keeping the pregnancy and its outcome a secret are apparently succeeding, though Evelyn's exile from the city has not diminished press interest in her and her entanglements as he had hoped.

White visits occasionally to check on his "ward," despite a back-breaking schedule of professional commitments. Among the most remunerative and demanding is a magnificent mansion for William Whitney's son Payne, which will take five years and many millions to complete. Jack Barrymore, still desperately in love, also makes the trip to New Jersey but is turned away and reduced to pinning tear-stained letters and poems to the trees. Nor has there been any letup in Thaw's assiduous pursuit. In the weeks following the Barrymore debacle, while Evelyn was waiting for school to open, Thaw had managed to insinuate himself into her good graces despite her initial unfavorable impression and the stern warnings to stay away from him from both her mother and Stanny.

On his best behavior with Evelyn during those weeks, Harry had convinced her that he had "a kind, sweet, generous and gentle side." That would have surprised the Tenderloin madam who would later sign an affidavit describing a very different Harry. In her sworn statement she characterized Harry as a sadistic pervert who was notorious in the Tenderloin for paying a premium to obtain underage girls and subjecting them to brutal whippings. *That* Harry, who used the alias Mr. Reid, was nowhere in evidence as the "gentle" Harry put his "finer qualities" on display for Evelyn, slyly exploiting her resentment against her mother and Stanny for treating her like a delinquent child. He had been a gushing fount of empathy and solicitude, and she had been receptive. Not only had his support made it easier to defy her mother, who seemed less concerned for her happiness than Harry, but perhaps there was some hope—however unlikely—that by letting Harry into her life, she could finally make Stanny jealous and rekindle their affair.

At some point during this interlude, when they seemed to be developing what Evelyn looked upon as a "genial friendship," Thaw had proposed marriage and she had declined. Dejected, Harry had left for a round of gambling and drinking in Monte Carlo and Cannes. Biding his time and plotting his next move, he has kept a steady stream of what he unabashedly calls "mush" notes crossing the ocean to his "boofuls."

When he returns to New York, Thaw has a plan. Taking the offensive, he persistently dangles the prospect of an extraordinarily rich son-in-law before Mrs. Nesbit, whose greatest fear is a return to the days when she depended on handouts from relatives. So grateful is she for the financial security White has provided for her and her family that she has banished any doubts about the appropriateness of his interest in her teenage daughter. But while Evelyn is perfecting her French and reading the classics, Harry, armed with his vast fortune and the information his spies have gathered on the "beast's" proclivities, is busy undermining Mrs. Nesbit's loyalty to White—and preparing to make her a better offer for Evelyn.

Then in April 1903, when Evelyn has been at school for almost seven months, Thaw's campaign gets a break. Mrs. Nesbit is suddenly informed that her daughter is "ill" with sharp abdominal pains and immediately calls White. When she fails to reach him she calls Harry, who leaps at the chance to accompany her to the school. When they arrive, they learn that Mrs. DeMille has managed to contact White, who has dispatched his friend Dr. Potter— the same who had examined Evelyn in New York—to take charge of the case. He diagnoses "acute appendicitis" and the school is evacuated while he performs an emergency operation in a classroom. Just before the ether takes effect, Evelyn looks up to see Mrs. DeMille, the doctor, and his aides standing around her, and Harry "on his knees beside the operating table," the image of unctuous solicitude, kissing her trembling hands.

Word of the operation gets out and again rumors fly, particularly among those who know of Evelyn's affair with White and her fling with Barrymore. White's swift move to see that his chosen doctor takes charge, the ad hoc operating theater, the missing father—all raise questions. Could it have been a belated abortion, perhaps precipitated by some complication? Was it a miscarriage, a premature birth, a stillbirth? Or was it, in fact, appendicitis? One thing is known: no birth is ever recorded.

With Mrs. Nesbit warming up to him—or so he believes—after their shared emotional moment, and Evelyn coming around, Harry senses victory. Nothing can drag him from the bedside of the ailing Evelyn, not even the spectacular wedding in Pittsburgh of his sister Alice to the foppish and impecunious Earl of Yarmouth, heir to the title of Marquess of Hertford. Even the usually indomitable Mother Thaw is powerless to pry him away to witness her triumph as Alice exchanges vows with a British aristocrat. Ever since the engagement was announced, the gossip mill has been grinding away, speculating on the price to be paid in this dollars-for-title exchange. With the country in the grip of a craze for forging marital ties with peers of the realm, such transactions involving marriageable heiresses have become so frequent that the *Times* periodically prints a list of the sums changing hands.

Negotiating for the deeply indebted Yarmouth, his solicitor had originally agreed to accept 200,000 pounds sterling as an appropriate dowry, according to the *Times* list. Then, on the morning of the wedding, while Harry remains defiantly at his "Angel-Child's" bedside, the groom is arrested in Pittsburgh on a writ from a London court for a debt of 300 pounds. To get him to the altar—forty-five minutes late—the deal must be renegotiated to cover the debt plus a few other pressing matters, and rumors circulate that the final price paid to the "Count de Money," as he is known in Pittsburgh, is over a million dollars.

Evelyn's operation, hastily performed in rather primitive conditions, begets complications. She is so weak and depleted that White arranges for her to be admitted to a private sanatorium in New York and even has a telephone installed in her room—a great novelty. Not to be outdone, Harry fills the room with flowers and gifts and hires the Waldorf's famous chef to cook and deliver whatever she craves. Both men visit, careful not to do so at the same time. Evelyn, still trying to make Stanny jealous, responds to Harry's overtures, hoping that White will take notice, but Stanny's reaction is not jealousy but a stern warning that Harry is dangerous company. While Harry's solicitude knows no bounds, White is caring but no longer shows any romantic interest in Evelyn.

Their affair has been the most passionate and long-lasting of any of White's many others, but even Evelyn could not hold his attention forever. White's closest friends had predicted that his infatuation would be over in a few weeks and were astonished when it lasted for months. They were familiar with how his affairs had almost always progressed—how the discovery of a new young beauty would fire him up, how he would win her over with his easy charm, surround her with beauty, and set an exquisite stage for seduction. Then for a while he would shower his new lover with gifts and tender attentions but before long complications would inevitably arise, cooling his passion and sending him back on the prowl.

It has taken longer with Evelyn but the time has come when her lively intelligence, her playfulness and her genuine appreciation of his creative work have not been enough to keep White from losing interest. Complications have, in fact, arisen. Evelyn has had jealous lapses, has entertained an illusory hope that White might abandon his wife, and the Barrymore episode has been a worrisome irritant in White's life. But in the end, for White, the affair has probably just run its course and it is time to move on.

Acknowledging, at last, that Stanny can never be hers in the way he once was, Evelyn is forced to contemplate a future without him. When Harry suggests a recuperative trip to Europe with Mrs. Nesbit as chaperone, she agrees and convinces her mother to come along, though Mrs. Nesbit remains reluctant to accept her daughter's change of allegiance from White to Thaw. Just before their party boards the SS *New York* in May, White appears at the pier and slips Evelyn a letter of credit for $500 in case of emergency, assuming—correctly—that she is headed for trouble.

15

THE DODGE-MORSE TANGLE

I was never served with a summons or complaint in the divorce action and
knew nothing about what was going on in reference to it . . .
—CHARLES DODGE

In the fall of 1903, Charles Dodge, a nondescript little man whose sole distinction is a gargantuan capacity for dissipation—particularly in the form of liquor, drugs, gambling, and women—is about to become the antihero of a long-running comic melodrama. Chased down in Atlanta in September by Abe Hummel's man Edward Bracken, Dodge is lured to New York to sign an affidavit swearing that divorce papers ending his marriage to Clemence were never served on him. A $5,000 bribe, the first of many Hummel will pay and Charlie Morse will fund before the "Dodge-Morse Tangle" unravels, has made it easy to convince Dodge that he misremembered receiving the papers making his divorce from Clemence official, that, in fact, he was unaware of the divorce until he read about it in the papers.

Everyone is happy, Dodge with his windfall, Hummel with his ingenious scheme and his hefty retainer, Morse with the miracle of the marriage that wasn't, and the chance to wed his true love, Katherine Gelshenen. Adopting a somber tone of lawyerly concern, Hummel advises his client Morse of the situation: "It is my duty to inform you that this decree is collusive and irregular, and it may be doubted that your marriage is a lawful one and whether Mr. Dodge could not set aside that decree and claim that your subsequent marriage to his wife was an alienation of her affection and that her action in becoming your wife entitles him to a decree of adultery against you."

Jerome, who has been waiting for Hummel to go too far and now has reason to hope that he will take Morse with him over the cliff, is also delighted. To expose their ludicrous conspiracy, he will bring Dodge before a grand jury and get him to testify that he lied when he claimed ignorance of the divorce. With the zest of a hunter about to corner his prey, Jerome has Dodge arraigned on the perjury charge but before he can be induced to talk, Morse sends Hummel another bundle of cash to bail him out and the chase is on. Dodge and Edward Bracken, his Hummel-appointed guardian, hightail it to New Orleans, then on to Houston and beyond. Staying just ahead of the law, the stalwart Bracken keeps his charge "entertained" with all the whiskey and women he can handle as they head off on a multistate debauch, a grand tour of Southern bars, racetracks, and whorehouses—all at Morse's expense.

One person who is not happy with Hummel's inventive extra-legal maneuver is William Sweetzer, the man who had actually served the divorce papers on Dodge in 1898. In October, determined to save his career by proving he had not been negligent, Sweetzer undertakes a thorough search of the records and comes up with documents confirming that Dodge had indeed been served. He hands them over to a grateful Jerome, who dispatches private detective Jesse Blocher to find Dodge and bring him back to New York to at last own up to his lie before a grand jury.

Once Blocher is on the case, the hunt for the elusive ex-husband intensifies, but with Morse's largesse, Hummel's network of bribable stooges, and Bracken's vigilance, Dodge and his minder manage to elude their pursuers, their path greased by well-rewarded local authorities, convenient jurisdiction squabbles, and extradition issues. Morse money pours into the pockets of enablers, with Hummel as paymaster, while Morse, sensing danger, sails off to Europe and the newspapers make hay with the tale of true love gone amok. Hilarious stories feature the loutish fugitive on the run, the fire-eating DA in hot pursuit, and a full cast of venal spies and corrupt provincial authorities dedicated to saving Dodge from the jaws of justice. The antics are a welcome distraction from dreary dispatches from the Russo-Japanese War and depressing political developments at home as the municipal election campaigns heat up amidst indications of deep dissatisfaction with Mayor Low and his reformers.

Low is renominated by the Fusionists, but the stout, earnest burgher, however honest, has shown that he has neither the temperament nor the views to appeal to those outside his own class. In the popular mind he represents the interests and smug views of his "silk-stocking" constituency. Nor does it help when Jerome, who dislikes Low personally and thinks his politics too close to Republicanism, writes to the secretary of the Citizens Union criticizing Low and the letter is leaked to the press. The public is shocked, as members of the Citizens Union surely must have been, to read that Jerome would look upon Low's reelection as "the wickedest thing that has been done in political life in my recollection."

Though not up for reelection himself, Jerome is a pivotal player in the political maneuvering and has much else to occupy him while waiting for the law to catch up with Dodge. As the man expected to eliminate small-time vice, crack down on corporate criminals, and bring change to a culture that has lost respect for the rule of law, he is much too busy to focus all of his attention on one case. With public pressure to follow through on his promises to pursue corporate higher-ups building, much of his energy is focused on efforts to penetrate the webs of obfuscation spun by their lawyers. Suspicions that the titans at the top of the insurance business are running a high-toned racket are growing stronger, while public outrage against the crumbling Metropolitan Street Railway system and its hated chiefs—William Whitney in particular—is even more troublesome for Jerome. Many are aware that Whitney has achieved his position as one of New York's richest and most powerful men as a result of joining forces with Tammany, and Jerome's failure to prosecute him and his ilk for their financial perversions has disappointed his supporters and energized his critics. But though Jerome has been combing the books of the Metropolitan for evidence of criminality, he has found nothing actionable, leaving him frustrated and allowing critics like William Randolph

Hearst, publisher of the *Journal* (and politically ambitious), to label him "the brass-buttoned bellboy of the trusts."

As expected, in November Tammany's mayoral candidate, George McClellan, wins by a wide margin, results that give Tammany almost full control of the city again. Gleeful crowds of McClellan supporters gather to celebrate, filling the air with the familiar refrain of the popular pro-Tammany street song, back again: "Well, well, well, reform has gone to hell!"

16

THAW UNMASKED

Every bit of humanity had gone out of him; he was a monster, a fiend, a demon.
—EVELYN NESBIT

As White watches the SS *New York* pull away from the pier, he is troubled by the risk Evelyn is taking with Thaw, whom he knows to be not merely disreputable, but dangerous. The $500 letter of credit slipped to Evelyn on the sly might at least help her escape in an emergency, but there isn't much more he can do. Even that is money he doesn't have with his debts now estimated at nearly $600,000. To get his finances under control and avoid a catastrophic bankruptcy, he is counting on Charles Barney to bring him back from the brink using the skills that have made him a leading figure in New York banking. Barney, though under some financial strain himself, and battling the city over changes it is imposing on White's design for a splendid new Knickerbocker Bank building, takes up the challenge for his old friend. On his advice, almost everything White owns is turned over to creditors or assigned as collateral for loans. Only what White is storing in warehouses is to be spared for eventual sale.

In a wrenching gesture of retrenchment, White vacates the West 24th Street loft and dismantles the exquisitely decorated rooms, stripping them of the sumptuous divans, the multiple mirrors, and carved antique furnishings that had once so awed Evelyn. The gorgeous red velvet swing is cut down, and the marble mantel, which had been hoisted to the top of the building in 1897, is lowered back down to the street and hauled off to storage. For six years these rooms above the F.A.O. Schwarz toy store have been a favorite trysting place, stocked with champagne and in regular use. But Jack Cheever, a broker at Henry Poor & Co. and co-signer of the lease, has been dunning White for his unpaid rent and there is no choice but to give it up. To console himself, and because the only thing that keeps him from worrying about money is spending it, White arranges to share the rental of a less elaborate space with Thomas B. Clarke, the art dealer and collector who is also his client.

For all his problems, White maintains a lively after-hours amorous life, seldom misses a society event, and never turns down a tempting commission. He has little time to worry about Evelyn, who is, in fact, discovering that a doting suitor with money to burn is a very satisfactory traveling companion. No extravagance is denied her or her mother, a reluctant chaperone who still favors White and worries that the European tour will be taken by the family's generous (though unbeknownst to her, broke) benefactor as a lack of gratitude for all he has done for them. Thaw is redoubling his efforts to win her over, but Mrs. Nesbit is horrified when they arrive in Paris to find that their party of three (including Thaw's valet) will be lodged not in a hotel, as they had been promised, but in an apartment on the posh Avenue Matignon. Evelyn, now an adult of eighteen, is dismissive of her mother's chronic concern with propriety, while Harry chips away at Mrs. Nesbit's disapproval with a show of stunning largesse.

He takes mother and daughter wherever they want to go, pays for whatever they choose from couturiers like Doucet, and wines and dines them at Voisin and La Perouse. The two women ride through the Bois de Boulogne in their own carriage and are gallantly saluted by the passing parade. At the races on weekends, they turn heads at Auteuil and Longchamps when they take their seats in Harry's box. In the cafés of the Latin Quarter they are entranced by the artful naughtiness of the cancan, the cakewalk, and the apache, and Harry also introduces them to the social set he had cultivated during his earlier European wanderings. At the brilliant Sunday-afternoon gatherings hosted by salonistes Elsie de Wolfe and Elizabeth Marbury in Versailles, the beautiful protégée of "the rich American from Pittsburgh" captivates the collection of French aristocrats and intellectuals, continentals and American expatriate millionaires who call her "La Bebé."

Evelyn is enchanted by their high-style living in Paris. Her immersion in the sensual pleasures of the European idle rich is like a dream, albeit one from which she is sometimes rudely awakened when Harry flies into one of his jealous rages. One day in a restaurant, when an American acquaintance approaches their table and inquires of Evelyn if she has heard from White, Harry, in a sudden fury, overturns their table with everything on it. The mere mention of White's name is enough to trigger a terrifying outburst, and if any man dares to look at her with admiration, Evelyn is helpless to prevent Harry from making "a mad dash for the unfortunate fellow," fists flying. If he is faced with real opposition, however, she has observed that he is quick to back off and reveal himself as "an abject coward." Evelyn, who could never share Harry's virulent hatred of White, chooses to humor him, though she is not above an occasional provocation to test her powers.

When he proposes in Paris and Evelyn turns him down, Harry is inconsolable despite her efforts to explain, as tactfully as possible, that she would be an unsuitable match for a man of his rank, hinting at something in her past. He weeps and wails and refuses to leave the apartment for days. Nor will he allow Evelyn and her mother to leave, which is too much for Mrs. Nesbit. She wants to use White's $500 to flee to America and pleads with Evelyn to come with her. But Evelyn has not yet seen London, Berlin, and Vienna and refuses. When at last Harry relents and they again venture out, there is a marked change in his mood. No longer the exuberant impresario of good times and shopping sprees, he is anxious and distant, sometimes sitting for hours without speaking, then flying into a rage. When his ravings subside, he is full of remorse and once again the humble supplicant, falling to his knees and pleading with his "boofuls" to forgive him. But no matter how many times Evelyn rejects him, Harry refuses to drop the idea of marriage. He proposes repeatedly and seems unable to understand how she could possibly refuse.

"Don't you realize what marriage to me would mean?" he asks. "Why, if the United States were a monarchy, I would be the Prince of Pittsburgh and the Duke of Allegheny!"

Each rejection is greeted by rage, then contrition. Sometimes Harry disappears for a day or so before reappearing in a strangely tranquil state. For long periods he sits staring into space, saying nothing. At other times he questions Evelyn into the night. Why won't she marry him? Is she a virgin? He is tedious, exhausting, odd, but he is desperately in love with her, Evelyn tells herself, and she holds the power. She believes she can handle Harry and there is so much more to see, so many more hats and gowns to add to her wardrobe, so many more soirées to attend where all eyes will be on *La Bebé*!

Then, on a summer night, long after Mrs. Nesbit has retired, an exhausted Evelyn, who has been fending off Harry's exasperating questions for hours, commits what she will call "the greatest, the most terrible, the costliest mistake of my life." She tells Harry about the night in the loft when White seduced her and about their subsequent intimacy.

"The beast!" he cries. "The filthy beast!" With each added detail he weeps hysterically. He sobs, he rages, he wrings his hands and insists she repeat the story again and again. Each telling puts him in the same frenzied state, though at one point he confesses to Evelyn that he already knew of her intimacy with White because his detectives had long been following her in New York.

Soon after, the trio moves on to London where Evelyn, lodged at Claridges, pampered and plied with gifts including "four lovely diamond brooches" from Tiffany's, puts the troubling confrontation out of her mind. They visit Thaw's sister Alice in the small but elegant Berkeley Square residence staffed and maintained by the money that the "Count de Money" billed the Thaws for her coronet. The visit goes smoothly, but Evelyn's quarrel with her mother comes to a head with Harry's discovery of White's letter of credit. He blames Mrs. Nesbit for hiding it from him and his screams of rage send her fleeing to bed, where she threatens to stay. Mother and daughter are barely speaking, and the impasse is only resolved when Mrs. Nesbit accepts Harry's offer to pay her way home and assures her, untruthfully, that he will provide another chaperone. Evelyn, unwilling to leave with her, chooses instead to return to Paris with Harry, where one afternoon when he has left her alone in the apartment, she spies a small metal box on a table and opens it. She is staring at its contents—a hypodermic syringe and several needles—when Harry walks in and reacts "like a man gone berzerk." The discovery cannot be a complete surprise to Evelyn, given her backstage education, Harry's odd absences, and his erratic behavior. Fortunately for her, he blames his butler, Bedford, for leaving the box where she would find it, and she does not bear the brunt of his rage. It is unpleasant evidence of what she surely suspected, but not so alarming that she regrets her refusal to return home with her mother.

Bedford's punishment is to be left behind, and, freed from Mrs. Nesbit's chaperonage and the butler's hovering presence, she and Harry continue their European tour, presenting themselves as a married couple. In late summer they arrive in the Austrian Tyrol where Harry rents an isolated castle, the Schloss Katzenstein, high above an Alpine valley and so remote and desolate it can only be reached on foot. One night, after the caretakers have left the two guests alone, Evelyn wakes in her high, four-poster "princess bed" to see Harry standing over her, stark naked. He has yanked the blankets from the bed, and when she screams, he claps his hand over her mouth and tears off her nightgown. Terrified, she struggles, but the more she fights, the more violent he becomes. He ties her hands behind her back and whips her repeatedly with a dog whip. Though she screams and screams, there is no one to hear her, and the beating goes on and on. Bleeding, covered with welts, and desperate to get him to stop, she tries making promises. This excites him and inspires him to suggest things she should beg for.

Then suddenly he stops, leaves the room, and returns with brandy and soothing words for Evelyn, but any illusions that she can control him have been destroyed.

It takes a week in bed for her to recover and more weeks for "the telltale marks of abuse" to heal. Nor is that the last time Harry will take out his whip. He repeats the sadistic attack while still at the castle and again in Switzerland and Paris. As they travel, Harry brings with him a locked bag in which he keeps his needles, various drugs, and a selection of whips. He no longer hides his use of cocaine and morphine, and when angry at Evelyn, he sometimes brings out his dog whip or the rattan cane and beats her. He sometimes succeeds in compelling her to share his cocaine but she resists, fearing the loss of whatever control she still has over Harry. Though his abuse invariably ends with a contrite and humble Harry on his knees pleading for forgiveness, Evelyn now wants only to escape, and her ticket from White is now gone. In October she gets her chance when, back in Paris, she and Harry are joined at tea by Elsie de Wolfe and Elizabeth Marbury, who are about to sail for New York. Inexplicably, Harry agrees to allow Evelyn to join them.

Three days after her arrival in New York, at 7:00 o'clock in the evening, Evelyn hears a familiar drumming on her door at the Savoy Hotel. It is Stanny there to welcome her home. "Oh Kittens," he says and gives her a hug. "Oh Kittens, where have you been?"

White, who remains protective of Evelyn but has found others to excite his passion, is relieved to find Evelyn unencumbered by Harry and looking chic with her four diamond brooches adding sparkle to her Parisian ensemble. He invites her to his Tower parties, but she seldom gets to see him alone. For too long she has no chance to tell him about her "nightmare," but when she does, he "boils over." He is horrified by the abuse she has suffered but also uncomfortably aware that, under duress, Evelyn may have said things that Thaw could use to destroy him. He insists that she immediately pay a visit to the one lawyer who can fix anything. Abe Hummel, he assures her, will see to it that she is spared "any further contact with that lunatic."

On October 27, 1903, guided by the gnomish "Little Abe," Evelyn signs an affidavit in which she swears to a horrifying list of abuses inflicted on her by Thaw and includes her statement that Thaw had tried, unsuccessfully, to get her to charge White with having raped her. Hummel files the affidavit, which, not incidentally, protects White, and sends White a bill for $1,000.

The affidavit proves useless in deterring Thaw, but at Hummel's prompting, Evelyn has confirmed that Thaw's repeated attempts to persuade her to betray White had failed. Her loyalty is a huge relief for White, whose greatest fear is that his erotic entanglement with a minor might become public knowledge with ruinous consequences for his reputation and his livelihood. Concern for Evelyn is not the only reason he is willing to pay Hummel's exorbitant fee for preparing the affidavit, the contents of which will one day be of great interest to prosecutor William Travers Jerome.

Though Harry is informed of the existence of the affidavit and told to leave Evelyn alone, he ignores the warning, and Evelyn soon finds it expedient to resume relations with him. Gifts and billets-doux arrive from Harry throughout the fall, addressed to Evelyn as his "angels, her tumtums, her tweetums, her boofuls." When on Christmas Eve Stanny hosts his annual party at the Tower, Evelyn is not among the guests. She instead accepts Harry's invitation to join him at Rector's and they spend the evening together, carousing into the wee hours of Christmas day, her nineteenth birthday. Since there is no longer any hope of reclaiming White as her own, she knows she must make other arrangements for her future. Her decision to risk it on an alliance with a fabulously rich psychopath testifies to her lost hopes for romance, her familiarity with the harshness of life without money, and Harry's dogged persistence.

17

JEROME'S SECRET

He was a bit of a swashbuckler.
—Arthur Train

McClellan's victory over Seth Low in the 1903 municipal elections gives Tammany pols and their corporate sponsors a breather but no permanent respite from the aggressively honest DA, William Travers Jerome, who remains in office and has lost none of his fire. Arthur Train, among the first to have signed on to his legal staff, marvels at the image the public holds of his boss—"a combination of Savonarola, St. George, and D'Artagnan." Train has no doubt that Jerome remains "the popular hero of the slums and Fifth Avenue alike" and that "the mob" would follow his "alert, square, high-shouldered figure anywhere." But, too much the maverick to be trusted by professional politicians and establishment powers, Jerome is also under attack.

As a birthright member of the wealthy society that "the mob" despises, Jerome's popularity among tenement residents is remarkable. If it is largely explained by his daredevil exploits and his attacks on the privileged, it also owes something to his lack of pomposity. In Jerome the masses recognize a relaxed appreciation for life's small comforts that is more closely aligned with their own outlook than with the grim puritanism of bluenosed reformers ever eager to "save" them from their pleasures. Like his father, Jerome disdains the stultifying social taboos against alcohol, tobacco, and cards and is fond of natty clothes and boisterous discourse. But while Lawrence Jerome, a sportsman and hedonist, lived only for pleasure, his son's tolerance for self-gratification is strictly limited. It does not extend to men like William Whitney and his clique of entitled voluptuaries whose gargantuan appetites are sated at the expense of the poor and the powerless.

As New York's self-styled incorruptible crusader and standard-bearer for civic virtue, Jerome, with his equally obvious aspirations for higher office, is assumed to be as free from scandal as anyone in his position could be. His political rivals—not to mention his prosecutorial targets—might have enjoyed exposing him as a hypocrite and a fraud by uncovering some secret breach that would reveal smoking and drinking to be the least of his sins. Jerome knows this. And yet, at some point during his tenure in the DA's office, Jerome does something that puts everything at risk. In his mid-forties, he falls in love with a woman who is not his wife.

Ethel Stewart Elliot is everything that Jerome's wife, Lavinia, is not. Twenty years Jerome's junior, she is beautiful, cultured, a lover of good conversation, witty, understanding, interested in politics, and in love with Jerome. For a warm-blooded, gregarious man who has chosen self-banishment rather than share his home with a woman with few interests outside her son and her two feckless brothers, Mrs. Elliot offers an unexpected chance at happiness. Divorced and the mother of a daughter, she had trained for a musical career, appeared as a concert singer with some success, and surrounded herself with a wide circle of friends in the musical world. She gives up a great deal when, with an extraordinary generosity of spirit and capacity for love, she accepts a life of clandestine domesticity with Jerome as the love of his life. It is at her insistence that nothing in their relationship be allowed to interfere with his political career. Those closest to Jerome—most importantly his son and eventually his daughter-in law—can see that, in fact, Mrs. Elliot is as ambitious for Jerome as he is for himself, and she soon wins them over.

Living a secret life, always wary of exposure and the uproarious scandal that would ensue, surely has its torments for Jerome, but divorcing Lavinia and marrying Ethel is apparently not an option he is willing to consider. Society frowns on divorce, and for a politician it can be ruinous, as he well knows. But when, years later, his daughter-in-law asked him why he had not taken that route, which would have been more in character and more just perhaps to both Ethel and even Lavinia, he offered a bizarre twist on the straitlaced code of personal conduct instilled in him by his mother. A divorce, he explained, would have been unjustifiable since the incompatibility that made his marriage to Lavinia a misery was neither her fault nor his. She had been the best kind of wife she knew how to be. Jerome was also surely aware that a legal divorce would become public knowledge, and that the stigma attached to it would likely derail his political career.

But if he cannot divorce merely because Lavinia is an obstacle to his happiness, neither is he prepared to sacrifice that happiness on the altar of this quaint code of behavior. He and Ethel share a house on East 36th Street like any married couple, and there is perhaps no greater testimony to Jerome's brilliance than his ability to manage his unconventional domestic arrangement in such a way as to avoid upsetting his family and upending his career.

Perhaps his enemies fear that the DA's extensive files hold enough damaging evidence of their own transgressions to bring them down with him. But although he can fight hard, even mercilessly, when principles are at stake, Jerome has a well-known disdain for personal vindictiveness. He is more likely gambling on a convention that would last well into the 20th century whereby a politician's personal life is considered off limits to the prying press. As family members later confirmed, many people knew about Mrs. Elliot at the time without making an issue of it. From Lavinia, Jerome apparently has nothing to fear. If she is aware of her husband's double life, she never lets on.

So Jerome guards his secret, but not without paying a price. Proud of his reputation for absolute integrity, he must put up a false front and face each day with the knowledge that it could be the one when someone does make an issue of his unsanctified relations with Mrs. Elliot, putting everything he has worked for at risk.

1904

18

SPIRALING DOWNWARD

Then upon his return to private life, after he had passed his fiftieth year,
Whitney's love of wealth and luxury got the better of him . . .
—Dixon Wector, *The Saga of American Society*

One month into the new year, on February 2, 1904, White's old friend and best client William Whitney, returning from a performance of *Parsifal* at the Metropolitan Opera, steps through the gates of his Fifth Avenue mansion and is never again seen in public. Rumors fly when the news of his sudden death at age sixty-two is announced, and the family issues a story attributing his swift decline to blood poisoning following an emergency appendectomy—all suspiciously treated at home by doctors who refuse to provide any details.

Was he shot? Was he stabbed? Was the killer an unhappy investor in the waterlogged stock of the Metropolitan Street Railway Company? A radical reformist for whom Whitney is the embodiment of corporate corruption? Or, more likely, one of the legion of cuckolded husbands whose wives have surrendered to the suave womanizer? A story that makes the rounds and is widely believed owing to the source's social bona fides is that Whitney was stabbed in the doorway and died from his wounds. But by whom? And why?

There are no answers. The *Times* prints a respectful obituary, though the reporter's frustration at the reticence of the physicians who refuse to provide any details is evident. The public announcement attributes his death to peritonitis and blood poisoning after a severe attack of appendicitis. There is a high-toned funeral at Grace Church packed with Whitney's highly placed friends and associates who pay solemn tribute to his "signal abilities" and "amiable qualities." Then the ten pallbearers—Grover Cleveland, J. P. Morgan, and Thomas Fortune Ryan among them—shoulder the flower-draped coffin and the mourning party heads to Grand Central Station, where a special train is waiting to take them to Woodlawn Cemetery.

As the *Times* reports, speculation about the fortune left by Whitney and its disposition is "rife" in the aftermath of the shocking news of his mysterious death. Wild guesses put the figure as high as $100 million, though the *Times*, after consultation with "an authority having ample opportunities for forming a correct opinion," settles on $20 million. What is clear is that Whitney's heirs are to inherit a vast fortune in money and real estate but not a single share in the Metropolitan Street Railway Company, which is headed for an ignominious collapse. After fraudulently pumping up the stock, Whitney and his cohorts, including pallbearer Ryan, had happily dumped theirs and then felt no obligation to actually build the modernized streetcar system they had promised.

For White, whose flexible morals bend toward tolerance for the privileged on whose wealth his income depends, Whitney's transgressions are easy to ignore. He will miss his friend, the companionable carouser who was also his best client. In addition to the huge sums Whitney was willing to pay for additions and alterations to his various residences, he had also provided White with access to substantial accounts to use for purchases on his behalf at White's discretion. These transactions have been White's private business, an important source of income in the form of commissions, customarily set at 10 percent.

The death of the patriarch does not, however, spell the end of all Whitney bounty. The house White is designing for Whitney's son Payne will be the most expensive of White's career, coming in at roughly $1 million, and he is once again authorized to scour Europe for its sumptuous furnishings.

As the impresario of such abundance, spending great sums vicariously on behalf of his hugely rich clients and friends, White, on the brink of financial disaster, finds it impossible to acknowledge his own precarious situation. Unwilling to show himself as any less generous than his wealthy friends, he and Bessie invite 250 guests for a musical evening at their Gramercy Park home a few weeks after Whitney's funeral. It is catered by Sherry's, the fashionable Fifth Avenue restaurant designed by White, where White's overdue bills are approaching $5,000. Restaurateur Louis Sherry, who presides over the legendary dining and reception rooms inspired by those of French palaces, has been understandably reluctant to pressure White for payment. Other creditors are less so, and White is constantly dunned by his florist, jewelers, decorators, booksellers, and photographers. Many are threatening legal action. Charles Barney, on whom White relies to devise ways of satisfying his creditors, advances him $100,000 and is able to consolidate many of his debts, relieving some of the pressure and prompting White to declare him "the best friend I have and the best fellow in the world."

One man who is out of patience is White's landlord, Henry Taylor. Since White moved into 121 East 21st Street in 1898, he has paid neither rent nor taxes, and now, in 1904, his debt to Taylor has ballooned to roughly $53,000, and Taylor wants to be paid. White has put a great deal of money into improvements during his tenancy, and even as he and Barney are negotiating with Taylor to credit those expenditures and accept a new payment plan for the rest, White is arranging to rent two rooms in the Bryant Park Studio Building for entertaining in private. (Hearst has helpfully informed his readers that "studio" is merely an artistic name for such love nests, and that men keep them not for the pursuit of art "but for the pursuit of sin and the ruin of human souls.") Even in his precarious financial condition, White can no more abandon his compulsive quest for such secret spaces than he can forgo his annual escape to Restigouche in the spring.

A fishing trip to one of the most expensive places on earth to catch a fish is hardly an exercise in retrenchment, but White is obviously exhausted—overworked and plagued with worry—and his partners, once again concerned for his health, urge him to go. To double his pleasure (and perhaps pay his way), Jimmie Breese goes along and White is soon feeling like the free spirit he once was and his friend Jimmie still is. In a letter to Bessie, who is traveling in Europe, White claims that he is at least belt-tightening in a literal sense by putting himself on a weight-loss regime. He writes that he is exercising, which Breese finds laughable, and reducing his alcohol consumption to just one whiskey before dinner, "but Jim says it is big enough to kill an ox." With Breese he is full of mischief and bonhomie, able to forget for the moment the mounting problems that await him on his return.

19

DEATH IN A HANSOM CAB

Battalions of reporters wrote millions of words; countless artists
drew countless pictures . . . It was a riotous journalistic jag and the
American newspapers have never had such a good time.
—NEWMAN LEVY, THE NAN PATTERSON CASE

When Charlie Morse steps off the gangplank onto the teeming New York waterfront on his return from Europe in February 1904, former mayor Van Wyck and a Tammany sidekick are there to meet him. While he was abroad, keeping clear of the DA and his questions, Morse had been cheered by a letter from Hummel advising him that the annulment of his marriage to Clemence had cleared the last hurdle and he was free to marry Katherine. Subsequent developments, however—the indictment and pursuit of the fugitive Dodge on charges of perjury, a grand jury, prodded by Jerome, sniffing conspiracy—have him feeling the heat. When Jerome calls him to testify before the grand jury, Charlie, uncharacteristically uncommunicative, cites his constitutional right against self-incrimination.

While Jerome is waiting for his men to catch up with Dodge, for Hummel to run out of tricks, and for the courts to rule that Canfield's high-rollers must answer his questions, a sensational murder case lands in his lap.

Early on the morning of June 4, 1904, Caesar Young, a notorious gambler, bookmaker, and racehorse owner, and his mistress, Nan Patterson, a former *Florodora* girl just like Evelyn Nesbit, pick up a hansom cab near the entrance to Central Park and instruct the driver to take them to West Fulton Street. The cab is to carry them to the pier from which the *Germania* is set to sail at 9:30 A.M. taking Caesar and his wife—Nan's implacable rival for Caesar's affections—to Europe for a second honeymoon. Nan has reluctantly agreed to see Caesar off secretly but has no intention of ceding her lover permanently to the obstinate Mrs. Young.

On this early June morning Nan and Caesar make a handsome couple, both conspicuously well dressed except for Caesar's shabby hat, a sartorial imperfection that he corrects during a quick stop at the Knox hat store in the Fifth Avenue Hotel. At Caesar's request, the cab makes another stop at the corner of Bleecker Street and West Broadway where the couple downs a drink or two at a saloon before again heading for the Fulton Street pier.

Then, shortly before nine, the driver hears the sharp report of a pistol coming from inside his cab. When the smoke clears, he finds Caesar Young sprawled across the lap of his mistress with a fatal bullet wound in his chest.

Nan claims that Caesar's death is a suicide, but it looks a lot like murder and she is taken to the Leonard Street police station for questioning. Suspicious details in the coroner's report end her hopes for release on bail and she is committed to the Tombs, New York's dark, dank, and unwholesome jail. A bailiff leads her from the coroner's courtroom back through gloomy corridors and over a narrow walkway known as "the Bridge of Sighs," connecting the Criminal Courts Building to the prison. In the courtyard below, condemned men once faced the gallows; ahead, the iron bars of the prison loom. Nan collapses and has to be carried inside.

The newspapers leap on the story. That night the *Evening Journal* fills half its front page with the headline "CAESAR" YOUNG, RICH BOOKMAKER, SHOT AND KILLED WHILE IN A CAB WITH *FLORADORA* SWEETHEART.

Jerome, perhaps influenced by the guaranteed public attention, takes a leading role in prosecuting the case, despite being fully aware of the challenges involved in prosecuting a beautiful young woman in a city besotted by sentimental notions of the weaker sex and apt to confuse youth and beauty with innocence.

Ecstatic at the opportunity Nan presents for whipping up public sentiment and selling papers, newspaper publishers print breathless descriptions of the beautiful chorus girl accused of murdering her man. The *Herald* rhapsodizes on the subject of Nan's dark brown hair "massed on the top of her head" beneath a "becoming hat." The *Evening Telegram*, also struck by Nan's "abundance of brown hair," praises her "blue eyes and fair complexion" and gives her measurements: five feet seven inches, 135 pounds. Is it possible that someone so pleasing to look at is capable of cold-blooded murder?

Jerome knows that it is the prosecutor who is more likely to be labeled cold-blooded for badgering a helpless woman, especially one who happens to be "decidedly striking," but he is temperamentally incapable of backing off from a fight for justice, particularly one that will be so closely watched. In court, two of his ablest assistants, William Rand and Francis Gavan, will argue the case under Jerome's close supervision and will have to demonstrate that no one—no matter how physically captivating and popular with the press—can get away with murder. In this case, with all the evidence pointing to homicide, Jerome is confident that in the end logic must and will prevail over emotion—a belief that will die hard.

20

EVELYN ASCENDANT

Joan of Arc would not have been a virgin long if Stanford White had been around.
—HARRY K. THAW

White, relaxed and almost carefree, has few thoughts for Evelyn as the Restigouche horses, three abreast, tow the club's luxurious houseboat upriver to prime fishing grounds. He believes he has done what he can to protect her. Guided by the incomparable Abe Hummel, she has signed a document so incriminating in its account of Thaw's abuses during their European tour that Harry has been warned by his lawyer and others to stay away from her. White puts the sordid episode out of mind here in these idyllic surroundings where he and Jimmie Breese, joined by a convivial group of millionaire sportsmen, pursue their favorite pastime. Waiting to stop where the fish are plentiful, they gather on the verandah dressed, as a guide once described them, "like they were going to Parliament."

The question of how to "protect" Evelyn has paradoxically also been plaguing Harry. While White has concluded that it is Thaw who poses the greatest threat to Evelyn's safety, Harry is convinced it is the "degenerate" White. Ignoring the affidavit and his lawyer's warnings, he has succeeded in convincing his "boofuls" to forgive him for his horrific abuse and to resume their intimacy. Once again, they are seeing each other regularly, though Harry broods continually about the wrong White perpetrated on Evelyn, oblivious to his own abuse, and is overwhelmed by paranoid fantasies. He tells Evelyn that he has detectives trailing White, and he employs others to protect her and himself from the Monk Eastman Gang, desperadoes out of Hell's Kitchen who, he claims, have been hired by White to kill him.

Harry has also allied himself with the Society for the Suppression of Vice, feeding the city's self-anointed anti-vice crusader Anthony Comstock his fantasies of orgies orchestrated by White behind the walls of his "dens" scattered around Manhattan. He hints darkly of lewd goings-on in White's Tower studio and has Comstock on full moral alert with his description of one of White's lairs where workmen outside claim to have "heard girls scream." The custom there, he confides, is "to drug the victim, usually an American girl, innocent and about fifteen years of age." He informs Comstock that in another hideaway White has "works of art"—always suspect—"and probably a vast collection of obscenity." He tells Comstock that, according to his calculations, White has "ravished 378 girls." If Evelyn is disturbed by Harry's hatred of White and his increasingly paranoid behavior, she does little to interfere. A hard look at her options has set her to thinking that Thaw's millions might be enough to compensate for his monomania.

Evelyn is not the only one who has noticed that Harry, always on edge, is especially overwrought. Mother Thaw has heard her son groaning and sobbing at night and has elicited his tearful avowal that his mind returns obsessively to Evelyn Nesbit, the crime that destroyed her innocence, and the beast who was responsible. The news that her favorite son, scion of the gilded Thaw dynasty, is obsessed with a common chorus girl with "nothing but her looks" to offer does not sit well with Mother Thaw. Nor are Evelyn's renewed relations with Harry acceptable to her mother, now remarried to her longtime admirer, Charles Holman. Mrs. Holman remains adamantly opposed to her daughter's having anything more to do with Thaw, whose erratic behavior in Paris had alarmed and frightened her.

Evelyn, however, seems resigned to the reality that her close relationship with White has ended. She moves into a hotel where Harry has rooms and is eventually persuaded to return with him to Europe. In June 1904, they sail for Genoa on the *Kaiser Wilhelm der Grosse*. Harry is carrying a revolver for protection against the Monk Eastman Gang and his behavior is increasingly erratic. Often drunk, he appears at times to be drugged. The mere mention of White's name provokes fits of rage and he threatens to kill Evelyn if she dares to pronounce it. But in Paris Harry's extravagance knows no bounds and Evelyn revels, as she had before, in the dinners, suppers, races, and nights at the opera or theater—with new hats and gowns for every occasion. During a five-week stay on the Riviera, they stop at Monte Carlo where Harry loses what Evelyn considers "marvelous sums" every night. Lodged in a suite at the Hermitage Hotel directly below Enrico Caruso's, Evelyn can hear the celebrated tenor practicing every morning when she wakes up.

During a trip by car through parts of France and Switzerland, Harry's lapses into irrationality persist, but Evelyn tolerates them because in Paris, as she later explained, "Our manner of living would have ruined an Indian potentate." Besides, she believes she has found new ways to handle his outbursts. After an episode, when he is full of remorse, she can make him bend to her will with slavish humility, prostrating himself at her feet whenever his fear of losing her overcomes his sneering sense of entitlement. She has even learned to enjoy sending him into paroxysms of rage against White, which is almost too easy. She has only to "forget" and utter the name Stanford White to experience a perverse pleasure in watching him work himself into a jealous fury.

Evelyn's mother does not share her daughter's belief that Harry is too fixated on possessing her to do her real harm again. When she hears that Evelyn has traveled to Europe again with Thaw, she writes to White and pleads with him to intercede. Though Evelyn is largely out of his life at this point, White continues to write her occasionally, showing an interest in her welfare. He still provides support for Howard Nesbit's education at a military academy and retains the loyalty of Evelyn's mother. The recently remarried Mrs. Holman still considers White her best ally in the struggle to keep her daughter away from Thaw, whom she denounces in her letter to White as "a scoundrel, villain, and a man with murderous intent."

A scoundrel, yes, but murderous? Seriously miscalculating, White brushes the accusation aside.

21

HARD WORK AND HEADACHES

If, as has been said, Waterloo was won on the playing fields of Eton, it can be said with equal truth that many murder trials at the beginning of the century were won in the pages of the World *and the* Journal *as much as in the courtroom.*
—NEWMAN LEVY, *THE NAN PATTERSON CASE*

On June 13, 1904, the day Nan Patterson is indicted for the murder of Caesar Young, she wears a heavy veil and is dressed in deep black—mourning presumably for her dead lover. Any hopes Jerome may have nourished for an unbiased weighing of her case at trial are shattered as the press immediately takes up the cause of the ill-fated beauty.

NAN PATTERSON IS A PHYSICAL WRECK the *Evening Journal* headlines a story that claims a week in the Tombs has turned the once "jaunty, self-possessed girl, sure of her looks" into a "jaded drooping woman," her skin "sallow," her eyes "sunken." When Nan's ancient father arrives and informs her that doctors believe her bed-bound mother would not survive the shock were she to learn of her daughter's predicament, the floodgates open to a tsunami of tear-jerking prose. On June 22, the *Evening Journal* describes the heartrending scene: "Gently the feeble old man broke the news, and with a shriek the girl fell to her knees, grasping him about the knees, and crying aloud. The girl swooned, and it was some time before the restoratives applied brought her to consciousness again."

The courtroom battle lies ahead, scheduled to open on November 15, but the propaganda battle is as good as lost. The maddening irrationality of the

sensationalized press, as always, adds fuel to Jerome's fire, and his trial preparations are intense. The darling of reporters when he was wielding an ax or
delivering a give-'em-hell speech, Jerome has never reciprocated with respect,
holding a predictably low opinion of the predominant yellow press. Among
journalists and their bosses, this rankles.

Jerome's distrust of the press is not the only reason he must be ready with
all the ammunition available to see that justice prevails and Nan is punished.
The humiliation will be hard to bear if he cannot convince a jury of the
absurdity of Nan's claim that Caesar, with the flexibility of a contortionist,
had managed to shoot himself in the back while stuffed into the tight space
of a hansom cab. As "the greatest cross-examiner of his time and one of the
greatest that ever tried a case" in the words of the popular writer Irvin S.
Cobb, he cannot afford to lose.

Adding to the pressure is Nan's choice of the firm Unger and Levy for
her defense. Henry Unger had opposed Jerome in his 1901 campaign for
district attorney, and Jerome certainly does not want to be trounced by the
firm of his late rival for office. No more than he would enjoy seeing his friend
and associate Arthur Train proved right in his assessment of Unger's partner,
Abraham Levy, whom Train has praised as one of the most brilliant criminal
lawyers in the country. Jerome has no intention of allowing Levy's brilliance
as a legal tactician to outshine his own.

While Nan is languishing in the Tombs, Jerome is frantically busy, working
sixteen- to eighteen-hour days throughout the summer and fall. In November
he receives word that the amendment to the criminal code allowing him to
force Richard Canfield's high-rollers to testify about their gambling activity
has been upheld. It is the weapon Jerome has been waiting for to send the
King of Gamblers to jail, but his euphoria is short-lived. Just as it seems that
Canfield will have to do time, Joseph Jacobs, who had so eagerly provided
Jerome with the evidence to justify the raid on Canfield's, has a crisis of conscience. All contrition and tearful remorse, he confesses to Canfield's lawyer
that his claim to have gambled at Canfield's place was a lie, one he is willing
to swear to in return for enough money to flee abroad out of Jerome's reach.

Canfield's lawyer takes Jacob's affidavit and promptly turns it over to Jerome, thwarting Jacobs's plan to profit from the deal he thought he had sealed. Jacobs is sentenced to a year in Sing Sing for swearing out a false affidavit. Canfield pleads guilty to being a common gambler and pays a $1,000 fine. And Jerome, bitterly disappointed that three years' work has yielded no more than a slap on the wrist for Canfield, must admit to himself that the collapse of his case is largely due to his own arrogance. When a Canfield regular had tipped him off that his star witness had never set foot inside the elite gambling house, he had been too eager to dismiss an unwelcome stumbling block on his march to justice. Instead of looking into the claim, he had denounced his informer as a liar and proceeded full speed ahead on false information.

Then, while Jerome is juggling the Patterson, Canfield, and Dodge imbroglios, a chain of events is set off by President Roosevelt's free-spirited daughter Alice that will at last give Jerome his long-awaited opportunity to put the old swindler William D'Alton Mann behind bars, shut down his scandal sheet, and put an end to his odious journalistic corruption.

On a visit to Newport, Alice's lively antics attract the leering attention of one of Mann's snoops assigned to sniff out scandal in society's playgrounds for *Town Topics*. Mann, whose sleazy business model has not stopped him from taking the moral high ground on matters of decency and decorum, somehow manages to reconcile the polar opposites of his modus operandi. Spurred to action by an apparently sincere disapproval of Alice's unconventional behavior and nursing old resentments against the president for perceived slights, Mann makes the dangerous decision to publish a thinly veiled attack on the president's daughter.

Writing as "The Saunterer" in his *Town Topics* column, Mann laments that not only was a nameless young woman (whose resemblance to Alice no one could miss) seen fancy dancing "for the edification of men," she was also "indulging freely in stimulants."

The attack provokes outrage not only among Alice's many admirers but among many others who are disgusted by what they refer to as Mann's "skunk journalism," some of whom have been targeted themselves. Robert Collier, son of *Collier's Weekly* founder Peter Collier (and the same Bobby Collier who fell under Evelyn Nesbit's spell), is particularly infuriated by Mann's poisonous pen, which has taken aim at his father on more than one occasion. Aware that his friend Jerome has long looked for a way to exterminate *Town Topics* and prosecute Mann, he arranges to meet with Jerome. Also invited to help frame a plan to end the Colonel's reign of terror are *Collier's* editor, Norman Hapgood, and a number of other friends and fellow clubmen, including Harry Payne Whitney, artist Charles Dana Gibson, and writer Finley Peter Dunne, creator of the endearing social critic Mr. Dooley.

Jerome, at the height of his powers, is working harder than ever as everything seems to be happening at once, including the call to trial of the Nan Patterson case. By the time the *People v. Nan Patterson* opens on the morning of November 15, Jerome has had to deal with fugitive witnesses as well as an unceasing stream of mawkish newspaper accounts pulling heartstrings on behalf of drooping, pitiful Nan, her despairing old father, and her claque of photogenic showgirls, so touchingly loyal, so very attractive. Assistant DA William Rand, with his colleague Francis Garvan, is arguing the case, but Jerome is closely supervising and in the courtroom almost every day despite the unremitting demands on his time. Then, suddenly, the trial comes to a halt when a juror suffers a cerebral hemorrhage. A mistrial is declared and the press pumps up the pathos as the fragile Nan, who must now endure the agony of a second trial, is returned to the Tombs.

By December 5, when the case is again called to trial, the public has been whipped into such a frenzy that the police have difficulty preventing the crowds from crashing into the courtroom. The Russo-Japanese War is raging and Port Arthur is in imminent danger of falling, but for the New York press, Nan Patterson is the big news. When she takes the stand, deathly pale and still dressed in somber black, she proves an ideal witness, never evasive, always to the point. Spectators sit breathless at the edge of their seats, their eyes fixed on Nan's face, when Nan's counsel Abraham Levy puts his client's poise to the test in an exchange that is the dramatic highlight of the trial:

"Nan, look at me," he instructs. "Did you shoot Caesar Young?"

"I did not," says Nan, her voice soft but steady. "I swear I did not. God knows that if I could bring him back to life I would."

The following morning the *Times* reports that Nan "bore herself bravely" and "did not falter a single time under the fire of Assistant District Attorney Rand's pitiless questioning."

The next day Rand's reasoned summation is widely admired and seemingly irrefutable in its presentation of the evidence against the possibility that a few minutes after buying himself a new hat, Caesar Young had suddenly decided to shoot himself in the back. But the sobs that can be heard in response to Levy's emotional appeal to let Nan "go and sin no more" are an indication of what is to come. The jury deadlocks, its holdouts unmovable in their view of Nan as a victim, ill used by the rampant evils of Sin City, and a mistrial is once again the outcome. Jerome, who is steadfast in his view of Nan as an amoral creature, and who is also no doubt loath to give up a fight that involves his ego and his professional pride, decides against dropping the case. Nan will have to be tried again and the date is set for April 18, 1905.

There is better news for Jerome in his chase after Charles Dodge. The running farce that has kept Dodge one step ahead of the law, boozing and whoring his way from one state to the next (an awed Texas Ranger reports that Dodge once consumed forty-six whiskeys in fourteen hours), is finally reaching a climax.

On Christmas Eve, with snow falling outside, New York's Criminal Courts Building swarms with tall-hatted, gun-toting deputy United States marshals from Texas, who have arrived with a delivery for the DA. They have brought him a wobbly Charles Dodge, who looks at least a decade older than his fifty-eight years and has lost all his teeth. With their mission accomplished, the deputy marshals head out into the snow, whooping with joy and hell-bent for trouble. Reports of their misdeeds arrive at Jerome's office for days afterward until they are finally packed off back to Texas.

Alerted to Dodge's arrival, Abe Hummel, in the midst of a holiday party for his theatrical friends, slips away to the Criminal Courts Building in hopes, however slim, that he can persuade Dodge not to turn state's evidence.

Dressed in evening clothes and swinging an ebony cane, he approaches the reception desk.

"I'm here to see my client Charles Dodge," he announces.

"He isn't your client any longer" is the brusque response.

Just as he fears, his ex-client is inside, telling all. For two days Dodge continues to talk while he is sobered up, nourished, and fitted for false teeth. Over the holidays Jerome works on Hummel to confess to the part he and his lovestruck client have played in the scheme, but Hummel stonewalls. Despite Jerome's relentless appeals, Little Abe stubbornly refuses to implicate Charlie Morse, whose late-blooming passion and insistence on the annulment of his marriage to Clemence are responsible for the whole series of illicit maneuvers that now threaten to put them both behind bars.

For his part, Charlie, who has reveled in his role as a romantic hero willing to risk all for love, is discovering the limits of his all-for-love valor. With Dodge in Jerome's clutches and Hummel under intense pressure to betray him and take a deal, thoughts of prison are having a decidedly cooling effect on his ardor. As Jerome sees to it that Dodge is happy and chatty and keeps the heat on Hummel, Charlie finds it expedient to douse his passion for Katherine and realign himself with the oddly compliant Clemence. Against Hummel's wishes, he orders the annulment annulled, and while Hummel argues against the decision to abandon the hard-won document, he does as he is instructed and continues to hold out against Jerome's efforts to tempt him into betraying Morse.

Is some code of loyalty among outlaws at play? Or does Hummel's stubborn refusal to squeal in exchange for a deal have something to do with a rumored "retirement plan" Morse has promised his able accomplice? Morse himself, having bought some time, finds himself back where he started, except that the whole circus, involving more than thirty lawyers—not to mention travel and treats for the insatiable Dodge—is estimated to have set him back upwards of $100,000.

Worse, a grand jury is showing an expansive interest in hearing testimony from Morse's family and associates, and this time his customary practice of

1. Charlie Morse has left Bath, Maine far behind on this day c. 1905 when he is photographed on horseback in New York City. Profits from his fraudulent schemes have made him wealthy enough to buy three homes in the 700 block of Fifth Avenue. He is a member of the Metropolitan, University, and Lawyers' Clubs, and has his own pew at the fashionable Fifth Avenue Presbyterian Church. CREDIT: *Maine Maritime Museum, Bath, Maine*

2. James Breese, a bon vivant with bohemian tastes, shares Stanford White's passion for elaborate entertainments, especially costume balls which give the two friends an excuse to suit up in britches, doublets and ruffs. CREDIT: *Self portrait by James Breese, courtesy of Mark Sink*

3. In a photograph taken shortly before his first rendezvous with Evelyn, the 47-year-old White is not yet complaining of stress and "corposity." He cuts a fine figure with his impressive moustache and carefully assembled wardrobe, which he replenishes each time he travels abroad. CREDIT: *The Library of Congress*

4. Jerome, in his element out on the hustings or pacing the courtroom, looks a little uncomfortable sitting still for this rather formal photograph. More characteristically, when he is at work in his office he can be found leaning back in his chair with his feet on the desk. CREDIT: *Courtesy William Travers Jerome IV*

5. In Robert Carter's celebrated caricature, Jerome appears as a nattily bow-tied, cigarette-smoking tiger, pleased with himself and with the day's exploits. Jerome inscribed the caricature to his son, William Travers Jr. CREDIT: *Courtesy of William Travers Jerome IV*

6. After Special Commissioner Hand found no grounds for removing the District Attorney from office and dismissed all counts in the complaint against him, an amused cartoonist rehabilitated Jerome with a pair of wings. CREDIT: *Courtesy of William Travers Jerome IV*

7. William Travers Jerome has the stern look of a prosecutor in this 1905 portrait. At six-foot-three, wiry and intense, he can be ferocious in the courtroom, but to his staff he is a witty, irreverent leader who always has their backs and seems to be happiest when is is engaging them in lively "bull sessions." CREDIT: *The Library of Congress*

8. Called "the Napoleon of the Western bar" for reasons that his portrait makes apparent, Delphin Delmas, Harry K. Thaw's lead defense lawyer in the first murder trial, was a lawyer of the old school. His ornate language sounded laughable to East Coast ears but he remained courtly and courteous throughout the trial in contrast to Jerome, who lost his temper and harmed his own case. CREDIT: *The Library of Congress*

9. This photograph of Evelyn Nesbit, c. 1900, is one of hundreds that were taken of the teenage beauty who was a favorite with photographers almost from the moment she arrived in New York. Stanford White began collecting images of Evelyn even before he arranged to meet her, and may well have possessed this one. CREDIT: *The Library of Congress*

10. Sometimes Evelyn vamped for the camera. At other times she appeared as a gypsy, a dancer, a fashion plate, or an innocent child cuddling a kitten. Here she looks like the young girl that she was, but with that certain hint of recklessness that Jack Barrymore saw in her eyes.

11. Nan Patterson, daughter of the very respectable supervising architect for the U.S. Treasury, heard the siren call of the city in 1898, became a Floradora girl, and made the mistake of falling in love with a married man. Nan's trials for murdering her lover revealed how easy it was for an attractive woman to sway a jury, a lesson Jerome was unwilling to accept. CREDIT: *The Library of Congress*

12. The Casino Theater on the southeast corner of Broadway and 39th Street, was an exotic temple of light opera, frothy revues and burlesque. On its stage, Evelyn beguiled dashing young men who came hoping for romance, and rich old plutocrats ready to offer the world to a willing Floradora girl. Here, New Yorkers are arriving at the theater for a Saturday matinee, which has attracted a less racy crowd. CREDIT: *The Library of Congress*

13. Colonel Mann used his society scandal sheet Town Topics to extort money from rich men who were willing to pay to keep their sexual adventures quiet. He apparently took decorum seriously but had no morals, and was one of Jerome's prime targets. With an outlandishly colorful wardrobe, he was a star at his own trial but his win was a Pyrrhic victory. CREDIT: *The Library of Congress*

14. However impeccably dressed, manicured and well groomed, there was always something odd about the way Harry presented himself, something Evelyn remarked on later when she described her impression of him at their first meeting as "a man whose face attracted and at the same time repelled me." CREDIT: *The Library of Congress*

15. Relying, as he always has, on the vast Thaw fortune to rescue him from the unpleasant consequences of his perversions and criminal acts, Harry enjoys the privileges money can buy, even in jail. Here the accused murderer enjoys a breakfast brought in from Delmonico's restaurant and elegantly served on a white tablecloth. In the background is the brass bed that spares him the indignity of sleeping on a prison cot. CREDIT: *Bettman/Getty Images*

16. A vast but orderly crowd watched as William Collin's Whitney's flower-draped casket is carried from Grace Church to Grand Central Station where a special train is waiting to take it to Woodlawn Cemetery. The family attributes Whitney's sudden death to complications from an emergency appendectomy but questions are raised. His doctors provide no details and rumors are rife that the death of the man many hold responsible for the derelict condition of New York public transit was a homicide. CREDIT: *The New York Public Library Digital Collections*

CRIMINAL COURT BUILDING & BRIDGE OF SIGHS, NEW YORK

17. Jerome's friend and colleague Arthur Train called the Criminal Courts Building "one of the gloomiest structures in the world." An architectural monstrosity, it was connected by the "Bridge of Sighs" to the even gloomier Tombs, where accused murderers Nan Patterson and Harry K. Thaw each languished while their many admirers clamored for their release.

18. "Boss" Croker is accompanied by reporters as he leaves the American liner pier after arriving from England. If Jerome turned up the heat on Croker's corrupt Tammany machine, Croker could always opt for a holiday on cooler shores and cross the Atlantic. He owns an Irish estate where he indulges his passion for racehorses, as well as three houses in England, where the king of graft takes on the airs of British gentry. CREDIT: *The New York Public Library Digital Collections*

bribing his way out of a jam will not be an option. When the word gets out that the list of people who will be called to testify ranges from Morse's lawyers and accountants down to the office stenographer, anyone with the where-withal arranges to be out of reach. Katherine Gelshenen takes off for Cairo. Charlie, traveling in Europe, sleeps uneasily, dreaming of prison gates closing behind him.

22

KEEPING UP APPEARANCES

. . . I am staggering under a load which I fear I really will not be able to carry . . .
—STANFORD WHITE

D espite the mountainous debt that has him sneaking out back doors and taking circuitous routes to elude bill collectors, White continues to spend as lavishly as ever, unable, or unwilling, to economize except in refraining from large-scale stock market speculation, which he cannot continue. When he is honest with himself, he realizes that his hopes of somehow paying off his debts and putting his life back on course are unrealistic, but he clings to his role as Stanford White, famous architect, society darling, extravagant spender, party-giver and tastemaker. His staggering losses following the Northern Pacific railroad panic had put financial recovery out of reach, absent a miracle, and, adding to his mental distress is the guilt he feels for having used some of Bessie's money in the venture, with her consent, and lost it. In low moments he acknowledges feeling "hopeless and desperate."

With his fifty-first birthday looming in November, White is also feeling his age. Distressed by his "growing corposity" and his susceptibility to repeated illness, he has acknowledged that it is the "driven" life he is leading that has eroded his physical and mental health. Yet slowing down is apparently only possible at Restigouche when he is out on the river casting for salmon or cruising along at a leisurely pace.

As soon as he is back in town he is rushing again to keep up with a frantic schedule of meetings with clients, project deadlines, high society events, and sexual rendezvous. With his sexual appetites undimmed, he has decorated the recently rented Bryant Park studio with the same attention to detail that he has lavished on his many other secret trysting places. Evelyn, whose evolution from lover to friend is now complete, is no longer among the guests, but neither is she still pining for Stanny. She is now Harry's constant companion, though still refusing to marry him.

In the late fall of 1904, when she and Harry return from Europe, a mob of reporters is waiting for them on the pier in New York, all under the misapprehension that they are man and wife and wanting to know where and when they were married. Thaw's arrest for speeding through Switzerland with his "wife," as he felt it wise to identify Evelyn to the police, had been reported in the Swiss papers, making the couple newsworthy again. Their denials do nothing to quiet the clamor, and reporters who follow them to the Cumberland Hotel are rewarded when Harry and Evelyn are asked to leave after refusing to register as man and wife. The press is again in pursuit.

Their passage, purportedly booked to bring them home in time for New York's "winter season," arrives, to Evelyn's dismay, too late for the season's mid-November opener, the spectacular Horse Show at Madison Square Garden. Timed to open a week before the opera, the ball that signals the start of the weeklong equine event is a glittering, glamorous affair that keeps dressmakers busy for weeks in advance. The whole Garden neighborhood is alive with anticipation as a parade of chariots, equipages, four-in-hands, hunters, jumpers, trotters, and pacers head for the vast arena with seats for eight thousand. Restaurants and hotels are filled with violets and chrysanthemums, the official flowers of the show. Shop windows display the blue and yellow colors of the Horse Show Association, whose members are among the anointed of New York society and pay hundreds of dollars to watch the equine entertainment from their private boxes. The promenade is a festival of fashion as women spectators, who are expected to wear a different outfit for every performance, proudly display their plumage and measure it against what the other women are wearing.

This is Stanny's crowd and he is the center of attention wherever he goes, surrounded by friends from the worlds of art and society, his very presence certifying the event's social significance. For Harry, a weeklong affair held in the magnificent Garden amphitheater designed by the hated Stanford White holds little appeal, a likely reason for his choice of return passage aboard a liner scheduled to arrive in New York just a little too late. Evelyn, in possession of a new Paris wardrobe, is deeply disappointed.

In the eyes of the fashionable spectators, many of them clients as well as friends, White is as charming and irrepressible as ever, a towering figure, in a hurry as always, exchanging greetings, laughing his full-throated laugh and moving on after a friendly clap on the shoulder to the next cluster of acquaintances eager for their chance to enter his aura. Only close friends like Charles Barney and Jimmie Breese are aware of the severe mental stress he is under as he grapples with his deteriorating finances. He is grateful to Barney for his heroic efforts to deal with the morass of overdue bills, bank overdrafts, and loans, but when the social whirl comes to a halt at the end of the day and he is forced to face his situation, he sees only one way to climb up from the abyss. He begins gathering together all the goods he has in storage and on loan to friends for a giant sale in 1905. He is pinning all his hopes on it.

1905

23

CORPORATE SCANDAL AND
A CAUTIONARY CASE

*There are no laws to cover ninety-nine out of a hundred cases of the crimes
committed every day in this era in the name of high finance.*
—WILLIAM TRAVERS JEROME

B y 1905, the rumbling against Jerome for his failure to go after the high
and mighty is growing louder. There is rising anger aimed at insiders
of the three big insurance companies— Equitable, New York Life,
and Mutual—for squeezing millions from their policyholders and using the
money to invest in securities for their personal profit or to reward legislators
for standing firm against industry regulation. Scandalous but not quite illegal,
the corporate pilfering is putting huge profits into the pockets of powerful
capitalists with access to the treasuries of the big three—men with names
like Vanderbilt, Frick, and Gould. Given the lack of regulatory legislation on
the books, Jerome, try as he might, is unable to find any evidence of the kind
required to take the corporate con men to court.

Pressure on Jerome intensifies when dissension within the Equitable Life
Insurance Society between the company's elderly president and 29-year-old
James Hazen Hyde, son of Equitable's founder and heir to a controlling
interest in the company, precipitates a major scandal. Determinedly cosmo-
politan and flashy, Hyde never misses an opportunity to flaunt his wealth and
high rank among the elite, most recently with a star turn at the Horse Show
with the president's daughter Alice on his arm. For his greatest social triumph,

he has chosen to host a magnificent costume ball for which no expense is to be spared.

The Equitable's old guard, upset by the prospect of young James putting the company's ill-gotten gains on display at a high-profile, high-cost ball at a time when the business is already in bad odor, would like very much to squelch the party, rid themselves of its irresponsible host, and get back to the business of quietly looting the company's coffers. But the newspapers have been reporting on ball preparations for weeks and there is no way to avoid the enormous publicity, which risks raising uncomfortable questions—questions that, if pursued, could shine a light on obscene corporate greed and its connection to high-society hedonism.

On January 31, 1905, at 10:30 P.M., a steady stream of carriages and electric vehicles rolls up to Sherry's to deliver Hyde's costumed guests. The host, splendidly attired in the uniform of the New York Coaching Club—coat of myrtle green, black satin knee breeches, black silk stockings, and an assortment of medals—is there to greet them and signal the way to the third-floor ballroom. Originally designed by Stanford White in full-on French palatial style, it is filled with roses, palms, shrubs, and arbors, a study in excess that recalls the splendor of the court of Louis XV, which is, in fact, the motif Hyde has chosen for his extravaganza.

When, with a tap of his baton, the conductor of the forty-piece Metropolitan Opera House Orchestra gives the signal and the music begins, the dance floor fills with swirling figures. Mrs. Fish's fabled turquoises, Mrs. Belmont's parure of emeralds, and Mrs. Potter Palmer's head-to-foot diamonds catch the light as they whirl around and twinkle like fireflies. Mrs. Palmer, encased in her glittering armor—diamond tiara, diamond dog collar, and diamond breastplates—moves with some difficulty, while Mrs. Clarence Mackay, encumbered by a train so long it has to be carried by two tiny pages, is completely immobilized, reduced to sitting out the all-night festivities on the sidelines. By the time the last stragglers head home in the early hours of February 1, photographers have already rushed their film to their respective newspapers. Photographs of the ultrarich frolicking in royal splendor can be counted on to sell papers, and there is no time to waste. The presses are rolling.

To the dismay of Hyde and his coterie, instead of arousing admiration and envy as expected, the images of foppish men and dowagers staggering under the weight of their jewels fuel public resentment against such mindless frivolity. When rumors circulate that the ball may have cost as much as $200,000, public outrage is such that the newspapers quickly shift gears for a far hotter story. Hearst wastes no time in adding firepower to the barrage of bad press in his *Journal-American*, and Hyde's social apotheosis dissolves in ignominy.

On February 16, the *Journal*, which had printed its original coverage of the party under the headline GORGEOUS BALL IN NEW YORK CITY takes Hyde to task on its editorial page for his "fancy costume ball and dinner." While he has money and "may spend it as he pleases," the writer observes, "the idea of a man who is head of a corporation controlling millions, upon the wise management of which depends the welfare of thousands of insurance beneficiaries, widows and orphans, strutting around in a Louis XV costume . . . does not appeal to insurers and the wise heads of the company have evidently begun to realize this, and to see that if the company is to go on forging ahead it must eliminate Mr. Hyde as a controlling factor."

Just as old-line management at the Equitable had feared, questions have been raised about the source of all that money, and the word on the street is that policyholders have unwittingly funded the frippery. Hyde is forced to resign, but the din in the press has led to calls for a state investigation of the whole insurance industry. Jerome braces for a new round of attacks on his failure to clean up the mess that an industry probe will surely uncover.

Four days before the ball, on January 27, Abe Hummel had been indicted along with Dodge and two others believed to have participated in a conspiracy to deceive the courts in connection with the Dodge divorce. But the latest development in the Dodge-Morse affair cannot compete in the news with stories of the obscene self-indulgence of the silly—and probably criminal—rich or the pathos of Nan Patterson, who is wasting away in the Tombs.

COMING TO TERMS

In justice to Mrs. Thaw, it must be said that she did everything that
she could do to prevent the marriage.
—EVELYN NESBIT

For a man as popular as White, distractions are always available and he seldom passes one up. Desperate to put aside his financial troubles and to get some relief from the effects of a harsh winter on his deteriorating health (admittedly half "due to nervous troubles and half to my diet and drinking at night"), he decides on a brief holiday. Toward the end of January he leaves for Florida with Jimmie Breese, the friend who has always been able to cheer him up.

As a sunny escape, the trip is a disaster. In a letter to Bessie, who is on her own four-month European holiday, White writes of catching a cold on his way south and enduring "a regular old-fashioned earache" that left him temporarily "quite deaf." After that it gets worse. He and Breese had arrived in Florida to find it "colder than I have ever experienced in my life," the aftermath of "a frightful blizzard" that had struck the whole country. With temperatures hovering around 20 degrees and winds howling at 25 miles an hour, "everybody froze to death," he writes, "except Jimmie Breese, who had his great big polar bear overcoat and all his winter paraphernalia." The automobile race at Daytona, which the two men had been looking forward to, was disappointing, but the chance to take a hair-raising ride in a friend's racer, covering "10 miles in nine minutes and 13 seconds . . . as near flying, I think as I will ever come to," was an experience that came close to salvaging the trip.

On his return to New York, White rejoins the social whirl and is conspicuously present at the Hyde ball, the repercussions of which will affect not only the future of the insurance business but the career of DA William Travers Jerome. To Bessie, White writes that the ball was "the most gorgeous affair I ever saw" with servants in magnificent livery, guards with drawn swords and spears, and the supper room "an absolute bower." He is dressed as a diplomat in white tie and tails, displaying a "Star Order" on his chest. His description of Mrs. Mackay's outlandish getup seems designed to amuse Bessie, who has never hidden her aversion to the self-indulgent high-society frolicking her husband is so fond of. Yet his admiration comes through when he describes for her Mrs. Mackey's splendid gown "of spun silver and gold all encrusted with turquoise," its ten-foot train, and the wee pages in "gorgeous gold dresses" who carried it. He is clearly delighted to have spent an evening in this fantasy world free of any reminders of his dire circumstances.

Back in reality, in another gesture at retrenchment, White decides to sublet his Gramercy Park house, fully furnished, for the four months that Bessie is away. He can charge his tenant $6,000 and move in temporarily with Charles McKim, who would do almost anything for Stanny and worries constantly that his old friend is self-destructing. As White contemplates further economies, he considers giving up his "little eagle's nest way up in the top of the Tower" but cannot summon the will to make such a wrenching sacrifice.

Then, just when it seems that White's financial situation cannot get any worse, it does. Having reached the difficult decision to settle some of his massive debt by auctioning off his immense collection of museum-quality objects, tapestries, furnishings, and paintings, he has been gathering them from around the city into a loft on West 30th Street. That task is just about complete when, on February 13, 1905, fire engulfs the building with terrible swiftness, destroying almost everything in it. It is a huge loss, and, to make matters worse, the insurance has run out on many of the items, while some of his most precious treasures, which he had only just removed from his house and added to those in storage, were not covered at all. He is devastated, though he mutes his distress in a letter to Bessie. After describing how "the floors fell in, and sheets of water were poured over everything, which froze in a solid mass," he goes on to acknowledge that it is "a hard blow after all the others but after all there are so many, many worse things that could have happened…" There is surely little comfort for Bessie in this sad attempt to soften the blow or in White's game insistence that he is "grinning and going back to work as hard as I can."

After two days of "stony misery" following the disaster, White does manage to rally, bearing up "like a soldier in the loss of his things," according to McKim. He writes to Larry at Harvard, cautioning him not to upset his mother in his letters. Give the fire "the most casual and slight mention," he instructs his son. He also writes Jimmie Breese, who is in Naples, warning him to "say nothing but to make light of it" should he run into Bessie. But he is candid with his friend, admitting that it is "about as bad as it can be" and asking for another loan to meet his most pressing debts.

It is hardly a good time to take on new financial obligations but on the day after the warehouse fire White receives news that leaves him no choice. On February 14, he is visited at the office by a man who identifies himself as P. L. Bergoff. A private detective, Bergoff claims to have information that White is being followed by spies on bicycles and by car. To prove his claim, he has White leave the office for a walk while he keeps watch. Whether inexpert or simply overconfident, White's shadows—two men on foot, one man on a bicycle, and a woman—are easily spotted. As Bergoff had no doubt hoped, White signs on as his client, instructing him to find out who is paying his stalkers. It will turn into a long-term, very expensive arrangement, with Bergoff sending two or more of his men out daily to track down the truth. Eventually, at a cost to White of several thousand dollars, they will identify the person who is bankrolling the surveillance as "the Pittsburgh Pug," Harry K. Thaw. White complains to his lawyer that he is being "persecuted by Thaw," then dismisses the lawyer's warning to take precautions. "That dude won't attack me with a pistol," he says. "He hasn't nerve enough. All he is trying to do is scandalize me."

More than a year has passed since the Christmas Eve of Evelyn's nine-teenth birthday when White had invited her to his annual holiday party and she had instead celebrated with Thaw. The decision had marked the end of her romantic illusions, her acceptance that her lover and patron had moved on, and that Harry might be her best option. Since then, refusing to give in to jealousy and despair, she has drawn on survival skills learned long ago when she had assumed responsibility for her mother and brother. Now, with no wish to return to a life of poverty, and aware that she must look out for herself, she is weighing the advantages of solidifying her alliance with Harry, whose riches promise not just future security but security in high style. Countless rich old men have offered as much, but Harry is young, extremely generous, and capable at times of showing genuine concern for her welfare. She is constantly reminded that in Harry's mind she and White remain linked by Harry's dual obsession—with her, whom he is determined to marry, and with White, for whom he is consumed with hatred for having her first. She is prepared to tol-erate Thaw's ugly obsession but could never become his partner in hate. Her lingering feelings for White, obvious to Thaw, fan the flames of his rage and sometimes lead to violence. She has been in no hurry to marry him, content to humor him and string him along.

Sometime that February Evelyn, in pain for what is later described as "intestinal adhesions," undergoes another operation (mocked by skeptics as "a second appendicitis") in the private New York City sanatorium of Dr. Clement Cleveland. For the next six weeks, during which Dr. Cleveland over-sees her recuperation at the sanatorium, an attentive Harry sees to it that her every whim is satisfied. It is he, not White this time, who installs a telephone in her room. Roast partridge and champagne are delivered from the Waldorf, and he fills her room with flowers. He continues to implore her to marry him, makes daily visits for a week or so, then disappears for a few days.

On her release from the sanatorium, Evelyn convinces Harry that she must have a quiet place of her own to complete her recovery. She takes a small apartment just off Madison Avenue on 38th Street where she can be free from Harry's importunities whenever it suits her. Toying with him, she alternates between admitting him with a great show of delight or refusing to see him, leaving him to torture himself imagining whom she might be entertaining behind the closed door.

When his frustration becomes unbearable, Harry does what he has always done when he needs help. He sends for his mother to come to New York from Pittsburgh and plead his case. Neither she nor Evelyn's mother has favored the marriage, but Mother Thaw is incapable of resisting the pleas of her favorite son and eager to believe that marriage will calm him down. Evelyn's mother, lately estranged from her daughter because of her disapproval of Thaw, also drops her resistance to the alliance. There are rumors, almost certainly exaggerated, that she has been offered $100,000 for her daughter's hand.

Under increasing pressure, Evelyn agrees to meet with Mother Thaw and the two women sit down to negotiate over tea. Worn down by Harry's relentless pursuit, his declarations that he loves her—and only her—and a clear-eyed assessment of the limits of a career on the stage, Evelyn is ready to deal.

"My son is very much in love with you, Evelyn," declares Mrs. Thaw in her opening argument, "and I wish you would marry him." Evelyn responds by pointing out that Harry's love has not always deterred his odd behavior. True, counters Mother Thaw, Harry has always been a cause for anxiety, but now that he has found love she holds renewed hopes for him. Nothing would please her more, she says, than to see Harry happily married and settled into a quiet life in Pittsburgh—a prospect that can only fill Evelyn with dread. On the other hand, if marriage were to include frequent escapes for nights on the town in New York and travels abroad on a limitless budget, shopping and socializing with the cream of European society, then perhaps life with a somewhat domesticated Harry might be worth the gamble.

Like sovereigns signing a treaty, the two women come to terms, and on April 4, 1905, Evelyn returns to her native Pittsburgh to be joined in holy matrimony to Harry Kendall Thaw in the rectory of the Third Presbyterian Church. The bride wears black.

25

"THE BIG SPIDER"

*Within the past decade or so there has arisen a new class of crime, rather subtle crimes
which do not come within the pale of the law.*
—WILLIAM TRAVERS JEROME

By the time the *People v. Nan Patterson* is called for trial the third time on April 18, 1905, journalistic and public interest is feverish. Again, police reserves have to be called in to restrain the crowds clamoring for a glimpse of Nan, who has abandoned her grim widow's weeds in favor of a becoming steel-gray dress specially made for the trial. Those lucky enough to gain admission to the courtroom are dismayed to see that the choleric John Goff is presiding as judge and has banished Nan's ancient father to spectator seating, leaving poor Nan to face her fate without him at her side at the counsel table.

After the usual preliminaries, Assistant DA William Rand calls his medical experts who confirm what he and Jerome consider the most vital proof in the case: that the nature of Caesar's wound proves conclusively that he could not have committed suicide. Abraham Levy counters for the defense with a parade of his own experts, who testify to the feasibility of suicide, and the trial devolves into confusing and contradictory analyses of the anatomical possibilities. Spectators yearning for Nan's return to the stand to slice through the baffling medical testimony and deliver the drama they came for are disappointed. Fearful that the grueling year in the Tombs has put Nan's nerves on edge, making it risky to try her luck once again, and alerted to the possibility that some damaging evidence may have surfaced since the last trial, Levy decides against having her testify and rests his case.

In the final round, with Jerome at his side, William Rand sums up his case, arguing persuasively, and with considerable irony, against the possibility that a rich young man, a man who had just bought a new hat, would suddenly decide he might like to die. Can anyone really believe, he asks, that Caesar, with a pistol that happened to be handy, had suddenly chosen to kill himself and then, instead of aiming at the brain or the roof of his mouth for a quick death, had instead held the revolver upside down and pulled the trigger with his thumb—the contortion required, given the position of his wound? And if such a suicide seems to defy logic, finding motive for homicide on the part of a woman whose lover is about to sail off with her rival surely does not.

It is a rational argument but Abraham Levy, whose successful advocacy of all-but-hopeless defendants has earned him the nickname "The Last Hope," pulls out all the stops in his final argument. For more than two hours he pumps up the pathos, lamenting the sad fate of his young and virtuous client and interspersing his argument with homilies on the purity of womanhood, the lustful nature of man, and the fallibility of human testimony.

Once again, the jury is unable either to convict or acquit. Eight jurors vote for acquittal and four for conviction. Jerome, bitterly disappointed, calls the trial a miscarriage of justice and complains that the case was "misrepresented to the public." Then he asks that the defendant be discharged, as another trial would be "unavailing."

On May 12 Nan leaves the Criminal Court Building a free woman and is hailed by a cheering crowd of two thousand. Among them are children who sing a song set to the familiar tune of "Tammany":

> *Nan is free, Nan is free.*
> *She escaped the electric chair,*
> *Now she's out in the air…*

A few are heard to render the second line:

She deserved the electric chair.

Logic had proved powerless against the emotional appeal of a practiced performer and a pretty face—a lesson Jerome will continue to ignore at his peril. The loss hurts, but other matters demand his attention.

In the months since Bobby Collier, the young publisher of *Collier's* magazine, had hurled his copy of *Town Topics* onto his editor Norman Hapgood's desk declaring the attack on Alice Roosevelt by The Saunterer (a.k.a. Colonel William D'Alton Mann) "the most vicious paragraph that ever appeared in a magazine," hostilities have continued to simmer. Vowing to use the pages of his magazine to fight Mann, Collier had instructed Hapgood to write an editorial immediately excoriating Mann's methods. Hapgood had happily obliged, calling *Town Topics* "the most degraded paper of any prominence in the United States . . . a sewer-like sheet," and Collier himself had added the final sentence, declaring Mann's standing among the people to be "somewhat worse than that of an ordinary horse thief or second-story man." It was the first salvo in a months-long exchange of vitriol.

Since early in his first term as DA, Jerome has been looking for a way to prosecute Mann and put an end to his "skunk journalism," but solid evidence of extortion has been hard to come by. As he has explained to his clubmen friends who have joined him in an unofficial anti-Mann cohort, no one is willing to admit to having anything to do with Mann and his blackmailing con, nor can any basis for criminal libel action be found, so clever are the Colonel's hacks in making the identities of their targets obvious without naming names. A few "small fry" have been caught, but not the real culprit, the man Jerome calls "the Big Spider."

As Mann likes to boast, no libel suit has ever come to trial against *Town Topics* in all his years as publisher. Nor does he lose any sleep over future stains on his clean legal slate. It has been his experience, he once observed, that "ninety-nine men out of a hundred are moral cowards." With such favorable odds, he is ready in May 1905 to take a European holiday, leaving his loyal lieutenant, Judge Joseph M. Deuel, in charge. Deuel, a short, squat man with abundant curly white hair and an extravagant handlebar moustache, is presiding justice of the Children's Court and a part owner of *Town Topics* as well as one of its editors, but it is his legal cunning that has been most valuable to the Colonel in keeping *Town Topics* from crossing the line into libel.

As the SS *Majestic* pulls away from the pier and heads out to sea with a long, mournful blast of its foghorn, Mann waves from the deck to the receding figure of his friend Deuel, confident that *Town Topics* is in good hands. When the New York skyline disappears from view, he makes his way to the sumptuous suite he is sharing with his third wife, Sophie, mercifully unaware of trouble brewing.

On July 11, while the Colonel and Sophie are luxuriating among the splendors of Europe, back in New York, Edwin Post, a popular member of the New York Stock Exchange, is keeping an appointment with a certain Charles Ahle in the gentlemen's washroom at the Holland House on Fifth Avenue. Finding the dapper young man waiting for him, Post slips him an envelope with five $100 bills, and Ahle assures Post that he can now rest easy knowing the money will serve as insurance against exposure in *Town Topics* of some highly damaging revelations concerning Post and a mistress. The item, he informs Post, was to run in "Saunterings" if Post were to be a no-show at the Holland House. It would have informed readers that the Post family home in Tuxedo is not Edwin Post's sole residence and that he shares "a little white studio" in Stamford with "a fair charmer" who has a penchant for "white shoes with red heels and patent leather tips."

Their transaction complete, Ahle is heading for the door when Detective Sergeant Bernard Flood of the NYPD steps out of a cubicle and arrests him, charging him with extortion. As Post later testifies, he had been approached by Ahle earlier with an offer to keep any mention of his dalliance out of *Town Topics* in exchange for money. After asking for a few days to consider the proposition, Post had consulted his lawyer and been reminded that the DA had been trying for years to get just such evidence without success since none of Mann's victims have ever shown any backbone. Post had also consulted his wife Emily (later of etiquette fame) and gotten her consent to take the high road, turn his story over to the authorities, and participate in a sting.

The day after Ahle's arrest the scandal is front-page news and Post is a hero, while Ahle is consigned to the sweltering Tombs. When Post appears on the floor of the Exchange, fellow members greet him with cheers and applause. A few take him aside to murmur that they, too, have "been there."

When his office alerts him to the news of Ahle's failed attempt at blackmail, Jerome is in seclusion at his Lakeville summer home. Like every other New Yorker with a place to go and no compelling reason to stay, he has taken refuge in Connecticut from the scorching heat of the hottest July the city has seen in a decade. He has been taking advantage of the time away from the hyperactivity of his New York office to scrutinize a state commissioner's report on the Equitable insurance company. Combing it for evidence of indictable crime and finding none, he is bracing for the political embarrassment his inaction is bound to cause. William Randolph Hearst has his *Journal* reporters pounding away at Jerome, seizing on everything they can find to prove their boss's claim that Jerome is nothing more than a lackey of the trusts. With his course set on the same political path Jerome hopes to follow, leading to Albany and on to the White House, there is more to Hearst's attacks than a desire to sell papers. Hearst is gearing up for a run for mayor and intent on removing Jerome as a political rival, while Jerome dismisses Hearst's politically motivated harangues as contemptible journalistic demagoguery.

What grieves him most, Jerome will declare in a speech, is "that educated men should bark down the pike like half-bred curs, led away by a Hearst and other unspeakables." Jerome has been struggling to explain his inaction, citing the lack of laws on the books that would criminalize the egregiously unethical practices of the corporate looters, but the results have been discouraging. It is a relief to turn his attention to his pursuit of "the Big Spider" and what promises to be a break in his efforts to put Colonel Mann behind bars. There is even some respite from the press, which is shifting its attention, at least for the moment, away from the corporate scandals. They have become rather tedious now that the Hyde Ball and its outrages are fading from memory, and it is much more fun to focus on the very juicy scandal involving Mann and the sexual improprieties of his high-society victims.

On July 24, Jerome arrives back in New York on the same day that a tanned and chipper Colonel Mann descends the gangplank of the *Zeeland* to be greeted on his return from Europe by reporters from every newspaper in town, all eager to grill him on the Post affair and its aftermath as the press dives deeper and deeper into the workings of *Town Topics'* unique business plan.

To the Colonel's staunch defense of his publication as a clean newspaper despite the struggle he says he must wage to keep it that way given the deplorable state of public morals, Jerome has an immediate response. He has always considered *Town Topics* to be "a nest of skunks," he informs reporters.

The next day, *Collier's* editor Norman Hapgood, who happens to be a boyhood friend of Jerome's, pays the DA a visit, and with Bobby Collier on board, they map out a strategy for goading Mann into filing suit. *Collier's* will publish more editorials, written by Hapgood, that will denounce the Colonel and the whole *Town Topics* operation, including Judge Deuel's part in it. His words, though carefully chosen, will be so blunt that an enraged Mann will feel obliged to sue Hapgood and the magazine for criminal libel. If they are correct in their bet, Jerome as the prosecutor will be able to put Mann and Deuel on the stand as witnesses for the prosecution, and, using his legendary courtroom skills, Jerome will get them to expose their own criminality. Placed in the position of prosecuting his friend Hapgood on behalf of men he detests—Colonel Mann and Judge Deuel—Jerome will be required to turn the purportedly injured party into the villain and the accused into the hero, which will require some fancy footwork. He decides that he must take full charge of the case, the first he will personally conduct in his four years in office.

It is a serious matter but also an opportunity for some good fun at the Spider's expense—a game that Jerome and his two eager friends will play to win.

26

A SHOPPING SPREE

Perhaps because I am getting old, and still try to do so much and
can't do it, but I seem to get more and more behindhand on my work
all the time and to be in constant hot water . . .
—STANFORD WHITE

Boarding the SS *Lorraine* for a European buying trip at the end of May, White gets a boisterous send-off. As he ascends the gangplank, a chorus of jeers can be heard above the shouts of longshoremen, hawking vendors, and clattering horse carts. White betrays no sign that he is aware of the insults hurled at him and hurries aboard, but the incident is unnerving. His alarm increases when Detective Bergoff sends him a report informing him that the heckling was arranged by Thaw's private detective agency and that one of their number, traveling with a female friend, has actually taken passage on the ship with orders to trail him through Europe.

The trip is planned as a shopping spree to purchase antiques and artworks for Payne and Helen Whitney's Fifth Avenue mansion, already three years in the works and destined to cost even more than the opulent town house White had created for Payne's father. It is White's first trip abroad since 1900, a chance to indulge his insatiable acquisitiveness on behalf of the Whitneys, to rummage through the treasures of European antiquarians, decorators, and dealers and spend Whitney money with abandon. In London, Paris, Florence, and Rome, Payne and Helen Whitney, who accompany White part of the time, spend more than $300,000 on everything from wood paneling ripped from an Italian palazzo to a Louis XV mantel clock, and a Clouet portrait of Henry II.

White's customary 10 percent commission makes the trip worthwhile monetarily, and for his young friends it is great fun. White knows everyone, is a knowledgeable and amusing traveling companion, and gives his all to his job as escort, leading the young Whitneys down narrow European streets and into the rarefied domains of antiquarians, where dealers he has cultivated for years and who know his taste show him the best of their treasures. He hits more than fifty dealers and galleries galloping through Europe, keeping a pace that is probably not what his stalker had envisioned when he invited his girlfriend on a European holiday.

In Paris, White takes some time out from his frenetic shopping to meet with his longtime friend and client James Gordon Bennett, the *Herald*'s flamboyant publisher, to discuss plans for a mausoleum. Relations between White and the brilliant but obstreperous Bennett have not always been easy. The self-styled "bad boy" of New York, who had attached himself in his youth to the fast crowd around the Jerome brothers, has gone well beyond them in his disdain for the niceties of polite society. Fast women and horses, carousing and yachting are Bennett's passions. White had managed to please him with his decor for the 227-foot yacht *Namouna* that is Bennett's pride, but in 1895, when White had designed new offices for Bennett's *Herald*, the publisher had complained that the four-story building at Herald Square looked like "an Italian fish market."

The two men agree on a design for the mausoleum to be located on Riverside Drive. It is to take the shape of an enormous owl—the *Herald*'s symbol—sculpted in bronze on a scale to rival the Statue of Liberty. An interior stairwell is intended to take visitors past Bennett's suspended sarcophagus. Fortunately for White's reputation, the need is not urgent, the plan collects dust, and the monstrosity is never built.

On his return to New York in August, White writes that Europe was a "bully time," then adds, "but I worked too hard and did little else but work." His commissions on the Whitney purchases, though substantial, barely make a dent in his debts and his financial troubles remain overwhelming. Nor will there be any time to rest after his frantic race through Europe. During White's absence, Charles McKim, unwell for some time, has collapsed and is unable to work. White's already heavy workload gets heavier and his own poor health threatens to incapacitate him as well. Work on the Payne Whitney house, ongoing since 1902, helps to keep him from sinking under the weight of his debts, but the project is fraught with delays and headaches. Helen Whitney, who has run out of patience, grumbles to White that she feels like "chucking the whole thing and getting a nice ready-made house."

As summer fades into fall, White complains that the stress on his mind and body has made life "more like hell than anything else." His sciatica has worsened, necessitating prolonged medical attention, and he is desperately trying every conceivable remedy, from a diet of fermented cow's milk to "quack medicine," which seems sometimes to offer some relief, though at other times he feels "little better than a cripple." A photograph taken by eminent photographer Gertrude Kasebier reveals the ravages that time and reckless living have imprinted on the rapidly aging architect, who sits shoulders hunched, flabby-faced, his signature thatch of red hair thinned and gray.

27

MORE CHALLENGES

As a matter of fact, at this very moment I have cartloads of stories locked up in my safe that would turn New York upside down if they were published.
—COLONEL WILLIAM D'ALTON MANN

N ew Yorkers are wilting in the blistering heat. In the tenements, workers suffer through the sweltering days and crowd onto the rooftops at night with their families, desperate to catch a breeze and a night's sleep. On his return from Lakeville, Jerome had found New York as oppressively hot as ever. On July 17, when temperatures in the city had climbed to ninety-five degrees, 137 deaths from the heat were reported. The next day—the hottest on record at ninety-six degrees—75 more New Yorkers had succumbed to the heat. In the streets, vendors are shirtless, while office workers dare to remove stiff collars and struggle to carry on amidst whirring fans that bring little relief. Tempers are short and concentration impossible.

The heat is big news, but not big enough to have bumped the insurance scandals from the newspapers where reports on corporate skulduggery are again daily fare now that Nan Patterson has crossed the Bridge of Sighs for the last time and no sensational murder has come along—yet—to mesmerize the public. The daily hammering on the insurance issue is putting more pressure on Jerome, with some of the most strident attacks emanating from his political rival, publisher William Randolph Hearst. Collecting laurels as a defender of the "plain people," Hearst rails day after day in his papers against the victimization of the "little guy" at the hands of insurance titans and the millionaires who are milking the dilapidated streetcar system for their own profit.

Jerome, frustrated by the charges and aware that his arguments in his own defense are unsatisfactory, remains unshaken in his faith that he will win in the end. While he continues to seek a way around the inadequacy of the legal tools at his disposal, through his spies he is keeping tabs on his other top targets whose plots promise to lead to indictable criminality.

Colonel Mann's arrival back in New York aboard the liner *Zeeland* had received heavy coverage in the press. With a Mediterranean tan to set off his snowy white beard, and waving an oversized Panama hat to the crowd of reporters gathered to grill him on the Post/Ahle sting, the Colonel had descended the gangplank with a springy step and dismissed any concern over the matter, leaving reporters with the impression of a man without a care in the world.

The Colonel's high spirits, despite the botched blackmail attempt by Charles Ahle, are soon explained. After stewing in the hellishly hot and fetid Tombs since his arrest and finally making bail at the peak of the heat on July 18, Post's would-be blackmailer had taken only enough time to sell all his belongings before heading with his wife for the cooler shores of the Continent. Jerome, after believing that Colonel Mann and his scandal sheet— the real culprits behind the blackmail—were at last in his grasp, must now accept that he has been given the slip. Ahle is enjoying life abroad. Mann is free to cast his veiled aspersions on those who won't play his game and to spare his roster of paid-up "immunes."

And then, in an exasperating twist to the sorry tale, Jerome learns that when Ahle made his move in the men's room of the Holland House he was acting as a free agent behind the Colonel's back. Jerome can only imagine that Mann, secure in his innocence of this particular crime, has had a good laugh at the fuss over his anticipated demise and at Jerome's frustration. The whole fiasco is another disappointment for Jerome, but he is left with at least one thing to celebrate: Mann may have survived this time, but the newspapers have shone a light on his smarmy operation, and now the lid is off. Jerome, who has never doubted his own abilities, remains confident that sooner or later the plan hatched with his friends Bobby Collier and Norman Hapgood to lure the Big Spider into their trap will pay off.

Meanwhile, his spies assigned to monitor Charlie Morse's activities have informed him that Charlie, though under attack from every direction, is still buying up coastal steamboat lines, aiming to become the "Steamboat King" by using the same underhanded methods he had employed in building his ice empire. At one point, cocky as always, Morse has even offered to buy J. Pierpont Morgan's popular and profitable Fall River Line, a foolhardy move that has so angered Morgan that Charlie now has the most powerful man in New York vowing to make shipping as difficult as possible for him.

Then, as the scorching July heat persists, Charlie's uncle Jim, portrayed in the press as the saltiest of Down East mariners, descends from Maine to take the blame for Charlie's love-driven folly. With his mea culpa, uncle Jim dashes any hope that by offering leniency to Hummel, whose indictment on suspicion of conspiracy is hanging over his head, Jerome can get Little Abe to admit that Morse is his client and has been funding the harebrained—and illegal—scheme to uncouple him from his wife.

Someone, perhaps Morse, though more likely Hummel, has come up with the inspired idea to put the blame for the whole mess on Uncle Jim, who is happy to oblige. To the delectation of reporters, Captain Jim, who is all Yankee forthrightness and crusty integrity, makes the preposterous, yet impossible to disprove, claim that the tightly knit Morse clan disliked Clemence and had considered her an entirely inappropriate spouse for Charlie. As the family's representative, he claims to have approached Hummel to find a way to break up the marriage and says he paid cash for the deed—all presumably without telling Charlie, who is innocent, says Captain Jim, of any involvement.

A relieved Charlie, free to carry on with his unscrupulous schemes, packs Clemence off to Europe, ostensibly to spare her the torrid summer heat, but remains in New York, perhaps to dally with Katherine Gelshenen. A frustrated

Jerome is obliged to abandon plans to prosecute Morse—for the time being—but at least Hummel is now almost his.

At 8:00 P.M. on July 31, 1905, Jerome dashes from his private office in the Criminal Courts Building out to the huge rotunda where a scrum of reporters assembled under the building's soot-encrusted glass roof is expecting to hear the DA confirm what many have speculated—that he is planning a run for New York City mayor.

Instead, the next morning's edition of the normally staid *New York Times* carries a story that leads with uncharacteristic hyperbole. "Last night," readers are informed, "District Attorney William Travers Jerome threw a bomb into the political arena." The *Times* story goes on to quote Jerome's announcement:

"I do not desire and never have desired to be a candidate for the office of mayor of this city," Jerome had declared, his words reverberating beneath the immense dome. Having once again defied expectations, he had paused to savor the moment before dropping a second bomb. Not only was it his intention to run for a second term as DA but he would do so without seeking the support of any major party. "Running wildcat," he planned to appeal directly to the people, whom he believed he had "served efficiently" and knew he had "served honestly." With their signatures on a nominating petition and their votes on election day, he was looking forward to four more years of rooting out lawlessness free of the evil influence of machine politics, fighting for the people with no debt to "those groups and individuals" accustomed to using their power in a way that is "wholly selfish, almost entirely irresponsible and not infrequently corrupt."

In conclusion, Jerome stated that he was "simply making public a purpose formed and communicated to a number of my friends as early as February of this year." And with that, reported the *Times*, he "picked up his grip and started out of the building without further ado."

Reaction to Jerome's announcement among reformers is predictably positive and considerably less circumspect in identifying Tammany's troops as the "groups and individuals" under attack. Citizens Union president Robert

Fulton Cutting weighs in with a blast at Tammany and the "horrible conditions" created by its "supreme dominance," which, he asserts, were actually understated by Jerome. Nor does Republican senator Chauncey Depew, among the most celebrated orators of his day, pass on a chance to exercise his eloquence on behalf of the candidate of righteousness.

"Jerome is the only man in New York who could take such a position with any hope of success," Depew tells the *Times*. "He is the most original and picturesque as well as the most honest and able figure we have had in municipal life for a generation." Other eminent Republicans are not so keen. In their eyes, Jerome is "unsafe"—too apt to challenge their bedrock beliefs, too undiplomatic and uncontrollable. No one can question his dedication to the office of district attorney, but, among those who know him, there can be no doubt that the prospect of higher office is never far from his mind.

Over at the Democratic Club, the *Times* correspondent finds Tammany men "inclined to make light of Mr. Jerome and his statement." They may believe that by rejecting any support from the powerful forces that conventional candidates rely on to push them up the political ladder, Jerome is sabotaging his own efforts. Or, as seems more likely, their show of unconcern is merely a cover for their panic at the prospect of four more years of Sir Galahad.

If their studied indifference disappoints, newsmen, avid for drama, know where to turn for more lively copy. Never impressed with the "little tin soldiers" of the reformers' brigade and the "silk stocking high hats" supporting them, "Big Bill" Devery, beloved of reporters for his unabashed amorality and inspired mixed metaphors, remains characteristically free of doubt. No one wants a return to reform's "panty-waist rule," he proclaims and predicts a clear Tammany victory.

As Jerome begins to plan for his campaign, he gets the good news that Colonel Mann has taken the bait and is ready to avenge his vilification in the pages of *Collier's* in court. Originally inclined to regard the attacks as an acceptable aspect of the business he's in, Mann has allowed himself to be persuaded to sue by Judge Deuel, who has felt the sting of Hapgood's pen and is adamant that only a lawsuit will end the attacks and punish the perpetrators. On August 21, the Colonel announces to the press with a flourish that he, Judge Deuel, and the Town Topics Publishing Company are suing *Collier's* and Hapgood for $100,000.

There is a dizzying flurry of maneuvers and counter-maneuvers, during which Jerome and Hapgood, unsatisfied with a civil suit, work to goad the Colonel and the judge into elevating their complaint to criminal libel. Hapgood continues to blast *Town Topics* with his vicious, but carefully worded, attacks while accusing the Colonel of deliberately delaying the legal proceedings he himself initiated.

Affecting a false gloom, Bobby Collier confides to a reporter, "We have no hope that the suit will ever come to trial" and slyly suggests that if the Colonel were truly convinced that a crime has been committed, he would file charges of criminal, not civil, libel. The next issue of *Collier's* includes reprints of all Hapgood's editorials attacking *Town Topics* "in compact form for the Colonel's convenience," and Bobby Collier announces that he will be in his office every afternoon awaiting arrest.

The taunt hits its target, and the same Detective Flood who had arrested freelance extortionist Charles Ahle arrives at *Collier's* and arrests not Bobby Collier as expected but Norman Hapgood on charges of criminal libel filed by Mann's loyal sidekick, Judge Deuel. A delighted Hapgood is arraigned the next day in Jefferson Market Court and indicted on October 26.

The next day, at their county convention, the Republicans decide to back Jerome's candidacy for reelection as district attorney after their first choice as a nominee declines to run. His opponents for reelection are James W. Osborne, Tammany's candidate, and Clarence J. Shearn, counsel for William Randolph Hearst, who is himself running for mayor against George McClellan. Hearst, self-proclaimed champion of "the common man," cuts a stiff figure in his long, somber frock coat. He continues to live the life of a playboy but runs hard, appealing to the poor, who suffer under "the soulless greed" of the rich.

One observer describes Jerome's campaign for reelection as "the most remarkable in the history of popular elections." Proposed by himself, relying solely on the voters and not on support from the powerful, he attracts throngs of supporters who are disgusted with corrupt machine politicians and corporate criminals and still believe that Jerome is the only man who can stand up to them. In a rousing windup at Carnegie Hall, Jerome does nothing to soften his stance against the financial and commercial powers capable of derailing his political future, claiming that the corruption found in public life, in large measure, "simply reflects the corruption of our business life."

When the votes are counted on November 7 Jerome is reelected by a comfortable margin. Hearst loses to McClellan and claims he was robbed. At midnight, the Briggs Military Band strikes up a victory march at Jerome headquarters where the windows are thrown open for all to hear. A crowd reported at "many thousands" brings all traffic to a standstill outside as shouts of "Jerome, Jerome" ring in the air.

There is no time for the victor to rest on his laurels. Hummel has run out of delaying tactics, and his trial on a conspiracy charge is on the docket for December 13, while the Hapgood trial is set to open on January 15, 1905.

It is a pale and nervous Abe Hummel who arrives at the courthouse for the first day of testimony with his lawyers, Delancey Nicoll and John Stanchfield. As the trial gets underway, Nicoll objects to every question posed by the prosecution led by Jerome, and every objection is overruled. There is little drama until Dodge takes the stand on December 17. Looking dapper, his wide smile revealing a fine set of $40 false teeth provided by the DA, Dodge, eager to keep his bargain for leniency, testifies volubly. He relates in detail how he was suborned to perjure himself in the divorce case and then was virtually kidnaped to keep him from falling into the hands of the DA. In an attempt to crack Dodge's surprising composure, Nicoll confronts him with his many lies, only to have Dodge cheerfully confirm that he has "lied and lied." Once he had accepted the money, he explains, he had felt honor-bound to keep lying to earn it.

Nicoll's closing argument, which brings tears to Little Abe's eyes, makes a passionate appeal to the class resentments reliably present in most New Yorkers, portraying Hummel as its victim. "It is high time for the men who own gas plants, insurance companies, railroads and steamships and walk by our courts contemptuously to be brought to justice. They laugh at the efforts of the court to convict them of wrongdoing. Something must be done!" he roars. "It isn't right to oppress the weak and leave the rich and powerful to go and do as they please."

It is a good effort but Hummel's case is hopeless. Implicating Morse for his role in the conspiracy would only confirm its existence. Nor would the argument that Dodge is a known perjurer be of any avail. On the contrary, as the prosecution is well aware, the whole case against Hummel hinges on the fact that Dodge is a perjurer and Hummel hired him to commit perjury. An attempt by Stanchfield to argue that the Morse clan really did think there was something wrong with the divorce proves as ludicrous as it is irrelevant.

On December 30 it takes the jury just eighteen minutes to find Hummel guilty. At a little after 3:00 P.M. the twelve jurors file into the courtroom and the foreman reads the verdict: "We find the defendant guilty of conspiracy as charged in the indictment." Sentenced by Jerome to a year in jail and a $500 fine, Hummel crosses the Bridge of Sighs to the Tombs. A few hours later, after a dinner of cold lamb and bread, he is released on bail and is soon finding creative ways to delay doing time in one of the eight hundred fetid, overcrowded cells of the forbidding penitentiary on Blackwell's Island (later Welfare, then Roosevelt Island) for the foreseeable future.

28

PARADISE LOST

'Something terrible is going to happen in your life,'
my subconscious mind seemed to warn my conscious one. 'A cataclysm that
for a time will overwhelm you. But you will survive . . .'
—EVELYN NESBIT

Dashing off a quick note to his old friend Gus Saint-Gaudens, now living in Cornish, New Hampshire, White puts his cares aside and writes with undiminished passion and playfulness. On the page he is the same fun-loving, beauty-obsessed Stanny of three decades earlier, the exuberant traveler who had raced through Europe with Gus and McKim, "the three redheads" giddy with youth, ardor, and mischief. What has sparked his excitement is a photograph of a Greek Venus that, as he reminds Gus, had left him "perfectly ravished" years ago when he first saw her. To his immense regret, he had failed to obtain a photograph at the time, but now, at last, he has found one and is enclosing a copy.

Does Gus agree that "she is the 'most beautifullest' thing that ever was in this world!" Also included for Gus's artistic appraisal is a photograph of another Greek antiquity, "a wonderful statue of Paros marble and of the most beautiful color you ever saw." Having selected "Dear Gusty," from his stock of affectionate salutations reserved for Gus, who is sometimes hailed as "Dear Old Hoss," sometimes "Gustibus" or "My Beloved Snooks," White signs the note, dated October 25, 1905, with a simple "Affy, Stanford."

The memories evoked will be bittersweet for Gus, who is ravaged by the cancer he has been fighting for more than five years. Known in his youth for his sunny outlook and love of good times, especially those that involved "whooping it up" with Stanny, Saint-Gaudens, with his health rapidly deteriorating, is now plagued by depression. His many youthful affairs, one of which has given him a son and a second household to support, have strained his marriage, and, unlike White, he suffers from remorse. A fire that swept through his Cornish studio in 1904, destroying much of his work of recent years, nearly destroyed him as well.

White has his own serious health problems and is tormented by fear of a forced bankruptcy that would be ruinous for his livelihood and his prized role in society. In a document signed in May, White had agreed to dissolve the equal arrangement of profit sharing with his partners McKim and Mead, recognizing the burden his indebtedness was placing on the firm. As an employee, he has been receiving a salary of $1,000 a month. Mead and McKim, his true friends, have been at pains to keep his reduced status a secret and to help when they can. Yet, despite his precarious position at the edge of financial disaster, White still refuses to curtail his spending. And though he is often in pain, afflicted with crippling sciatica, kidney problems, and digestive disorders, and admits to feeling "very much discouraged" about his physical condition, he is working as hard as ever. He is able to function professionally and socially without betraying the turbulence of his personal life, but his nerves are frayed as he moves about the city, aware that wherever he goes the bill collectors and Thaw's hired spies are on his trail. In the office, he has gone so far as to hang a mirror aimed at the door allowing him to catch sight of an approaching creditor in time to make a quick exit through a back door.

To his friends White complains of the stress of his professional burdens, but it is apparent to most that he needs constant work to survive. Among the many projects making demands on his time is the house for Helen and Payne Whitney, which is nearing completion. When, after almost five years, it is ready for occupancy, it will not only turn out to be the most expensive private project of White's career but it will also be hailed as one of the best in every respect. Helen Whitney will forget her frustration and lavish unreserved praise on the home she had feared would never be finished and on the man responsible for its magnificence. The triumphant outcome owes much to White's remarkable ability to seal off his worries when immersed in creative work. Just as he is able to insulate himself from feeling remorse for the pain he inflicts on others when he is in the grip of amorous passion.

Evelyn, who had accepted her sentence to "live forthwith in the charmed circle of a Presbyterian home" as part of her marriage vows, is now occupying a wing of the Thaw family manse in Pittsburgh. After returning from their cross-country honeymoon, during which their train was besieged by reporters at every stop, she is enduring life at Lyndhurst, a hideous monument to Calvinist gloom that is Mother Thaw's dreary domain. Covered in black lace and interested only in her charitable church work, Mother Thaw is a joyless presence. Like cordial but distant acquaintances, she and Evelyn cross paths beneath the huge chandeliers that hang over rooms cluttered with ugly overstuffed furniture but empty of life.

After marrying off Harry's older sister to a Carnegie and Alice to a titled Englishman (albeit a weasely fortune hunter), Mother Thaw has been forced to accept her favorite son's choice of a showgirl, a disappointment Mother Thaw is ready to tolerate in the hope that domestic life with the woman he loves will put an end to Harry's perversities. And now that Evelyn is her daughter-in-law, Mother Thaw is grimly determined to rehabilitate her among residents of Pittsburgh's mansion elite, a campaign that is not going well. According to a newspaper account, Pittsburgh society is refusing "in spite of the efforts of Mrs. William Thaw, to receive Evelyn Nesbit."

Evelyn, having made her decision to marry Harry with few illusions, is also prepared to do her part to make the best of the situation. She doesn't complain but takes mental notes on life at Lyndhurst, which, from her perspective, is both more boring and funnier than she could have imagined. She is stupefied by her mother-in-law's tastelessness, her cultural ignorance, and the rigidity of her views. She observes with amazement the rituals of a family "that finds a joy in the little things that do not matter—the appearance of a

new minister, the comforts of a pew, the profits of a church bazaar . . ." There
are few visitors, but those who come arrive from the inner circle of pious Pres-
byterians. The ministers and their wives—predictably benign, intellectually
wanting—are a species for study. The wives speak "with a monotony and a
sameness" that suggests to Evelyn the existence of a school for ministers' wives
where they are taught "to say the same things in identical terms."

At first, Evelyn finds them interesting as a type she has never encountered,
and she suspects their act is a pose. Only with time does she conclude that
no, they are in earnest—that "their atrocious taste in dress . . . their terrible
triteness" is genuine. Dinners with these people are excruciating. Dinners *en
famille* are no better. Evelyn claims to have seen Mother Thaw animated on
only one occasion "when she suffered a heart attack from eating too much
mince pie and ice cream."

In these early days at Lyndhurst, Harry is on his best behavior. Evelyn
credits him with being the only member of the family with any taste and with
shielding her from the hostility she sometimes faces from a society that shuns
her. That Harry also shares his mother's interest in church work is to her
"a standing wonder." She claims admiration for his efforts on behalf of the
church but mystification when she hears him "enter so heartily into the details
of an organ fund or the work of this guild or the other."

The sociological study of these aliens amuses Evelyn and keeps her from
making heartbreaking comparisons between the dull purgatory she now
inhabits and the lost paradise of life with Stanny, but she is relieved when
plans are made to accompany Mother Thaw on a trip to Europe in the spring
of 1906. Plans that Harry may have no intention of carrying out.

29

ANOTHER PROBE, A NEW HERO

*Thousands of New Yorkers are entirely blind on the moral side and
only know that an act is immoral when it is written into the law as a felony.*
—WILLIAM TRAVERS JEROME

T he first meeting of the Armstrong Committee investigating charges
against the big life insurance companies is gaveled to order on September 6 by Counsel Charles Evans Hughes. Members of the Committee will continue to meet throughout the year at the elegant Bretton Hall
apartment hotel on Broadway. Hughes, who is considered a bright young
lawyer on the rise, has been garnering praise for his tireless efforts to chip
away at the defenses of the Big Three—The Equitable, New York Life, and
the Mutual Insurance Company—and get at the facts. Under his guidance,
the committee has been untangling interlocking directorates, uncovering
security-buying syndicates, and exposing the thievery of greedy insurance
magnates who routinely dip into corporate funds for their personal use while
paying themselves magnificent salaries. Bribery expenditures are enormous,
lobbyists obscenely well paid. For sheer brashness, the man hired by the
Mutual Life Insurance Company to manipulate legislation in Albany has
few rivals. Andrew C. Fields has been living large in the capital, occupying
a sumptuously furnished residence known as the "House of Mirth" and
charging its upkeep and accoutrements to "legal expenses"—a staggering $2
million-plus between 1898 and 1904.

The newspapers, which have been conducting their own informal investigations into the obscene extravagance of the insurance company grandees and the plight of their exploited policyholders, will have much for readers to feast on when the facts uncovered by the committee are released for public consumption. They are already putting increasing pressure on Jerome, reminding him constantly of his vow to send "corporate criminals" up the river to Sing Sing. While he remains a hero to the masses who voted for him, in political circles even some early supporters are raising doubts about his effectiveness. They grumble that rather than immersing himself in the painstaking lawyerly work required to bring corporate criminals to justice, he seems to prefer the excitement of leading dangerous raids against easy targets and the drama of the courtroom when there is a high-profile murderer to prosecute. Jerome can hardly deny that close study of the obscure language of legal and corporate documents bores and frustrates him, though it has not, in fact, stopped him from spending many fruitless hours at the task.

The constant needling wears on him. Over and over again he argues his case, explaining that the actions of insurance executives, however "immoral, unethical, dastardly," are not necessarily illegal as the law stands. It is one thing for the layman to recognize obvious corruption, quite another for lawmakers to define it and prosecutors to prove it and punish it.

So Jerome is criticized while praise is heaped on Hughes—brilliant, high-minded, handsome, and expected to go far. There is talk of running him for governor, a run Jerome himself still hopes to make.

Jerome is braced for a fresh barrage of criticism when the Armstrong Committee issues its report after the New Year. But for the moment he is eager to extricate himself from the miasma of capitalist corruption and resume his role as courtroom warrior prosecuting his friend Norman Hapgood for criminal libel—though he has no intention of convicting him.

1906

30

GATHERING SHADOWS

That dude won't attack me with a pistol. He hasn't nerve enough.
—STANFORD WHITE

I n February 1906 Stanford and Bessie White are among the seventy guests at a costume dinner hosted by Charles and Lily Barney that the *New York Times* calls "one of the few distinctly original entertainments of the Winter." Guests have been asked to come as 16th-century notables from the courts of Europe, and White, who likes nothing better than to create an elaborate costume for an evening of extravagant revels, is photographed nobly posed and resplendent in an ermine-trimmed velvet jacket, embroidered tunic, tights, and feathered cap.

The Barney mansion at 38th Street and Park Avenue, remodeled and redecorated by White, is considered one of Manhattan's most magnificent, though it has not always given Barney much pleasure. Work on the town house had dragged on far longer than expected, and the long exile to a hotel had put Barney in a deep depression. The delays and cost overruns—always more common than not with White—had put a strain on the men's long friendship. Then, shortly after the Barneys moved into their splendid new home, it, along with neighboring houses, began to sink, its foundation damaged by Barney's own company. The Interborough Rapid Transit (IRT), blasting for the subway tunnel leading to Grand Central Station, is the culprit. A prime backer of the underground rail line, Barney is caught between concern for his investment and, as the *Times* reports, the fear that his residence might "fall into the subway."

The bond between the city's foremost tastemaker and the financial wizard, who also happens to be a generous and passionate patron of the arts, has survived the tensions between architect and client, and White has become heavily dependent on Barney. In his old friend he has the one person he can count on to understand the chaos of his finances and to do what he can to bring some order to them. Barney, a sportsman in the less strenuous fashion of his times and his class—he enjoys yachting, hunting, pistol-shooting—has interests that White has no time for, but highly choreographed soireés involving costumes are a shared passion, and White would never miss one.

When at 8:30 a trumpet sounds the call to dinner, the Whites join the kings, queens, and infantas in the Renaissance Tapestry Room, to be seated at tables decorated with boars' heads and stuffed birds, where they will consume a meal of 16th-century viands. It is a scenario usually guaranteed to lift White's spirits, but his pleasure is dimmed by suspicions that Thaw's detectives are lurking outside, perhaps craning their necks for a peek at an orgy that is, in fact, a gathering of the silly but respectable rich. In his obsession with White, Thaw has been relentlessly deploying his spies, directing them to report back with accounts of what his anti-vice ally Anthony Comstock has denounced as the "awful and disgusting" behavior of the dissolute social elite. What he has learned is that evidence is elusive, that no one is willing to come forward to confirm his claim that White and his friends are "moral perverts" who ravish young girls with abandon and impunity.

After a difficult winter, White writes to Gus in early May about a proposed visit to Cornish accompanied by McKim, whose recuperation is progressing. "BELOVED!" he salutes Gus, who has accused him of being more interested in seeing a fine New England spring than in seeing him. Not so, writes White, "You are not only mistaken, but one of the most modest and unassuming men with so 'beetly' a brow and so large a nose 'wot is.'" The visit may be hard to organize, he admits: "I am a pretty hard bird to snare; and as for Charlie, he varies ten thousand times more than a compass does from the magnetic pole; so all this may end in smoke; but the cherry blossoms are out, and to hell with the Pope!"

There is no trip in the end, but the two old friends see each other in June when Gus comes to New York for X-ray treatments.

Shortly before leaving for Restigouche in June, White visits a young friend who is hospitalized. He confides to her that he is unnerved knowing that Thaw always carries a pistol and has threatened to kill him. But when she advises him to have Thaw arrested, he scoffs, "Oh, Thaw is crazy. He is a 'dope' fiend. He lives on the stuff but he won't hurt anybody. I don't fear him." Barely two weeks later, on his return from Restigouche, which has not had its usual calming effect, White, in a high state of anxiety, has changed his mind. He tells Bergoff, his hired detective, that the constant surveillance is making him "a nervous wreck" and that he plans to take the matter to the courts and put a stop to it.

He finds some relief on the weekend of June 23 with Bessie, his son Larry, and Larry's two young houseguests at Box Hill, where he is able to relax and enjoy the beauty of the countryside and the elegant home he has created from a simple farmhouse. One afternoon he drives out to Southampton, the seaside resort where, for the past ten years, Jimmie Breese has been doing something similar, turning a farmhouse into a mansion with Stanny's help. Work is in progress on what the *Southampton Press* will describe as "one of the most artistic music rooms on Long Island." White's opulent tastes are reflected in high, carved gilt columns, a painted Italian ceiling, and the usual artful clutter of tapestries, antiquities, and animal skins. Breese's daughter later recalled watching White, "his red hair *en brosse*, lying flat on his back on the elevated platform showing the Italian workers how we—he—wanted the work done."

Once again Breese has quite literally lifted his friend from the depths. But on Monday White will have to return to the city and an ominous reality.

·31·

A HIGH-WIRE ACT

If I should ever pen by chance some actionable skit,
And by a luckless circumstance, get hailed to court for it,
I hope that William T. Jerome will try the self-same plan
Upon the people's witnesses he works on Colonel Mann.
For as he's run the present trial of Hapgood up to date
I'd rather be defendant than the witness for the state.
—James I. Montague

As the date set for Norman Hapgood's trial on charges of criminal libel draws near, Jerome is in high spirits. If all goes according to plan, his performance in the courtroom will be as entertaining as it is astonishing—a high-wire act that will require him to establish the accused as a paragon of integrity and expose his own chief witness for the prosecution, Colonel Mann, as the villain. Cocounsels John W. Osborne and Edward M. Shepard will be responsible for defending Hapgood, though with the prosecutor on defendant Hapgood's side, their contribution is hardly necessary.

The newspapers have gotten wind of what is to come and are primed for what is anticipated to be "the best show in town." Seats in the dilapidated courtroom, with its buckling walls and flaking paint, will be hard to come by. The courtroom regulars who treat trials as a free-admission spectator sport will have to compete for seats with Hapgood's society friends, who are in on the joke and looking forward to the fun, as well as Colonel Mann's family and flunkies. Unaware of Jerome's duplicity, Mann's camp will be out in force, anxious to witness Hapgood's humiliating comeuppance.

As expected, on the morning of January 15, 1906, opening day of the trial, throngs fill the dingy corridors of the Criminal Courts Building long before court is called to order at 11:00 A.M., with Judge James Fitzgerald presiding over a trial that promises to be every bit as carnivalesque as Nan Patterson's. All eyes are on Jerome when he strides into the courtroom looking every bit the stern prosecutor, tall, square-jawed, and unsmiling. Exhilarated by his starring role and the twists of the script that will allow him to put his tactical brilliance on display, he takes the stage with the confidence of the folk hero he knows himself to be. Nor is he the only one supplying an avid press with colorful copy. Reporters can hardly believe their good fortune as the corpulent Colonel arrives in court each day carrying a high silk hat, wearing pin-striped trousers, and sporting a bright red or yellow vest under his Prince Albert coat. His long white beard, worn in the outmoded split-chin fashion, excites much comment; the *American* reports that it gives him "a fierce, buccaneering air." Once seated, he makes his presence felt by reacting histrionically to each turn of the testimony, groaning, grinning, pulling his whiskers. Judge Joseph Deuel, his right-hand man and the official complainant in the case against Hapgood, is a less compelling addition to the colorful cast but a picturesque presence nevertheless, short and stout with an outstanding head of curly white hair and a classic handlebar moustache. Usually jovial, he has adopted a more sober countenance, glaring angrily across the courtroom at the accused.

Defendant Hapgood, though conventionally attired and without exotic facial ornamentation, has the look of a "lean, keen, ascetic student," according to the *Journal-American*. At thirty-seven, he has abandoned a career in the law, choosing journalism instead. His reputation at *Collier's* is of a cautious rather than crusading editor, a stance gently mocked by Finley Peter Dunne, Hapgood's colleague at the magazine, who has his fictional Mr. Dooley deride "Norman Slapgood" and his motto "Yes . . . and no." Until he actually takes the stand, Hapgood is careful to hide whatever happy anticipation he may be feeling in advance of his friend Jerome's performance.

Spectators have no such compunction, particularly those social and literary celebrities for whom privileged seats have been reserved by Hapgood, Bobby Collier, or Jerome. Presiding Judge James Fitzgerald, perhaps intimidated by their social cachet, seems loath to use his gavel to curb their exuberance. The muted hilarity coming from one corner of the room is especially interesting to the press, present in force to report daily on the city's number-one attraction. While hundreds of the less favored are turned away every day, Mrs. Robert Collier, who happens to be the granddaughter of Mrs. Astor, and her retinue of society matrons take their seats in what the *Times* designates "the Royal Box." From this "fetching coterie" can be heard tittering and the occasional gasp whenever an indelicate reference comes up in testimony. After each recess they pose for the press, "dressed as if for the theatre."

On January 16, Judge Deuel, the first to take the stand, has no satisfactory defense when presented with evidence that he has been serving *Town Topics'* shady interests from the bench and accepting large payments for removing unflattering items from the scandal sheet. Then, on January 19, when Mann is called to the witness chair, a memo inscribed with his initials, suggesting that pressure be exerted on certain persons who would probably rather their affair not be exposed in *Town Topics*, elicits an embarrassing, and ultimately fatal, lie. Mann denies the obvious fact that he had signed off on the memo, a position that becomes increasingly untenable when the socialite and former congressman Oliver H. P. Belmont, "wearing the highest standing collar that was ever seen in public," as the *Journal-American* noted, takes the stand. A visibly nervous Colonel Mann is obliged to hear Belmont testify that after refusing to "lend" money to Mann, he had become the subject of some fifty abusive items in *Town Topics*.

When Hapgood is finally called as the last witness and asked by attorney for the defense Edward Shepard to divulge his source for the damning editorials he aimed at Mann, his response—that his source was the district attorney's office—sends ripples of laughter through the Royal Box. "The consensus between the DA and myself," he states, "was that the important thing would be to strike at the root of the trouble and get the man who was the fountain-head. We were entirely in accord."

"Then your judgment was based on the district attorney's?" asks Jerome, rising for cross-examination. "Then it turns out *I* am the writer of this article?"

This, according to the *Tribune*, provokes such uproarious laughter that Justice Fitzgerald, his patience at an end, is obliged to rap "violently" for order.

After a recess, Shepard delivers a two-hour closing address for the defense. Hapgood, he declares, has "rendered the best, the truest, the divinest service to this city and to this nation" in taking on the Colonel and his sham journalism. It is a biting denunciation of *Town Topics*, which he calls "a conspiracy to produce money" by making use of "sneaks in the clubs, sneaks in the kitchen, sneaks in the churches." He dismisses Deuel as "a corrupt judge" and Mann as "the master craftsman of blackmailers."

The next morning Jerome delivers the closing address for the prosecution. Besides making it obvious that he never meant to convict Hapgood, he takes a perverse pleasure in alienating the press. He declares that the criminal practices of *Town Topics* are standard procedure for all newspapers, that every paper in town prints atrocious scandal. It is the kind of righteous tirade that friends and supporters who are promoting Jerome for a gubernatorial run have come to dread.

On January 26 it takes the jury just seven minutes to acquit Hapgood. The "fetching coterie" in the Royal Box, despite a warning from Judge Fitzgerald, who has had enough of the carnival in his courtroom, rushes forward to throw their arms around Hapgood, who bears his "honors" easily, according to the *Journal-American*.

"Get out of here, you criminal—you've had your day in court," Jerome orders Hapgood, and the two leave arm in arm, headed for a victory feast at Delmonico's. The next morning Jerome starts proceedings to bring Colonel Mann to trial for perjury.

Mann's lawyer, the celebrated legal dreadnaught Martin Littleton—eloquent, handsome, considered Jerome's equal as a courtroom warrior, and reportedly being paid a whopping $75,000 to rescue the Colonel—puts up multiple hurdles on the path to justice. It will be almost another year before Mann's perjury trial will open in December, and then it will be rushed to a conclusion by the irascible Judge John Goff. The trial will be Goff's last case in the Court of General Sessions before he takes office as a justice of the New

York Supreme Court on January 1, 1907, and he will have no patience with delays, even going so far as to threaten to declare a mistrial if *People v. Mann* threatens to last beyond the end of the year.

When the perjury trial does finally open, Assistant District Attorney Francis Garvan suffers a major setback when Judge Goff prevents him from admitting Mann's testimony in the Hapgood trial. Garvan will nevertheless force Mann to admit having "borrowed" almost $200,000 from various Fifth Avenue and Wall Street swells with something to hide. Edward Post and several other grandees testify to Mann's underhanded methods of gathering "news" intended to satisfy his readers' appetite for scandal and collecting never-to-be-repaid loans.

Though the Colonel will be cornered and exposed as a perjurer and a blackmailer, Martin Littleton will deliver a summation that will have little to do with the law and everything to do with the brave old Civil War veteran and exemplary citizen under attack. The next day, the *World* will report: "When Littleton told how good a man he was, the Colonel wept, holding his hands to his face and sobbing." Everyone will weep for the old war hero, including the jurors who will deliberate for four hours and return with a "not guilty" verdict. The Colonel, overjoyed, will throw his arms around Littleton, "letting his tears of joy trickle down his coat" and in the next issue of *Town Topics* he will credit Goff for the gratifying verdict, writing that the triumph is a reflection of "the kindness of his great, fatherly heart," and naming him as his pick for the position of Chief Justice of the Supreme Court.

The old rogue will go free, another disappointment, but the trial will have exposed the Big Spider's true nature and put an end to his reign of terror. There will be little to celebrate, however, among the rich voluptuaries who have seen their tormentor defanged, only to realize they have traded one scourge for another. No longer victims of the Colonel's seamy but discreet swindle, they will be publicly attacked for their moral laxity day after day in the sensational press. There will be countless columns devoted to lurid tales—some true, some fictional—of their degeneracy, all designed to sell papers to readers with deep-seated resentments against the entitled elite and a robust appetite for scandal.

32

JUNE 25, 1906

This is a nightmare! It isn't true! It can't be true!
I will wake up and find it's all a dream . . .
—EVELYN NESBIT

The day is already unseasonably warm as White and his driver leave Long Island and head for the city early on Monday morning, June 25. By the time they arrive at the Manhattan offices of McKim, Mead & White the heat is oppressive. The summer of 1906 is off to a hot start, and it seems there's not a breath of air in all of New York. Hordes seeking relief are jostling for space in steamy streetcars heading for the beaches of Coney Island or the Rockaways. Word that the hippopotamus at the Central Park Zoo has collapsed from heat prostration is quickly followed by news of his death.

White has decided to postpone a quick trip to Philadelphia planned for Monday so that he can meet his son and Larry's visiting classmate from Harvard, Leroy King, for dinner in the city. At the office he tackles the huge workload that always awaits him, taking time to confer with Saint-Gaudens about their collaboration on a monument honoring James McNeill Whistler. Then, in the late afternoon, he takes a break and heads for the pleasure palace that has sealed his reputation as the undisputed architect of Gilded Age pageantry and festivity. Ever since its completion in 1891, Madison Square Garden has been central to White's life. Occupying a full block from 26th to 27th Street between Madison and Park Avenue, the building has been the setting for the entertainments around which fashionable New Yorkers—people like White himself—plan their social calendars. Its crowning glory, and White's destination on this muggy June day, is the 315-foot Moorish tower topped by Gus's scandalous nude Diana.

White takes the elevator up to the rooftop Garden Theater, where, as the Garden's architect, investor, impresario, and famous occupant of an exquisite tower studio, he is on home turf. After exchanging greetings with stagehands and staff, he bustles backstage to check on preparations for the evening's performance of *Mamzelle Champagne*, a particularly frothy musical in which he has invested. He is popular with the chorus girls who work the open-air theater in summer, serving up light comedy to audiences dressed to the nines. Finding the girls wilting from the heat, White asks that the water cooler be filled with ice and lemonade. Before leaving, he reminds stage manager Lionel Lawrence that he wants to be introduced to one of the new girls, "a little peach" named Maude Fulton.

As he heads home to dress for dinner, White is conscious of Harry's hirelings following not far behind. The thermometer has dropped into the seventies by the time he takes the wheel of his electric car—one of his great pleasures—and heads for Martin's, a haunt favored by fashionable bohemians, with Larry and his friend. They take a table on the balcony, which is fitted out as a French café, and spend about an hour in the restaurant. After dinner, White drops his young guests at the New Amsterdam Theater for a revue more to their taste, then stops at the Manhattan Club to write a quick note to a young actress in Atlantic City. After posting it at 9:15, he lingers awhile at the club before walking the short distance to the Garden. Arriving at the Tower shortly before 11:00 o'clock, he takes the elevator up to the theater, where he finds the show in its final act, and struggling.

∽⌒∾

A few blocks away, Harry and Evelyn have been staying at the Lorraine Hotel, where they have booked a suite for two weeks before sailing for Europe. Not one of the fashionable hotels like the Waldorf or the Astor, the Lorraine takes pride in its family-style accommodations. A bit old-fashioned and staid, it has none of the glamor that would have pleased Evelyn, who had been looking forward to some city fun and excitement. Instead, she is followed everywhere by Harry's detectives and forbidden to see most of her friends. Harry has made it clear that the only people she is to see in the city are May Mackensie, her chorus girl confidante, and Mrs. J. J. Caine, who had once sheltered Evelyn overnight when Harry was convinced that thugs from the notorious Monk Eastman Gang were after them. He has exempted the two women because "Mrs. Caine is a decent married woman, and May MacKensie," he declares to Evelyn's astonishment, "is a virgin."

The oppressive heat and Harry's obsessive monitoring have put a damper on their New York stay, but Evelyn's spirits improve when Harry proposes a night out on the Monday before their scheduled departure. Craving a refreshing soak, she has her maid draw a bath at around six o'clock. To her relief, Mother Thaw has chosen to sail on an earlier ship with the goal, Evelyn suspects, of assessing the state of her daughter Alice's marriage to the "Count de Money," which is rumored to be "troubled." Happy to be free—for the moment—of both mother and son, Evelyn sinks into the tub, while Harry, confident of her whereabouts, sets off to walk the four blocks to Sherry's wearing a summer straw hat and a ridiculously unseasonable overcoat. After downing three whiskeys, he is picked up by Evelyn, who wears a white summer dress and a fashionably oversized black picture hat, and Harry's chauffeur delivers them to Martin's. They are joined at the restaurant by Thomas McCaleb, an aspiring writer, and Truxton Beale, an old friend of Harry's from Pittsburgh. Beale is of great interest to Harry chiefly because he is reported to have killed a man in California but was acquitted using a defense based on the spurious "unwritten law" that affirms a killer innocent of murder if his victim has seduced—or tried to seduce—his wife or his sister.

The Thaws find Martin's already crowded with stylish diners when they arrive at around eight o'clock. While the balcony café offers the best vantage point for viewing the fashion show below, the sumptuous main dining room, a marvel of Gallic excess—all gilt, silk, and huge chandeliers—is the place to be seen, and Evelyn is dressed to turn heads. Harry checks his absurd overcoat at the entrance, and the party of four is shown to a table where Harry, as host, takes a seat with his back to the room while Evelyn, seated opposite Harry, has the best view of the dining room and the balcony. The conversation is at first rather subdued, ranging from gossip to money, until Harry orders a second bottle of champagne. The sommelier, wearing his gold key and chain, performs the ritual pop and pour with professional aplomb, and the party grows livelier. Harry orders three cocktails for himself, and after drinking them in rapid succession he comes to life, speaking loudly and disjointedly on subjects as unrelated as his mother's dedication to charity work and the dangers of mountain climbing.

Amid the champagne-induced exuberance, Evelyn is able to hide her panic when she spots an impressive figure making his way through the sea of tables, trailed by two young men. If White notices Evelyn and her party as he passes through the main dining room on his way to the balcony, he makes no visible sign. Luckily, Harry and his friends do not see White, but Evelyn, apparently feeling duty-bound to report all White sightings, slips Harry a note. "The beast was here but has left" she informs him, half expecting him to fly into a rage, but Harry takes the news with odd equanimity. As they leave the restaurant at about nine o'clock, Harry reclaims his overcoat and they walk over to Madison Square Garden. As she has done so many times in the past with Stanny, Evelyn takes the elevator to the Roof Garden, this time, astonishingly, with Harry. That he would choose to spend an evening in the dazzling rooftop theater created by his sworn enemy baffles Evelyn, but she can only hope that his restrained reaction to her note is a sign that calm will prevail.

Seating in the Roof Garden Theater is at tables rather than rows, and on locating theirs, Harry removes his hat but not his overcoat and almost immediately leaves the others, preferring to wander until curtain time. Evelyn catches the occasional glimpse of his conspicuous overcoat as he moves restlessly around the vast open-air theater. Relieved to see that the table several rows from the stage, always reserved for White, is empty, she allows herself to relax. It is a bittersweet pleasure to feel again the spell cast by such splendid surroundings—the illuminated tower crowned by Saint-Gaudens's stunning Diana, the undulating strands of tiny, loosely strung lights that wink and sway in the breeze, the huge potted plants strategically placed to give the theater a feeling of intimacy beneath the vast sky. Harry returns for the first act of *Mamzelle Champagne*, which is almost immediately recognized as a flop. Members of the audience quickly lose interest in the action onstage and begin table-hopping and chatting rudely, putting police on evening duty on the alert. Without a word to Evelyn, Harry leaves the table and joins the the milling crowd, quickly disappearing from sight.

Then, suddenly, Evelyn is aware of a disruption in the theater. Attention is directed to the back of the theater, where the tall figure of Stanford White is making his way to the table she had hoped would remain empty.

❧

By the time White steps out of the elevator and into the theater, he has missed Maude Fulton's rendition of "Can I Fascinate You," which earned her a rare round of applause, and tenor Harry Short is giving his all to a song titled "I Could Love a Thousand Girls." Twenty dancers are kicking and prancing onstage, but some among the nine hundred in the disgruntled audience have progressed from rude chatter to hissing and booing. White's entrance causes a ripple of excitement in the restless throng as he cuts a path to his table, nodding to friends, stopping for a word or two with acquaintances, waving to someone at a distant table. He seems to carry a corona of energy around him, charging the air and distracting momentarily from the vapid business onstage. When he finally reaches his table, Harry Stevens, the Garden's caterer, joins him, and the two carry on an animated conversation. White is so amused at something Stevens says that he throws his head back and laughs with the uninhibited delight that fills Evelyn, who cannot help watching and remembering, with nostalgia. When Stevens gets up to leave, White gives him a clap on the arm—a warm, easy, man-to-man gesture.

Alone again, White turns his attention to the stage and the silly spectacle of the show's closing number, waiting it out perhaps only because he is expecting Lionel Lawrence to deliver on his request for an introduction to Maude Fulton. With his fist tucked under his chin, he is a pensive figure, presumably entertaining thoughts of the pleasurable evening ahead, which he hopes to spend with "the little peach." Preoccupied, he is oblivious to the unsettled atmosphere around him. Oblivious, too, to something stirring close by. As the chorus joins the tenor for the final verse, a darkly muffled figure steps out of the shadows, moves to within three feet of White's table, pulls a revolver from his overcoat and fires three shots in quick succession.

White half rises, as if to stand, then slumps forward, taking the edge of the tablecloth with him as silver scatters and the jagged shards of a shattered wineglass disappear into a rising puddle of blood.

For a few seconds the audience assumes the gunfire is part of the show and is still. Then what Evelyn senses instantly dawns on the crowd as those nearest White scatter to reveal the toppled body of Stanford White. The music comes to a fitful halt, a woman screams—a long, piercing wail—several women faint, and there is a panicked rush for the exit. Evelyn watches in a state of shock as her husband, standing over his victim, raises his smoking revolver high in the air for all to see, then calmly empties its chambers, sending the remaining bullets clattering to the floor next to White's body. She elbows her way through the surging mob and reaches Harry just as he has been apprehended.

"Oh Harry, why did you do it?" she asks, throwing her arms around his neck to the astonishment of those close enough to witness the scene and hear his reply.

"It's all right, dear," Harry assures her. "It's all right. I have probably saved your life."

To the official who finally seizes the weapon he is still holding, Harry has a different answer: "He deserved it," he says. "I can prove it. He ruined my wife and then deserted the girl."

33

BEFORE THE STORM

Poor Stanford White labored through his life under a heavy hereditary handicap of sensuality. There is no reason why anybody should attempt to disguise that now that he is dead, seeing that he never made the slightest pretense of disguising it when he was alive. He had not that hypocrisy which is the homage vice pays to virtue.
—OPEN LETTER SIGNED "ANTI CANT"

Jerome, who has been working sixteen-hour days while under constant pressure to do more, is on vacation when the news reaches him of Stanford White's murder. When reporters finally catch up with him in Atlanta, they are taken aback by his insistence that the case is no more important than most homicides.

"What is there important about one man killing another for jealousy?" he asks. "It happens nearly every day in the week. In this case the defendant happens to have money, but in the eyes of the law that does not add luster to his situation . . . why it's just an everyday police court story."

Nearly everyone else disagrees. If people had ever believed in the moral superiority of the rich, the muck recently raked up confirming their cheating, thievery, and depravity on a grand scale has shown them otherwise. Irvin S. Cobb, the writer and correspondent for Pulitzer's *Evening World*, recognizes immediately that the story has everything: "Wealth, degeneracy, rich old wasters, delectable young chorus girls . . . the abnormal pastimes and weird orgies of over-aesthetic artists and jaded debauchees." The secrets of wicked Gotham, with its cast of rich and beautiful and famous sinners, will make a fine banquet for the masses, with their rapacious hunger for scandal.

If Jerome's initial attitude of studied boredom at another jealousy-inspired killing seems obtuse to the excited reporters, one explanation for the absence of his customary appetite for the fight may be more personal than professional. Though he would never compare his romance with Ethel Elliot to the philandering of men like White, the role of prosecutor in a case that is bound to focus on White's illicit affair with the murderer's wife is problematic. Jerome is, after all, involved in an extramarital affair himself, and with a woman twenty years his junior. He has been extraordinarily successful in preventing the truth of his unusual domestic arrangement from reaching the public at large, but the risk of exposure is always present.

Whatever the reasons for Jerome's phlegmatic reaction to news of the murder, his reticence in Atlanta is unsustainable in New York where the press, recognizing the story's potential to sell papers, is wasting no time in whipping the city into an emotional frenzy. Not only has one of New York's best-known figures been murdered in a crime of passion over a showgirl but the accused murderer is fabulously wealthy, the woman at the apex of the love triangle is spectacularly beautiful, and the rumors of illicit sex and bacchanalian behavior that have swirled around the victim promise to provide sensational copy.

In her panic immediately following the murder, Evelyn takes refuge with her friend May MacKenzie, but late on that same night, coming out of her shock, she takes stock of her situation and decides to act. While the city sleeps, she returns to the Hotel Lorraine to gather up letters left in her luggage—presumably letters from or about Stanford White. Meanwhile, Stanny's friends are taking similar precautions. Early in the morning on the day after the murder, Charles McKim, still physically frail and now emotionally devastated over the loss of his oldest and dearest friend, instructs some trusted members of the firm to enter White's private office, gather up any pornographic photographs, and burn them. A little later, one of White's private secretaries sends some 160 books of erotica and various photographs, paintings, and letters from White's office to Jimmie Breese for safekeeping.

Among the oddest of the pretrial maneuvers is one involving Harry's loyal retainer, Bedford, who contacts Evelyn to ask for the concealed and always-locked suitcase containing Harry's whips and other paraphernalia. Evelyn remarks that he looks unwell, and a few days later she learns that Bedford has died, "out of a clear sky," of acute appendicitis—a kind twist of fate for Harry. Had Jerome been able to put Bedford on the witness stand, Evelyn reckons that all of Harry's perversities would have spilled out and made front-page news.

In the early days of Thaw's imprisonment after being charged with murder and denied bail, throngs of New Yorkers gather daily in the courtyard around the Tombs, hoping for a glimpse of Evelyn, "the faithful wife," come to console her husband, "the playboy killer," in the melodramatic parlance of the press. One reporter, who manages to talk his way into the Tombs intending to photograph the wretched prisoner, is astonished to find Harry enjoying the preferential treatment a confessed murderer can command if he happens to be the millionaire "Harry K. Thaw of Pittsburgh." Opening their papers the next morning, some are amused, others outraged, to see Harry, not in the usual prison garb but nattily dressed, seated behind an elegantly set table about to tuck into an elaborate meal from Delmonico's. There will be champagne to wash it down, thanks to an accommodating doctor who has prescribed it for "medical purposes." Visible behind Harry is the brass bed that will spare him the indignity of sleeping on a standard prisoner cot.

While Thaw's "widowed mother" is reportedly making frantic arrangements to rush back from Europe to save her son, Evelyn is Harry's first visitor. Arriving in a chauffeur-driven electric hansom, she and her driver find the area around the Tombs so jammed with rubberneckers that mounted police have to clear a path for them to proceed.

"Give us a look at you!" someone shouts from the crowd, which has come for a glimpse of her "angel face" only to find that she is wearing a veil. Unnerved by the mob, Evelyn hurries inside where she is searched by a guard before being led to the tier of cells known as "Murderers' Row." There, Harry greets her, looking "cheerful and buoyant." It is obvious to Evelyn that he has no doubts about the righteousness of his act or the wisdom of carrying it out. Why should he regret killing a man who deserved to die? And what does he have to fear when his mother will pay whatever is necessary to spare him any unpleasant legal consequences—just as she always has? There is nothing to worry about, he assures his boofuls.

Immediately upon her return from Europe, Mother Thaw, draped in black lace and looking the picture of mournful maternal concern, confirms her son's faith in her by making her intentions clear: "I am prepared to pay a million dollars to save his life," she announces. Without delay, she makes her first purchase, hiring a press agent whose instructions are to present Harry to the newspapers as the avenging hero he believes himself to be.

If Jerome has any lingering doubts about the importance of the Thaw murder case—for the rule of law and for his own career—they do not survive Mother Thaw's ringing endorsement of the power of money. Now fully engaged and full of passion for the pursuit of justice, he has fighting words for Mother Thaw and her plan to buy her son's freedom: "With all of his millions," he thunders, "Thaw is a fiend! No matter how rich a man is, he cannot get away with murder!"

Thaw shot White point-blank before scores of witnesses, but Jerome has no illusions that convicting him will be easy. Not only will he be up against the mighty power of a mighty fortune with all the legal, medical, and press talent money can buy, but, in a culture corrupted by money, there is little respect for concepts of decency and justice. To bring Thaw to justice in a trial that will be watched all over the world, he will need all of his fighting mettle and tactical brilliance—the courtroom mastery that had prompted Irvin S. Cobb to call him the greatest cross-examiner of his time. It is his chance to reverse his slipping public support, to prove the cynics wrong, to uphold the dignity of the law and his own role in preserving it.

While the two sides are looking ahead to their clash in the courtroom, a report is issued by doctors who had conducted an autopsy within a day of White's murder. They state that his death by natural causes would likely have occurred within a year or so, so ravaged was he by disease. They find evidence of kidney disease, incipient tuberculosis, and severe degeneration of his liver in addition to the three bullets they remove from his body. Had Thaw only left for Europe as planned, or had White not postponed his planned trip to Philadelphia, the city might have been spared the expense and trauma of a murder trial, and White would no doubt have been buried with the pomp and ceremony due a cultural hero.

34

A DISCREET FAREWELL

The service was in very good taste but I do not remember a sadder one.
—A. W. Drake

The sun has not yet risen over the tops of Gramercy Square's graceful old mansions when Stanford White's friends begin arriving outside his 21st Street home. Still in shock, they gather in the early-morning gloom before being ushered into the dazzling interior of the White residence, so heartbreakingly representative of its owner's exuberant nature and eclectic taste.

One by one, they file by the open coffin placed in the great drawing room beneath an antique Roman statue of Venus. By eight o'clock, when the undertaker arrives to remove the coffin, the house is filled with mourners.

A *Times* reporter, reduced to peering through a window, describes the scene as White's mother takes "a last look at her son," followed by Bessie and Larry. Then the coffin is carried to a hearse "on the shoulders of six men employed by the undertaker." The departure has been ordered an hour in advance of the time given out to the press to avoid the expected crowd of sensation seekers drawn by lurid press accounts of the murder.

By the time the "morbidly curious" converge outside the Gramercy Park house, requiring two policemen to bar the doorstep, the funeral party is already on its way to Long Island, where the service is to be held in St.

James Episcopal Church, the "quaint old worshipping place" near the White home, Box Hill. The family's original choice for a more public funeral honoring New York's preeminent architect was St. Bartholomew's, the imposing church at 44th Street and Madison Avenue with an entrance porch designed by White. There were to have been ten pallbearers, but with the media hoopla intensifying and the newspapers offering more and more scandalous details related to White's personal life, that plan has had to be scrapped to avoid the inevitable mobs. It has fallen on McKim to announce the change. Always extremely fond of Bessie, the person he calls "the dearest friend I have on earth," McKim has stepped in as her protector. Bearing his own heavy burden of sorrow, still in frail health, and brokenhearted to see Stanny's reputation in ruins, he has somehow summoned the strength to handle the funeral arrangements and do everything in his power to assure that Stanny will have a dignified farewell.

It is still early when the hearse carrying White's coffin arrives at the 34th Street ferry and some 250 mourners who have followed board a special train in Queens to make the journey out to St. James. The absence of many of White's close friends is conspicuous, but a saddened and subdued Jimmie Breese is there, along with Thomas B. Clarke, William Mead, and others unafraid to be identified as White's friends. There is no sermon, no eulogy, but the altar is banked with orchids, lilies, and roses, and light filtering through stained-glass windows commissioned from White's friend John LaFarge pay silent homage to White the artist. A brief prayer offered by the church rector asks for strength for the afflicted family. The choir sings "Asleep in Jesus" and then precedes the coffin down the long avenue to the churchyard, singing and chanting hymns until they reach the gravesite. There White is buried near his infant son, Richard Grant White, whose small tombstone was designed by McKim. It is just noon.

Breese lingers awhile at the gravesite with Bessie, Larry, and McKim. Then McKim accompanies Bessie and Larry back to Box Hill, strangely still on this June afternoon, while Breese boards the train with the others for the sad journey back to the city.

THE PRESS POUNCES

Here were all the intimate things of life in the million mouths of New York.
—EVELYN NESBIT

I n full battle mode, Mother Thaw proceeds to open her purse to all and any who will join in her campaign to tarnish the image of the golden boy of the Gilded Age and raise her reprobate son to hero status as the righteous slayer of a lecherous rogue. Press agent Ben Atwell has never had such a client or made so much money as he does as the source of a continuous outpouring of scabrous stories about White's private life. Day after day, they fill the front pages with vilification and mud-slinging aimed at the victim while presenting his murderer as the chivalrous avenger of his wife's honor. Columns devoted to White's Tower studio and his numerous dens of unspeakable iniquity, his weakness for Tenderloin beauties, and his gluttonous stag parties featuring lewd entertainments flood newspapers engaged in a competition to see which can print the most scandalous stories.

Most egregious are the sensationalist papers led by Hearst's *Journal-American*, which portray White as a monster of depravity and see their circulations leap by hundreds of thousands. Nor does White's old friend James Gordon Bennett hold back. From Paris he cables his editors at the *Herald*: "Give him hell!" A headline in *Vanity Fair* declares, STANFORD WHITE, VOLUPTUARY AND PERVERT, DIES THE DEATH OF A DOG. Even the *New York Times* prints a letter, purportedly sent to Evelyn by an angry mother whose daughter had been "pure and good" until she met "that moral leper" White and disappeared. Colonel Mann, with no further payments to be expected from the deceased, adopts a tone of pained disapproval in *Town Topics* and declares primly that "some such deplorable incident has been anticipated."

Throughout the summer and fall the campaign of slander fills the front pages, and though many of White's friends keep their silence—several actually flee the city and hide from reporters—not everyone does. Some of the actresses whom White had helped come forward to praise him and defend his parties at the Tower as great fun and "always respectable." From Paris, Charles Dana Gibson writes of his outrage at the attacks on his friend and makes plans for a memorial gathering.

Richard Harding Davis, the novelist, journalist, and dashing proponent of clean, adventurous living, is the most outspoken in publicly defending White. In an article in *Collier's* he condemns the "yellow press" for presenting a "hideous" image of White that has left his friends "stunned and silent." The real White, he writes of his friend, was incapable of "little meannesses. He admired a beautiful woman as he admired every other beautiful thing that God has given us..." Though he is being painted as a voluptuary, Davis observes, "his greatest pleasure was to stand all day waist-deep in the rapids of a Canadian river and fight it out with the salmon..." Gus Saint-Gaudens, sick with cancer and sick at heart, writes a heart-wrenching letter to *Collier's* from his home in Cornish, New Hampshire: "You have no doubt read in the newspapers of the death of White by an idiot fool who imagined himself wronged . . . an idiot that shoots a man of great genius for a woman with the face of an angel and the heart of a snake!"

Saint-Gaudens's sympathetic reading of Davis's article is not widely shared, and the idolized author is suddenly subjected to the same virulent attacks as the man whose reputation he sought to defend. A New Jersey librarian gathers Davis's books from the shelves and dumps them in the gutter. The headmaster of a prep school warns students against reading Davis's books, calling them the "foul emanations of a depraved romancer."

When Evelyn's mother, initially eager to attest to White's character and to supply letters and other evidence in his favor, suddenly finds herself unable to follow through owing to her "delicate health," rumors fly that Mother Thaw has paid for her silence. There is talk that Evelyn has substantially outdone her mother and has been promised as much as $1 million from her mother-in-law for agreeing to stand by Harry and blacken the name of the man she had once fallen "head over heels" in love with. The same man who, as a friend and not a lover, had once warned her about Thaw. Also soaking up a tidy sum is a hack writer hired by press agent Atwell to melodramaticize the battle waged by the chivalrous hero, Harold Daw, against the deplorable lech Stanford Black, ravisher of young girls like the innocent angel Emeline Huspeth. The play, which opens at the Amphion Theatre in September, strings together scenes taken from newspaper columns purporting to expose the depths of dissipation among society roués who prey on innocent females and thumb their noses at the conventions of decent society. The curtain comes down as Harry Daw, imprisoned in the Tombs, declares, "No jury on earth will send me to the electric chair, no matter what I have done or what I have been, for killing the man who defamed my wife. That is the unwritten law."

In this climate of unreason, no one is disposed to take to heart Assistant District Attorney Francis Garvan's warning that "it is ridiculously easy to besmirch the character of a dead man who cannot reply or institute a suit for libel." It is far easier still to be swept up by the sentimental image of Harry and Evelyn as naive youths whose lives are ruined by a suave and insistent seducer. Irvin Cobb, covering the story for the *World* and well aware of Mother Thaw's role in turning the story on its head, observes that money, the irresistible force for Harry's salvation, is being "poured out by the Thaw family, and sucked up, like water in a sand bed."

It's a double win for the yellow press, with gratuities flowing from Mother Thaw's purse and skyrocketing circulations.

36

GIRDING FOR BATTLE

Justice is equally as great in comedy in America as it is in Italy . . . instead of centering on the crime and the criminal or the problem of responsibility, [the trial] will likely enough seek to discuss whether the victim did not really provoke his aggressor to madness.
—EXCERPTED FROM AN ESSAY IN *LA VITA* OF ROME

Forced to abandon his initial opinion that White's murder did not rise above so many others committed in a jealous rage, Jerome has quickly recognized the trial's potential as a stage on which he can demonstrate his brilliance as a prosecutor. For the next six months he throws himself into preparing for his time in the spotlight. He puts himself through a cram course in abnormal psychology, reading every available authority on mental diseases, especially those dealing with paranoia, and combing through all legal precedents that may have bearing on the case. But the more he learns, the more troubled he is by the idea of sending Thaw—a man just about everyone but the accused and his mother knows is insane—to the electric chair. It is clear that should Harry be freed, his paranoia and perversities will make him a danger to others and that locking him up for life in an asylum for the insane is the best way to remove him from society. Not only would executing Thaw violate Jerome's sense of justice but it would almost certainly make him look bloodthirsty.

With that in mind, Jerome puts aside thoughts of delivering the dramatic courtroom performance that might have burnished his image and perhaps silenced his critics and instead uses his newly acquired knowledge of mental diseases to urge that Harry be locked up for life in a mental institution. He arranges to confer with a member of Harry's defense team, and the two sides agree that Thaw is insane and that a sanity commission should be appointed to examine him. If its members declare him insane, Harry will be sent immediately to a mental institution and a costly, time-consuming trial can be avoided.

But Mother Thaw, as determined to see her son a free man as Jerome is to lock him up, dismisses the plan and the planners, firing the whole defense team for suggesting anything less than a fight for Harry's complete freedom. Having favored justice over glory, Jerome gets his chance to shine anyway. Harry is too pleased with his role as a hero to spoil it by being called crazy. Both he and his mother are totally opposed to a traditional insanity plea, which would end Harry's social aspirations and taint the proud family name. A buoyant Harry tells reporters that he is looking forward to his trial and the chance to expose the "set of perverts" who prey on young girls.

Mother Thaw's search for a new defense team, despite the fortune she is willing to spend, is not easy. The opinion of her original lawyers, that the only way to spare Harry's life is to plead insanity, is widely shared. Finally she extends an offer of $50,000 to Delphin Delmas, and the famous San Francisco courtroom spellbinder—dubbed the "Napoleon of the Western Bar"—cannot resist. A representative of the Western school of silver-tongued oratory with a remarkable resemblance to portraits of the emperor of France, Delmas is considered all but invincible, boasting a record of nineteen acquittals in nineteen murder cases.

The prosecution will face a fierce fight. Making Jerome's preparations for battle especially difficult are the laws of New York, which do not require a specific plea of insanity when the defense enters a general not-guilty plea. This means Jerome must devise a two-way, all-purpose case. As Arthur Train observes, "He has to prepare to prosecute the case not only upon its merits but upon the possible question of the criminal irresponsibility of the defendant."

Approaching the challenge with characteristic intensity, Jerome has little time to celebrate Abe Hummel's suspension from the practice of law in July or his subsequent disbarment. Still defiant, Little Abe has rejected repeated offers of leniency in exchange for telling the truth about Charlie Morse, but perjury charges still hang over his head and, as prison looms, Jerome hopes the odds are improving for a change of heart.

At the end of a long day of study, Jerome often heads for Pontin's chophouse on Franklin Street, just steps from his office in the Criminal Courts Building. A favorite with lawyers and politicians, Pontin's is the place to tuck into a mutton chop and chew over the latest political and courtroom news. Lawyers and judges gather in the dimly lit, old-fashioned dining room to rehash the day's legal maneuvering while political operatives, hunched over corner tables, plot their next move. Supporters who are urging Jerome to run for governor and have been working to pave the way know they can usually find him there, and on August 11 they bring him something to celebrate. After noting on its editorial page that word has reached the *Sun* that "Mr. William Travers Jerome is considering the propriety of offering himself as a candidate for the governorship of this state," the paper declares: "If Mr. Jerome runs, Mr. Jerome will be elected."

On August 19, with his moment to shine on the world stage drawing near, and feeling confident, Jerome takes a break from the books to announce that he will seek the Democratic nomination for governor.

The only other prominent candidate for the nomination is Jerome's archrival, William Randolph Hearst, publisher of the nation's leading Democratic paper, wealthy champion of the little guy, relentless agitator against thieving insurance magnates, capitalist pillagers of the decrepit streetcar system, and William Travers Jerome, whom he attacks as unable or unwilling to prosecute the high and mighty. A self-styled raging reformer, twice elected to the House of Representatives and an unsuccessful candidate for mayor of New York, Hearst has an uneasy relationship with the Democratic machine, which he holds responsible for thwarting his mayoral bid. This time, however, Tammany chieftains are forced to choose between two hated enemies—the DA who has a long record of inflicting serious damage on their operations, and the publisher whose newspaper has printed cartoons of Tammany's current boss wearing prison stripes.

In the end they opt for Hearst as the lesser of the two evils and shed few tears when he loses the governorship to Charles Evans Hughes, the brilliant, high-minded Armstrong Committee counsel who had garnered praise for his conduct of the investigation into the insurance scandals, reminding Jerome that it is easier to ferret out corruption than to prosecute it. That the highly dignified Hughes will serve as governor, a prize Jerome has long coveted for himself, is a blow, but not a devastating one. He is, after all, still only forty-seven. And there will be other elections.

1907

37

PEOPLE V. HARRY K. THAW I:
THE PRELIMINARIES

. . . the Thaw trial is being reported to the ends of the civilized globe.
—THE *NEW YORK TIMES*

S etting the stage for what is expected to be the most sensational trial ever to unfold in an American courtroom, Hearst's *Evening Journal* declares, "The flash of that pistol lighted up an abyss of moral turpitude, revealing powerful, reckless, openly flaunted wealth." For six months, the press, with no fewer than fourteen dailies covering New York City, some with both morning and evening editions, has been priming the pump. Most of the papers have joined in the character assassination of White, playing to the public's fascination with the beautiful woman/child he robbed of her innocence and the tormented husband who avenged her deflowering. Notably absent from the feverish coverage are any stories exposing the perversities of the murderer, about which the madams of the Tenderloin could give reporters an earful. But the madams are on shaky ground with the law, are no fans of Jerome, and besides, reporters, who have their marching orders, don't want to hear from them. Mother Thaw has made sure of that. Nor are any of the young actresses and dancers who had been pleased to have White's attention and grateful for the boost he was able to give their careers in any position to come forward. The vilification of writer Richard Harding Davis, who had defended his friend and paid a high price, was a warning to everyone: no one who has known Stanford White and called him a friend will be spared.

At the same time as White is being pummeled in the press, Jerome's own press notices are becoming increasingly negative. After building him up as the people's savior, the press is now closing ranks against him with the exception of the *Times* and the *Globe*. His heroics in pursuit of gamblers and vice peddlers had been the stuff of lively copy, but now that he has failed to deliver on his promise to move up the chain and prosecute the men at the top, it is more interesting to attack him. The big fish continue to elude justice, the people's anger is rising, and the press the masses depend on for their news has pivoted. With few exceptions, and with Hearst's papers leading the pack, admiration has given way to professed disillusionment and a constant drumbeat of criticism aimed at Jerome. To which Jerome, who has never made any secret of his lack of respect for the press, has responded with one of those inopportune bursts of unbridled hostility that so exasperate his friend Arthur Train. With no thought of the power the press will wield during the upcoming trial, and no idea of how righteous and arbitrary he sounds, Jerome had only recently blasted his journalistic critics in a speech. Singling out Hearst's *Journal-American* for his most scalding invective, he had called them "exponents of the vulture that seeks the carrion—and seeks it with a sense of recognition."

Thaw's new team of lawyers, led by the suave and courtly Californian Delphin Delmas, acquiesces to the Thaws' demands and arrives at a strategy that meets with their approval. The defense will argue that Harry was perfectly sane before the murder and perfectly sane afterward but temporarily deranged when he pulled the trigger and shot Stanford White. It will require convincing the jury that at that precise moment he was in the throes of a delusion, experiencing a brief bout of temporary insanity provoked by the intolerable stress of dealing with the knowledge of his wife's deflowering some five years earlier, well before their marriage.

As challenging as that may be for his famous adversary, Jerome has no illusions about the added difficulties he faces now that the jury must decide either to acquit the accused, whose temporary insanity might just strike a jury as excusable given the murderer's emotional torment, or find him guilty of cold-blooded murder. Faced with this novel—and, to Jerome's mind, bogus—argument, the prosecution will have no choice but to make its case for murder in the first degree even as a torrent of adverse publicity continues to portray the victim as a depraved monster who deserved to die, and his killer as the only man courageous enough to do what had to be done. Still, Jerome is confident in his abilities and unwavering in his belief that Thaw must be removed from society, one way or another.

Jerome sees the case now as he had when he first learned of it: Thaw killed White out of simple jealousy and was not Evelyn's savior. Jerome's detectives, deployed in the Tenderloin, have provided him with ample evidence that Thaw is anything but a savior and that his reputation for debauchery, including the criminal abuse of women, is well earned. Nor would Jerome's investigators have failed to discover the existence of the affidavit Evelyn signed in Abe Hummel's office. Jerome, who has at least an idea of its contents, is thought to be dangling leniency for the beleaguered Hummel in exchange for his help. If Hummel were to to turn over to Jerome a copy of the affidavit with Evelyn's sworn statement testifying to the horrendous abuses she suffered in Austria, it would be within Jerome's power to offer Hummel leniency in his own criminal case.

With a promising stockpile of ammunition and never one to doubt the virtue of his positions, particularly when they involve upholding the rule of law, Jerome offers some fighting words to the press. Defiantly—and unwisely—he informs reporters that if Evelyn seeks to portray her deranged and dangerous husband as a hero, he will "tear her limb from limb and exhibit the interesting remains triumphantly."

If his outburst is meant to strike terror in Evelyn's heart, it probably does, at least momentarily. Jerome's reputation for ferocity in the courtroom has not escaped Evelyn's notice, but when a sympathetic acquaintance suggests she skip town and avoid an ordeal in the witness box, she demurs. She is committed to playing the role she has promised to play in the trial, though she admits to her terror at having to face this "remorseless man," this "square-jawed lawyer, all brain and ice-cold logic."

When the trial opens on January 23 in the Criminal Courts Building before Judge James Fitzgerald, there can be no doubt that this is to be a mammoth media event. With the sins of the rich as its main theme, the trial has electrified the public, but spectators have been barred from the courtroom. To keep them informed, one hundred reporters from papers all over the world have been assigned to cover the trial. A Western Union telegraph office has been installed in the main hall, and a great cable of wires descends from the sooty skylight. One hundred policemen have been assigned to keep order.

During the tedious business of questioning six hundred prospective jurors, who are to be sequestered for the first time in history, reporters fill their notebooks with detailed descriptions of the scene in the packed courtroom and deliver a daily flood of florid prose to their readers. The somber procession of Thaw family members into the courtroom is rich with descriptive possibilities. The dowager matriarch, "veiled and dressed in unrelieved black," leads the way, followed by her daughter the Countess of Yarmouth, "a pretty young woman with a tip-tilted nose" and an absent husband. The Count de Money is reportedly in Monte Carlo, and rumors of a separation are quickly followed by talk of an annulment.

Mrs. George Carnegie, the countess's rather plain sister, gets less attention, and all eyes turn to the tiny figure of the murderer's stricken wife, a "deathly pale" and "hollow-eyed" Evelyn. With her is her friend May MacKenzie, a canary among crows, resplendent in a purple suit, purple gloves, and a rakish feathered hat. Presiding Judge James Fitzgerald, the same whose patience was tried by the antic atmosphere of Norman Hapgood's libel trial, is also given his due. Fat, with a chubby face and no neck, his girth lends him a ponderous appearance, though he is known to be quick-witted and strong-minded.

When the clerk calls, "Harry K. Thaw to the bar!" the accused, who has crossed the Bridge of Sighs from his cell, makes his entrance dressed in a blue serge suit and smiling broadly. After taking his seat at the defense table, he sits back in his chair, relaxed and barely seeming to listen as the judge instructs him on the procedure for challenging prospective jurors. It is a long, tedious process, and by the time twelve jurors have been selected and seated, reporters have exhausted their stock of adjectives in detailed descriptions of just about everyone involved—their height, weight, the tilt of their nose, the cut of their clothes. Already familiar with their famous fighting DA, the public is informed that his counterpart for the defense, Delphin Delmas, is equally celebrated on the West Coast. Short, stocky, and crowned with a Napoleonic coiffure, he makes his appearance in a frock coat, gray-striped trousers, and an Ascot tie.

Missing from the scene are Bessie White, who has announced that she cannot bear even to read newspaper accounts of the proceedings, and Evelyn's mother and her husband, Charles Holman. It has been widely reported that Mother Thaw had only consented to Harry's marriage after extracting Evelyn's pledge to sever all relations with her mother, a stipulation that has reportedly caused Mrs. Holman to have bitter feelings toward her daughter and son-in-law. No one was surprised when the Holmans announced on January 2 that they planned to attend the trial and offer testimony in vindication of Stanford's good name, but an alarmed Mother Thaw had dispatched her personal lawyer immediately to Pittsburgh to head off the Holmans. On January 5, her emissary had returned with news that Mrs. Holman's "delicate state of health" would not permit her to testify at the trial and a rumor began making the rounds that, after some haggling, Mother Thaw had met the Holmans' price. Satisfied that they will not be speaking out at the trial, Mother Thaw seems unaware that there are more devious ways for the Holmans to have their say.

Evelyn's brother Howard, not included in any transactions requiring his silence, is present. Accompanied by a former employee of Stanford White, he tells reporters that he has come from Pittsburgh "to do what I can to vindicate the memory of Mr. White." Seated apart and exchanging no words, brother and sister have taken opposite sides in this contest. While Howard is loyal to his family's benefactor (White had continued to pay his tuition even after his relationship with Evelyn ended), the benefactor on whom Evelyn now must rely is Mother Thaw.

On Monday morning, February 4, Jerome has Assistant District Attorney Francis Garvan deliver a seven-minute opening statement declaring that Thaw's shooting of White was "a cool, deliberate, malicious, premeditated murder, and we shall ask for a verdict of murder in the first degree." After several witnesses testify to the events of June 25, followed by a break for lunch, the opening speech for the defense is delivered not by Delmas, the orator of opulent phrases and biblical cadences whom everyone has been waiting to hear, but by John Gleason, a man totally lacking in eloquence or court-room charisma. Gleason presents a muddled, long-winded argument meant to elucidate the defense's complicated contention that Thaw is sane now and always has been except for that moment when, in a burst of madness, he killed White under the delusion that he was "an agent of Providence." His end-less ramble, during which he insists that a temporary aberration sometimes gets confused with a congenital state, baffles his listeners and visibly upsets Harry, who can be seen wincing at each reference to his mental incapacity. The hapless Gleason has apparently not fully grasped the fine points of his own argument, and after two and a half hours of his aimless ranting, neither does anyone else. A correspondent for the *Morning World* comments that of the many murder trials he has witnessed, "in none have I heard a forecast by the defense so wandering, so purposeless, so lame, so halt and straggling as the opening address of Thaw's counsel."

An inauspicious start gets worse the next day when the first "expert" wit-ness for the defense, called to clarify Gleason's bumbling attempt to explain the unique form of lunacy experienced by Thaw, gives Jerome a perfect opportunity to display his instinct for the jugular by subjecting the hoary "sci-ence" of old-time alienists to ridicule. Thanks to the many hours spent buried in medical books, Jerome is the true expert, and the "former Poo Bahs of the popular lunatic asylums along our eastern seaboard," as Irvin Cobb calls the herd of physicians-for-hire, are exposed as ignoramuses. Of Jerome's mode of attack another observer writes that he is "quick as a panther to spring and as ready to strike as an adder…" It is a good day for Jerome.

The next day the *Times* reports that the disastrous showing has left Harry in a "mingled state of rage and terror." Gleason's responsibilities are reduced, and Delmas introduces the jury to the concept of the "unwritten law," a hoary convention from the past when it was sometimes used to exonerate a murderer whose victim had seduced his wife or sister. Thaw's friend Truxton Beale's claim to have beat a murder charge by using the "unwritten law" had been of great interest to Harry, who had no doubt repeated his story to Delmas. Reliance on the spurious "unwritten law" and the novel notion of temporary insanity is risky, but with the help of the Thaw-funded PR campaign to blacken White's reputation, Delmas is ready to take the gamble. As confident in his legendary ability to manipulate a jury as Jerome is in his own brilliance as a tactician, Delmas plans to convince the jury that White's murderer should not just be forgiven but applauded—and certainly acquitted—for killing so loathsome a man.

One observer of Delmas's ability to manipulate a jury describes his manner as unctuous but appealing to jurors, who are given "a subtle hint of good fellowship and yet a deference which intimates, 'You are the twelve and I am merely the thirteenth. If you will permit this lesser being for a short time your gracious attention, I shall be most honored…'" He is a consummate courtroom performer, but Evelyn's testimony will be crucial. No one is in a better position to make the jury despise White, feel Evelyn's pain, and root for her savior. And whatever resentment she may feel at having to give the scandalmongers and the sensation-hungry public the titillating details of her past, Evelyn is stoic. She has made her choice and must put her faith in the promise that if she performs well and Harry is acquitted, she will be a rich woman.

38

PEOPLE V. HARRY K. THAW I:
THE "ANGEL CHILD"

The Thaw trial will have done a permanently valuable service if it destroys the veil of secrecy with which public modesty has surrounded certain vices . . . .
—THE *WORLD*

On the morning of February 7 Evelyn takes the stand to give the court and the world what they have been waiting for: a fulsome account of her torrid affair with White, of her life among the loose-living theater crowd and its hedonistic upper-crust patrons, and an answer to the question of why her relations with White had incited her husband to murder society's most celebrated architect and man-about-town. In anticipation of her testimony, a crowd estimated at ten thousand—the largest in the history of New York murder trials—has gathered outside the building.

As soon as Justice Fitzgerald has eased his mountainous bulk into his chair, Delmas orders, "Call Mrs. Evelyn Thaw!" and Evelyn enters dressed in the same schoolgirl outfit she has worn every day of the trial—a plain navy blue suit with a shirtwaist and Buster Brown collar. She is the image of betrayed innocence, and reporters have before them a beautiful child worthy of their most effusive prose. Among the special arrangements that have been made for the media are seats at the front of the courtroom set aside for four female reporters assigned by their papers to cover the trial from the woman's point of view. Their mawkish copy, heavy on melodrama and already a syrupy stream in the days leading up to the trial, will swell to a tsunami of treacle. Day after day, they watch Evelyn "lay bare her soul" and write tearfully of her tragic circumstances, an angel trapped in a web of debauchery and violence. Competing to tug at hearts and dampen eyes, they resort to such outlandish melodrama that they are commonly referred to as the "Sob Sisters" or, alternatively, the "Pity Patrol."

Evelyn's performance under oath is all that Delphin might have wished. Speaking with a "childish lisp," occasionally resorting to a whisper aimed at the judge's ear, she recounts her version of the events that brought her to where she sits in the witness chair. Prompted by Delmas, she describes her first visit to White's 24th Street studio and how White placed her on the soon-to-be-infamous red velvet swing and pushed her so high that her feet crashed through "a big Japanese umbrella on the ceiling."

Seeing all too clearly where this is headed, Jerome attempts to head off Delmas's end run around the inadmissibility of testimony concerning Evelyn's relationship with White as such. Addressing the judge, Jerome states his objection to the relating by the witness of "an occurrence," presumably Evelyn's description of what went on during that first visit to 24th street, when the question to be addressed concerns what she said to Mr. Thaw. Fitzgerald accepts the logic of the complaint, but Delmas is untroubled by the restriction.

Did you tell this to Mr. Thaw? he asks.

All of it, replies Evelyn.

The only effect of Jerome's objection is to oblige Delmas to frame his questions a little more awkwardly by directing Evelyn to repeat for the jury only what she had told Thaw. Since she claims to have told him everything, a public airing of the affair's intimate details is now assured, and Jerome is faced with the difficult task of proving either that the frail beauty in the witness chair had lied and had not told Harry what she claims she had told him, or that her story had not affected his mind. Adding to his frustration is that nothing Evelyn says with regard to the story will be subject to refutation. If she has fabricated the details, her lie is irrelevant. The issue, after all, is not whether what she told Harry was true but whether she had told him the story at all and, if so, what his reaction had been.

Delphin has thrown the prosecution off balance, and not for the last time. Pleased with his strategy, he steers Evelyn through some of the most compelling evidence of the trial—a recitation of the conversation with Thaw in 1903 during which she had confessed to him the details of her sexual relations with White. In answer to Delmas's questions, she testifies that the conversation took place in Paris after she had rejected Thaw's latest proposal of marriage when she had claimed that she was not worthy to be his wife. Asked to elaborate, she recalls that Thaw had questioned her so relentlessly about her relations with White, whom he blamed for her refusal to marry him, that he had finally succeeded in wearing her down. Wanting only to put an end to his badgering, she had told him everything about her seduction by White and their subsequent intimacy.

Delmas, no less relentless than Harry, prods her for details until she pleads that she can take no more. Her champions in the front row are aghast as Evelyn falls back in a swoon, moaning, "I can't go on! I can't."

Judge Fitzgerald halts the proceedings, the Sob Sisters emote, windows are opened and restoratives applied.

When she has recovered, Delphin resumes his questioning, asking her to tell the jury exactly what she had revealed to Harry that night in Paris and what his reaction had been. With his prompting, she recalls that she had told Harry of dining alone with White at the 24th Street studio and becoming groggy from the champagne, suggesting that she had been drugged. She testifies that she had been unable to tell Harry what followed, having lost consciousness, but that she had resumed her account by describing her horror when she woke up and realized that she was nude in a bed shared by White. Delmas persists. He has Evelyn repeat the shocking details.

Delmas: You say you found that you had been stripped. Did you
     describe to Mr. Thaw where White was?
Evelyn: Yes, he was right there beside me.
Delmas: Where?
Evelyn: In the bed.

Delmas: Dressed or undressed?

Evelyn: Completely undressed.

Delmas continues to prod. She must describe Harry's reaction.

Delmas: What was the effect of this statement of yours upon Mr.
Thaw?

Evelyn: He became very excited.

Delmas: Will you kindly describe it?

Evelyn: He would get up and walk up and down the room a minute
and then come and sit down and say, "Oh God! Oh, God!" and
bite his nails like that, and keep sobbing.

Delmas: Sobbing?

Evelyn: Yes, it was not like crying. It was a deep sob. He kept saying,
"Go on, go on, tell me the whole thing about it."

And what else had she told Harry on that occasion? Evelyn recalls telling
Harry about White's arrival at her hotel the next day, his assurances that
"everybody did these things," that she was too beautiful to resist, that "he
would do a great many things" for her and that the most important thing was
"not to be found out."

Jerome, as hotly indignant as his adversary is suave and controlled, protests
vigorously against Evelyn's account, "told when Mr. White is dead and in his
grave." Pacing before the bench and the jury box, nearly shouting, he asks,
"Are there no limits to this? There is no way in which we can controvert a
single bit of this testimony." It is all "nothing but gossip of the Tenderloin,"
he fumes, unworthy of belief by any thinking juror.

Jerome is not alone in his outrage. There is an uproar when Evelyn's shocking
testimony appears in print. The *Sun* expurgates the accounts, primly referring
to "conditions which cannot be described in a family paper." The sensationalized press, however, is only too happy to play the story for all it is worth—
which is a lot in boosted circulations and profits. The *World* acknowledges that

the material is salacious but asks, What ought the newspapers to do? Suppress the evidence on which Thaw's life depends? Print the evidence verbatim, as British newspapers are compelled by law to do? President Roosevelt enters the fray, professing such disgust at the frankness of the press accounts that he asks the postmaster general if it is possible to exclude it from the mails. Apparently it is not, and Brooklyn's *Standard-Union* wonders if "the president of the United States has undertaken publicly to edit the newspapers."

Delmas makes one more attempt to offer medical evidence of the effect Evelyn's lurid confession had exerted on Thaw's mind. He calls Dr. Britton D. Evans, who testifies that he has visited Thaw in the Tombs and found that the accused "exhibited the condition of a man who has just passed through an explosive and fulminating condition of the mind." He cites a certain restlessness of the eyes and incoherence of speech, along with several other symptoms. There are situations, claims the accommodating expert on the fairly new science of psychology, that cause a mind to "snap on an instant," a phenomenon he calls a "brainstorm." A few humorists comment that psychologists are evidently now meteorologists, but Jerome is far from amused by this venture into brain theory.

When Delmas calls Dr. Charles Wagner to the stand, he poses a question that takes sixteen minutes to read and describes in high-flown language Thaw's nearly blameless life up until the night of the murder, emphasizing his tender treatment of Evelyn following her surgery at Pompton. The jury does not get to hear the answer Delmas anticipates from Dr. Wagner—that such a history would make a man crazy enough to kill his rival. A furious Jerome interrupts with a dozen objections, assailing, among other things, the reference to Thaw's gallantry toward Evelyn after her operation, which he asserts has impressed him and others as being "of a criminal character."

After the uproar among the spectators has subsided, an indignant Delmas demands to know how the district attorney happens to know so much about this operation.

In fact, Jerome knows everything about the operation and calmly replies that his information comes from Evelyn's mother, Mrs. Holman. It seems that the unscrupulous Mother Thaw has met her match in Evelyn's devious mother, who had been "persuaded" by Mother Thaw to abandon her plans to defend White's good name at the trial but has been feeding the DA ammunition to use in challenging her daughter's version of her relations with him. Mrs. Holman's fury at the Thaws for insisting that Evelyn sever all relations with her mother once Evelyn had joined the Thaw household might explain her desire for vengeance, but people are horrified to learn that the woman who had all but sold her daughter to Stanford White is now conspiring with the DA to expose her as a liar.

Before turning Evelyn over to Jerome for cross-examination, Delmas also attempts to offset any evidence of Evelyn's continued relationship with White after her marriage to Thaw by establishing that White had pursued her against her will. Evelyn can offer only the flimsiest testimony of White's supposedly unwanted attentions but is helpful on the question of Harry's reaction to any hints that White had approached her. She recalls that he had flown into a rage when she had told him that White had addressed her by name on Fifth Avenue: "He said the dirty blackguard had no right to speak to me."

At the end of his session with Evelyn, Delmas is justifiably pleased with her performance and his own. She has impressed almost everyone as the wronged child taken advantage of by a selfish voluptuary. The mirrored bedroom, the drugged champagne, the glamor of White's celebrity were too much for an innocent girl from Pittsburgh to resist, and the melodrama is everything reporters had hoped it would be. Sob Sister Nixola Greeley-Smith declares that Evelyn "has laid down everything that womanhood holds precious to save her husband," and Irvin Cobb writes that "Harry Thaw sobbed unrestrainedly as his wife half whispered the story of her degradation."

Even Cobb, usually among the most clear-eyed of journalists, seems to have fallen momentarily under Evelyn's spell, though his Sob Sister tone hints at parody. He writes that she could never have counterfeited "the tortured twitch of the red, vibrant lips literally shrinking away in physical revulsion from the words they must frame, the eyes crying out of their glazed depths with a mute appeal for mercy, the gasp and the choke and the shudder that shook the childish voice." Then, after watching her exit the courtroom, swaying and "tottering precariously" before collapsing into the arms of a defense lawyer, he tips his hat to a superb performance, observing that "the best emotional actress in America couldn't have done it as well." Among the crowd of thousands gathered outside, some are surprised to see Evelyn, apparently fully recovered, make her way briskly through a cleared lane to the car that will take her and her escort of defense lawyers out for lunch—a meal that may be more celebratory than recuperative.

Evelyn has performed brilliantly, and it is generally felt that Jerome has been outmaneuvered. If he is to overcome such breathless admiration and pity for White's victim and turn the tide of the trial, his only hope may be to show that beneath the demure exterior lies a sophisticated woman who is well aware of her beauty, its effect on men, and how to use it to get what she wants out of life. It may be time to act on his threat to "tear her limb from limb."

39

PEOPLE V. HARRY K. THAW I:
JEROME, THE INQUISITOR

. . . Mr. Delmas' calm, suave, lengthy, painstakingly polite replies drove Jerome frantic.
—EVELYN NESBIT

Jerome's cross-examination—or inquisition, as many would call it—lasts three days, during which Evelyn proves a worthy adversary. With no avenue for challenging Evelyn's version of a conversation that took place four years earlier in another country, or questioning her opinion of Thaw's state of mind then or since, Jerome takes a risk and sets out to sully the reputation of the woman the press is portraying as a brave little fighter for her husband's life. If it can be shown that she had lost her innocence before she met White and had continued her affair with him after she claimed he had so brutally wronged her, then perhaps the jury will see that her alliance with Thaw and her testimony in his defense is a sham inspired by her instinct for self-preservation.

Conspicuously referring to a sheaf of unidentified documents as if they hold hard-and-fast evidence, Jerome raises the possibility that White was not the first older man to trespass on her purity. He seems to indicate that there is evidence that before she ever met White Evelyn had been listed in a divorce suit brought against one James Garland as a corespondent, a term applied to someone guilty of adultery with the defendant. Jerome believes that Evelyn and her lawyers are by now aware of Mrs. Holman's treacherous aid to the prosecution, and his obvious attention to the documents is clearly intended to suggest that he holds in his hands information to refute any denial.

But Evelyn reacts to the charge that she is a homewrecker with perfect sangfroid.

"It is not true," she protests. Yes, the kind Mr. Garland had entertained her on his yacht, but "Mama always went along too."

And when Jerome suggests that, as an artist's model, she must have posed "with exposed bosom," the charge prompts an indignant denial. He does get her to acknowledge that White gave her money "a number of times during 1901, during 1902...over a year in all, I think." And in another exchange, when he feigns shock at Evelyn's willingness to keep seeing the man who so brutally robbed her of her innocence, she cooly admits to their continued contact.

> Jerome: Did you, after being wronged, continue to go out to dinner and to dinner parties with Stanford White?
>
> Evelyn: Often. Sometimes every day; sometimes two or three times a week.
>
> Jerome: So he called on you at your home and at the theater often?
>
> Evelyn: Yes, he came nearly every day.

On one occasion, forced to recall those happy times with White, she appears almost ready to abandon her bargain with the Thaws, admitting that "outside of that one terrible thing," she thought Stanford White "a very grand man . . . Everybody says the same thing about him that knew him. He was kind and considerate and exceedingly thoughtful . . . much more thoughtful than most people. He had a very peculiar personality. People liked him very much. He made a great many friends and always kept them . . ."

It is a unique moment, the only time during the trial when Stanford White's spirit is palpably present, improbably summoned by his killer's most persuasive defender. But almost immediately Evelyn squelches the unbidden surge of true feeling by adding that "people are unwilling to believe the bad things" about White. When Jerome asks her point-blank, "Did you love Stanford

White?" her answer is no. And yes, she affirms in response to his next question, she hated him.

Stymied by the curious ambiguity of Evelyn's testimony, her evasiveness and denial of things he knows to be true, Jerome is increasingly irritable. Again and again, Evelyn makes him lose his temper, and his clashes with Judge Fitzgerald become more and more frequent. His snappish performance, in stark contrast to Delmas's oily solicitude, plays into the Sob Sisters' narrative that casts Jerome as a heartless bully and Evelyn as his helpless victim. He looks bad when he wins a point, worse when he loses.

Evelyn has proved extraordinarily adept at countering Jerome's attempts to undermine her credibility. Whether by outright denial or artful equivocation, and aided by Delmas's frequent objections, she manages to suggest that Jerome has become obsessed by his animus toward her. He is so anxious to "wipe up the floor with me," she tells reporters, "he seemed to lose sight of Harry Thaw completely." Jerome, placed in the extraordinary position of cross-examining a witness who swore to tell the truth but is permitted to lie as long as she sticks to what she told Harry, is confounded in his attempts to entrap her. Steadfast in her responses to questions asked and often angrily repeated, Evelyn cannot be induced to contradict herself or the agreed-upon narrative of the defense. Her tale of White's depravity and her own victimization may be "a magnificent lie," as Jerome and not a few others believe, but it is a lie well told by a beautiful woman who is also an actress, and if it is the lie she told Harry, the truth is irrelevant.

Jerome, running out of options for putting Evelyn on the defensive, turns at one point to her romance with Jack Barrymore in an effort to plant the suspicion that Barrymore, not White, was the man Thaw ought to have been jealous of. He calls Dr. Carlton Flint—the physician alleged to have been consulted by Barrymore and Evelyn for professional services of a questionable nature—to come forward for identification. Evelyn denies ever seeing him before and the doctor is dismissed, but Jerome presses on, hinting broadly that Evelyn's involvement with Barrymore had led to a pregnancy and an abortion. The tastelessness of the assault causes much consternation among

Evelyn's female champions in the front row, but Jerome plunges ahead, eager
to present the possibility that, in her confession to Thaw, Evelyn had placed
the blame for her ruination on White because she wanted to spare her true
love—the handsome young actor Jack Barrymore.

> Jerome: Did you ever go out with Barrymore and remain all night
>   away from home and send a telegram to your mother?
> Evelyn: When you say all night, I do not remember ever being out all
>   night with Mr. Barrymore. I have been out to supper with him.

Then, with surprising bluntness, Jerome asks if the operation performed at
Pompton was "a criminal operation."

Delmas springs to his feet to object: Evelyn was under an anesthetic and
could only know what she was told—that it was an appendectomy. There
are objections on both sides, and the discussion is thrown into confusion
over technicalities. Barrymore, who had appeared reluctantly at the trial only
after Jerome had had him subpoenaed, flees town to avoid further entanglement.

Jerome decides it is time to introduce his ace in the hole, a photographed
copy of the affidavit Abe Hummel had drawn up for Evelyn's signature in
1903 after her return from Europe in which Thaw is portrayed as a perverted
monster. Evelyn repudiates the affidavit and everything in it.

> Jerome: Did you tell Hummel that while at the German castle in 1903
>   Thaw had beaten you with a whip?
> Evelyn: I did not.
> Jerome: Did you tell Abe Hummel that Thaw had wronged you there
>   against your will?
> Evelyn: I did not . . .
> Jerome: Did you tell him that Thaw was terribly excited, that he tore
>   the bathrobe from you with his teeth, that he threw you on the
>   bed entirely nude and that you were wronged then and there?

Evelyn: No, I never did . . .

Jerome (showing Evelyn the document): Is this your signature?

Evelyn: I never remember signing anything like this.

Jerome is flustered, not so much by Evelyn's repudiation of the affidavit and everything in it, which he must have seen coming, as by the effect it appears to be having on the twelve men in the jury box, whom he doesn't trust to question the veracity of the beautiful, childlike witness. It seems that every time he tries to undermine one of Evelyn's untruths, it is the same story. Venting his frustration in an aside to a female reporter, he complains, "That girl is lying. I know she is not telling the truth. She knows that I know she is not telling the truth, but somehow I can't completely break her down. I don't know what to do next."

There is one thing he can do, and when he recovers his equilibrium, Jerome calls a witness whose testimony may be the only legally admissible evidence he has against Evelyn's mendacity. He introduces what the press calls "the most remarkable exhibit ever introduced in a New York law court" and calls Abraham Hummel to the stand. The "remarkable exhibit" is a copy of the affidavit, signed by Evelyn in October 1903, and drafted by the same Abe Hummel Jerome had tried for years to remove from circulation and had most recently tangled with in the Dodge-Morse fiasco. Hummel and his notorious law practice have always been of interest to the press, which has spread the word of his recent indictment on the very charge of procuring false affidavits. His appearance as Jerome's witness—to defend the admissibility of an affidavit of which he is the author—is sure to raise eyebrows, trouble the judge, and put Delmas in a fury. It's risky, but Jerome sees no alternative. The affidavit is his ace in the hole.

The ever-dapper Hummel, who has been summoned to confirm that Evelyn had sworn to the terrible catalog of Thaw's abuses, makes his appearance looking as jaunty as ever. This despite the fact that he is about to serve time himself. As a witness, Hummel comes with a serious credibility deficit, but Jerome needs his help, and Hummel has apparently recognized an opportunity for himself. There are rumors that in exchange for aiding the prosecution, Hummel's confinement to Blackwell's Island prison will be shorter and less onerous than it might otherwise have been.

If Jerome knows that Evelyn has been lying, and Evelyn knows that he knows it, so, too, does Delmas know that his client lied and her signed affidavit will prove it. He will fight as hard as he can to exclude the affidavit as evidence, to keep Hummel from testifying, and prevent Jerome's gambit from ruining his case. Because everyone knows that Hummel is himself an outlaw and so not the most reliable witness, Delmas enters the fight with a considerable advantage. Before Hummel can answer Jerome's first question, relating to the exact date of Evelyn's visit to his office, Delmas is on his feet with an objection. Hummel has no right to consult his office records, he argues, and the objection is sustained. Jerome next asks Hummel whether Evelyn had signed a statement in his office and Delmas again objects, insisting that before the question can be addressed, Jerome must first prove that such a document exists. Again his objection is sustained by Judge Fitzgerald, as is every one of Delmas's objections, effectively silencing Hummel, until Jerome finally snaps. Flinging his copy of the affidavit to the floor, he snarls, "We will have to excuse this witness for the time being."

Evelyn continues to hold up well, performing admirably as the defense's star witness, maintaining her composure as Jerome has not. He can hardly be pleased with his own frequent bursts of temper, which have made him look churlish and bullying, but he has succeeded in pointing up the ambiguity of Evelyn's emotions, and cast some doubt on her tale of betrayed innocence. A few publishers, eager to distance their newspapers from the yellow press, even treat Evelyn's testimony with mockery. The *Times* calls her story "preposterous," and the *Sun*'s correspondent ridicules the notion that she and Harry were young innocents wronged by White when, in fact, they had traveled together as intimates before they were married and at the time of her so-called "ravishment" Evelyn was a chorus girl, not married to anyone, with no home whose sanctity was in need of protection.

Jerome welcomes the rare sniping at Evelyn but has no doubt that the public still loves her. In the end, he has failed to shake her story that her seduction by Stanford White and her recital of its details drove Thaw to the madness that made him commit murder. Now he can only hope that a vigorous attack on the irrationality of a defense based on an unwritten law and an undocumented mental condition will fare better. At the outset, when Delmas had acceded to the Thaws' adamant rejection of an insanity plea, Jerome had seen no alternative to seeking a conviction on first-degree murder, though he remained convinced of Harry's overall insanity. He had accepted his duty to prosecute Harry for murder, despite his reservations, believing that the jury was unlikely to convict someone so obviously insane but that an acquittal was equally unlikely. With the introduction by the defense of the novel argument that the mind of an otherwise sane man could be susceptible, temporarily, to a flash of violent madness, and suspecting that the jury is buying it, raising the possibility that Thaw might well leave the courtroom a free man, he has seen the need for a new strategy, one that would discredit the ludicrously unscientific "brainstorm" defense. Determined to see Thaw locked up, he has been directing his efforts to proving Thaw insane, both at the time of the murder, before, and at present. Much as he likes winning, it would violate his most deeply held principles to wage a vigorous fight for a first-degree murder conviction knowing that Thaw is insane. And, not unimportantly, the execution of a deranged man would only feed the public's increasingly negative view of him as ruthless and heartless.

Jerome presents a series of questions to Evelyn that many take as an acknowledgment that he has failed in his attempt to discredit her and has decided on a change of strategy. He brings up the matter of Thaw's alleged insanity and encourages her to testify to several instances of Thaw's irrational behavior before the murder. She acknowledges that once, when she and Harry had passed White on Fifth Avenue, he had sobbed and babbled and "seemed to have a fit." She relates that on another occasion, in 1903, Harry had insisted that people were following him "to do harm to him . . ." and had explained that he carried a revolver for protection. Courtroom observers register with some surprise that Jerome's final questions seem to be aimed at getting Evelyn to confirm that well before Harry shot White, his behavior had shown him to be mentally unstable. And, in this, the DA succeeds.

> Jerome: You thoroughly believed that he was irrational?
> Evelyn: Yes, but then I knew what was the cause of his excitement—
>   that it was always Stanford White..."
> At this point, Jerome announces: That is all.

The day after her cross-examination ends, Evelyn is called back on the stand. Delmas has questions for her that are intended to show that it was her mother who made the monetary arrangements with White and to describe, once again, Evelyn's miserable childhood. Then Jerome recalls Dr. Evans, who had diagnosed Thaw with a "brainstorm," as well as Dr. Wagner, another lunacy expert for the defense. In his questions to Dr. Wagner, Jerome is so insistent in attempting to maneuver him into calling Thaw either sane and culpable or crazy and a danger to himself and society that he exasperates everyone. The judge is so angry that his big face turns bright red, and Harry, furious at the insulting references to his mental incapacity, hands a statement to reporters that announces, "I am not crazy, I was not crazy when I shot Stanford White. I'm glad I did it. I was justified when I shot him. I was never insane and never said I was."

In denying he was ever crazy, Thaw gives Jerome a brief moment of satisfaction by complicating Delmas's task. To exonerate his client Delmas must show that Thaw had experienced at least a moment or two of excusable madness when he murdered White to avenge his wife's ravishment. But if Harry refuses to swallow his pride and admit to being crazy, however briefly, the defense has a problem.

Happily for Delmas, his next witness is his greatest ally in the defense they have plotted together. When he summons Mrs. William Thaw to the stand, Harry's stately, white-haired mother enters the courtroom with all the dignity that might be expected of the Dowager Empress of Pittsburgh. Dressed, as always, in her widow's weeds—black dress, black furs, black gloves—she delivers her testimony in the quiet voice of a stricken mother overwhelmed by her son's plight, a self-portrayal distinctly at odds with her unscrupulous campaign to rescue him at all costs. With Delmas's prompting, she describes how Harry had confided in her before his marriage that he was so obsessed with Evelyn he was unable to sleep knowing that she had been victimized by "the wickedest man in New York." When Mrs. Thaw's voice breaks with emotion at the recollection of Harry's pitiful sobs over "the girl whom he loved," Delmas flutters with solicitous concern for the saintly old lady's suffering and holds his questions while she presses a black-bordered handkerchief to her lips.

When she has recovered, Mother Thaw describes Harry's emotional breakdown on the eve of his 1904 trip to Europe with Evelyn, and acknowledges that the doctor evaluating her son's mental condition at that time thought it worrisome. This brings Jerome to his feet to protest the absurdity of assuming that Harry was insane in 1904, as his mother has just suggested, insane in 1906 at the time of the murder, but not insane at the present time. For his pains he is rewarded with a scowl of impatience from the judge and a suave rejoinder from Delmas: "No presumption of the sanity or insanity at the present moment can have a part in this trial as it is now constituted."

After Delmas winds up his questioning of Mother Thaw, Jerome conducts a perfunctory cross-examination and the witness is excused. Her performance gets raves from Sob Sister Nixola Greeley-Smith, who writes, "The second great occasion of the trial had come and gone and Thaw's mother met it, determination written large on her placid forehead, the light of battle in her mild blue eyes…" Others agree that Delmas has been masterful in his handling of Mother Thaw, whose stoicism had crumbled in a heart-wrenching emotional breakdown that had jurors dabbing their eyes.

Delmas has little time to savor the accolades. Jerome, having promised only to excuse Abe Hummel "for the time being," announces that he is calling him back to the stand to help him expose Evelyn's lie in denying the existence of her sworn affidavit—one lie that will not be protected by the trial's strange constraints. By the time Hummel makes this, his second, appearance at the trial, he has to be summoned from prison. Almost two years after his conviction, he had been escorted to Blackwell's Island but not before throwing a farewell party the previous evening at his home on West 73rd Street. It was a spectacular send-off, and reports are already circulating that he is enjoying unusual privileges as a prisoner.

Unlike his first effort, Jerome has carefully prepared for his second attempt to use the affidavit in support of his case. He has brought in a new series of witnesses, including Thaw's private counsel, Frederick W. Longfellow, whom he asks whether he had represented Thaw in a suit brought against him for allegedly whipping a woman. Longfellow's response is so evasive as to convince everyone that the answer is yes. He looks like a liar and his client looks suspiciously like a man with a vicious perversion. Another witness, Stanford White's brother-in-law James Clinch Smith, who had been at the Garden Theater on the night of the murder, gives a chilling account of Thaw's odd behavior that night. While a visibly distressed Thaw squirms in his seat, others in the courtroom listen attentively.

Jerome is optimistic that his perseverance in chipping away at Thaw's supposed heroism may be paying off. The testimony he has elicited from his latest witnesses has advanced an uglier image of the defendant—Thaw as a flagrant abuser of women, Thaw as a murderer capable of engaging in amiable, if disjointed, chatter with Stanford White's brother-in-law just minutes before shooting White dead. Jerome detects an opening in his fight against the exclusion of the affidavit, sensing some sympathy from the jury, the spectators, and perhaps even the judge, all of whom are naturally curious about the information in the affidavit, which has been denied them.

Indeed, this time Fitzgerald finds reasons to overrule Delmas's objections, giving Jerome one of his most important victories. Hummel testifies that in 1903, in his office, Evelyn had denied that White had drugged and wronged her and had confirmed that Thaw had told her he "wanted to injure White." She had alleged that Harry "was addicted to the taking of cocaine" and described in terrifying detail the night in the Austrian castle when Thaw had approached her with "his eyes glaring and his hands grasping a rawhide whip." She had asserted that Thaw had tried to choke her and that his brutal attacks had continued until she was "unable to move." She had gone on to describe more beatings and abuses as they had continued their travels.

Hummel identifies Jerome's document as a copy of the original affidavit. Fitzgerald allows it to be read to the jury, and it is introduced in evidence as People's exhibit No. 76.

The unflappable Hummel gets a predictable grilling from Delmas, who makes sure that the jury is fully informed of Little Abe's criminal past. But Evelyn had told him the facts—many of them verifiable—and Jerome has had a good day.

On March 8, the defense closes its case, and ten days later the state does likewise, but Jerome is facing a dilemma. He has succeeded in casting doubt on Evelyn's character but not on her story of having related to Thaw the details of her sexual assault by White and seen him react with unbalanced rage and despair. If the jury accepts that story, as seems likely, then Thaw will leave the courthouse a free man. Jerome's charge as DA is to convict Thaw of murder and see him sentenced to death, and he dutifully calls several more doctors, ostensibly to prove that Thaw had been sane at the time of the murder. They are countered by Delmas's doctors, which Jerome had probably anticipated, and, in any case, both alternatives—either freedom or death for Thaw—are repugnant to Jerome. Once again, he had initially underestimated the current climate of sentimentality and emotionalism, so consistently encouraged by the sensational press. Despite his experience in the Nan Patterson case, he could not quite believe that the jury would view Evelyn only as a wronged innocent and would fail to recognize her "savior" as too mentally unsound to be either executed or freed. Believing that confinement in an asylum is the only sensible outcome, Jerome opts for a reverse in strategy.

In a surprise move that disrupts the proceedings and delays the final arguments, Jerome submits seven affidavits from doctors who have been observing Thaw in the courtroom and have concluded that he is incurably insane. Supported by their statements, Jerome renews the previously rejected request for a lunacy commission to determine whether Thaw is fit to stand trial. Having failed to make a dent in the overwhelming public sympathy for Evelyn, he sees a declaration by the commission that Thaw is mentally unfit as his best hope for removing Thaw from society.

Showing himself capable of all the histrionics the occasion requires, Jerome actually weeps in his impassioned plea that an insane man should not be tried for his life. The defense has held back facts about the accused's mental condition, he charges, facts that "forced me to put him on trial for murder though the man is insane."

His attack leaves the courtroom in an uproar.

Spectators, anticipating the oratorical fireworks promised by dueling final arguments, groan their disappointment at the delay.

The defense rages against the charge of unprofessional conduct.

Thaw is indignant at having his sanity questioned yet again and protests in a statement that he is "perfectly sane, and everybody who knows me knows I am sane."

Judge Fitzgerald is furious at Jerome's inconsistency, insisting at first that Thaw was sane on June 25 and thus culpable for White's murder, then pivoting and making a tearful argument against condemning an incurable lunatic to the chair. He orders that any evidence of unprofessional conduct on the part of the defense be produced by Jerome, who is obliged to make an awkward retreat. In defending himself against charges of inconsistency, Jerome further confuses the jury by declaring that Thaw "is a paranoiac, and while he is insane, he is not insane in the eyes of the law, for strictly speaking he knows the nature and quality of his acts."

40

PEOPLE V. HARRY K. THAW I:
CLOSING ARGUMENTS

An effort to inflame your passions and to turn the real issue aside
to the trial of another is not, as we conceive it on the Atlantic seaboard,
the professional manner of presenting to a jury a case.
—WILLIAM TRAVERS JEROME

He could not, he would not forget—great, courageous, indomitable man,
who believes he has a mission to fulfill—to make one more effort to rescue her
from the hands of vice into which Stanford White had lured her.
—DELPHIN DELMAS

On March 26, Judge Fitzgerald announces the appointment of a lunacy commission, and eight days later the three appointees declare that Thaw is mentally capable of consulting with his lawyers and understanding the proceedings—not quite a clean bill of mental health but enough to recommend that the trial resume with final arguments. Of the drama about to begin, Irvin Cobb comments that pitting Delmas against Jerome is akin to a contest of "rusted rapiers against the very newest in the line of Gatling guns."

Belying the rusted rapiers allusion, the silver-tongued Delmas, pacing before the packed courtroom in frock coat and pince-nez, beams his spellbinding oratory at the jury, justifying Thaw's act on the grounds of the "unwritten law." He is nearly tearful as he describes Evelyn's penniless childhood and bewails in resonant tones her betrayal by White, who lured her to his "gilded den" and there "committed the most hideous crime that any man can commit. To gratify his passion, he had crushed the poor little—the sweet little flower that was struggling toward the light and toward God."

Brought close to tears by his own eloquence, Delmas goes on to twist the knife in her tormentor's back, accusing Jerome of brutality in calling for the execution of Evelyn's husband, her last living support with her father dead and her mother siding with her attackers. He was anguished, he tells the jury, as he watched Jerome read from one of her mother's statements during his cruel cross-examination of the poor girl knowing that "every shaft that he aimed at her heart came from a quiver furnished by her mother..."

Thaw, Delmas suggests, was "an avenging agent of God" who, after firing the fatal shots that felled White, stood "facing the audience with his arms spread out in the form of a cross." If he is insane, declares Delmas, "then call it 'Dementia Americana!' That is the species of insanity," he says, his rhythmic cadences building and repeating like waves in a storm, "which makes every American man believe his home to be sacred; that is the species of insanity which makes him believe the honor of his daughter is sacred; that is the species of insanity which makes him believe the honor of his wife is sacred; that is the species of insanity which makes him believe that whosoever invades his home, that whosoever stains the virtue of this threshold, has violated the highest of human laws and must appeal to the mercy of God, if mercy there be for him anywhere in the universe."

Delmas's endless oratory drives Jerome from the courtroom to seek relief in a drink down the block at Pontin's. Nearly two hours of the Napoleon of the West's high-flown rhetoric strikes some East Coast ears as laughable, and most of the reporters seem to think that Delmas's melodramatic performance does not quite come off. But there is no denying that his courtroom audience, including the jury, had been raptly attentive from beginning to end. Nixola Greeley-Smith predicts that Delmas's words will have a "deep effect" on the jury and that now "Thaw's fate rests on whether or not the jury believes Evelyn Thaw or the perjured and convicted lawyer, Abe Hummel. I think," she concludes, "the twelve men will prefer to believe the woman."

Now it is Jerome's turn to take the spotlight and seize his chance to prevent justice from bending under the weight of the massive forces bearing down on it—the money, the sensation-mongering press, a citizenry that consumes a steady diet of sentimentality and scandal and has little interest in the truth. No less important for him, it is also his chance to redeem himself in the eyes of those who had watched as he was repeatedly frustrated by Evelyn's back-and-forth testimony and Delmas's cunning technicalities and are now questioning his effectiveness. He has been here before. The Nan Patterson case had demonstrated the power of irrational forces over hard facts when a beautiful woman sets out to sway an all-male jury. But he has never seriously doubted his own persuasive powers and doesn't now. Since the Lunacy Commission has declined to diagnose Thaw as a lunatic, allowing the trial to proceed, nothing remains but to put Thaw's fate in the hands of the jurors and convince them that Thaw cannot be allowed to leave the courtroom a free man. He is armed and ready to attack Delmas's overwrought appeal to unreason.

He aims his opening remarks at Delmas, his "learned opponent," reminding jurors that "however mellifluous sentences may flow from the lips of a polished orator, it is not on such things that the life of a human being is to be determined..." He speaks to the jury of Delmas's "indecent appeal to your passions" and delivers a biting challenge to the defense's claims that some "unwritten law" and some phantom form of mental illness they call "dementia Americana" justify Thaw's act, which was in fact nothing but "a common, vulgar, everyday Tenderloin homicide." And while White, the murder victim, "had his faults and his gross faults," neither was Evelyn the "angel child that Mr. Delmas would paint her..."

"Why what nonsense to come here and tell twelve men! She of the *Florodora* chorus! She, dragged into this den of vice and drugged! And drugged with what, pray?"

Energized and indignant, Jerome launches a vigorous assault on the testimony that flummoxed him when he had Evelyn in the witness chair. He asserts that "there is no drug known to science that could produce insensibility in two minutes" and wonders why Evelyn would go back again and again to "the great ogre" who had supposedly ruined her life. The answer, he says, "came from Evelyn's own lips" when she acknowledged never having known anyone who was "nicer or kinder than Stanford White . . . You may paint

Stanford White in as black a color as you wish," he argues, "but there are no colors in the artist's box black enough to paint" Harry Thaw.

Delmas's portrait of young Harry "paying honorable court" to Evelyn is treated with withering sarcasm.

"We find him wrapping fifty-dollar bills around the stems of American Beauties, sending them to a girl on the stage whom he did not know," he scoffs. We find him flaunting her "through the capitals of Europe for two years as his mistress," gloating at having won her back from the man he hates, the man "who had kept him out of the clubs . . . the man who had described him as a dope fiend…This is a case where a woman lay like a tigress between two men, egging them on. To Thaw she said White had wronged her. To White, she said Thaw had beaten her with a whip."

He warns the jury against being taken in by childish garb and a childish face, and, with a show of extravagant incredulity, asks, "Will you acquit a cold-blooded, deliberate, cowardly murderer because his lying wife has a pretty girl's face?"

Jerome's plea for reason impresses many who find it more convincing than Delmas's flight into fantasy psychology or the melodramatic tale told by Evelyn, whose flawed testimony Jerome had finally found a way to expose. The *Tribune*, not normally so admiring, has praise for Jerome's "hard-headed riddling" of Thaw's blatantly mawkish defense. One urbane observer of the proceedings expresses the view that Delmas's old-school courtroom histrionics are more suited to dampening eyes in old Western mining towns than impressing East Coast sophisticates.

But, legally speaking, Jerome's brilliant mockery of Delmas's outmoded style and his artful analysis of Evelyn's character are of no use. For a conviction, Jerome needed to prove the unprovable: either that Evelyn had not told Thaw the story she claimed she had, or that her story had not affected Thaw's mind. In his charge to the twelve men on April 10, Judge Fitzgerald reminds them that it is their duty to decide whether Thaw was insane when he shot Stanford White and had no understanding that his action was wrong—the only immunity from criminal liability recognized by the law. Additionally, he instructs them not to consider the truth or falsity of Evelyn's story about her relationship with Stanford White, which had been presented only to enable them to determine its effect on the defendant's mental condition.

As the jury begins its deliberations, Thaw and his camp appear confident, and the prediction is widespread that he will be promptly acquitted. By the next afternoon, with the jury still out, a crowd of some ten thousand gathers around the Criminal Courts Building expecting news. But when night falls and there is still no verdict, most return home disappointed. Not until 4:30 the next day does the jury return to the courtroom to announce that it is hopelessly deadlocked. Five jurors, it is later learned, had voted Thaw not guilty by reason of insanity, and seven had held out for a guilty verdict of first-degree murder.

The trial has cost the state $100,000, the Thaw family has spent at least three times as much, and the whole thing will have to be repeated. Jerome is exhausted but insists he is not discouraged. The *Times* reports that "persons close to him believed him elated" by the mistrial, and the article goes on to explain that "a conviction would have put the District Attorney in the unenviable position of having successfully prosecuted for murder in the first degree a man whom he himself believed beyond the pale of the law."

After observing Harry seesaw from empty-eyed apathy to extreme agitation as he sat through the trial, and with the views of doctors he trusts supporting his opinion, Jerome is more convinced than ever that Thaw is deranged and must be locked up for life—beginning immediately. When the Thaw family attempts to bring Harry home in the interval between trials, offering bail money rumored to be as much as $1 million, Jerome angrily refuses.

"Simply because this man has wealth," he tells reporters, "is no reason, to my mind why he should be turned out of jail. Let him stay there until a jury acquits him or a lunacy commission sends him to an asylum."

If Jerome is not devastated by the outcome, neither can he be entirely pleased. There can be little comfort in the *Tribune*'s assessment of Evelyn's testimony as "a triumphant bit of malignity" which, under the rules of evidence, could not be contravened. Her skillful vagueness and curious switchbacks had stymied him, and his most effective weapon—his fearsome cross-examination skills—had only made him look like a bully. In his frustration, he had lost his temper several times, while the beauty in the witness box had remained cool and clever. The opinion of many after the verdict is that the defense did better than the district attorney. Jerome will be on trial as much as Thaw this time around in the court of public opinion.

1908

41

PEOPLE V. HARRY K. THAW II:
A "PROPER VERDICT"

I contend that the District Attorney, by his attitude, his manner,
and the very tone of his voice, is seeking to discredit statements of facts,
which he knows under the rulings of this court, he cannot do.
—MARTIN LITTLETON

B y the time Harry's second trial opens on January 6, 1908, nearly nine
months after the first trial ended, the city and Jerome's place in it have
changed—and not for the better. The financial market, which had been
shaky all year, was sent into a tailspin in October 1907 by none other than
Charlie Morse, whose attempt to corner the copper market with a few shady
partners backfired spectacularly. A run on Charles Barney's Knickerbocker
Trust Company, which held a million dollars' worth of stocks in Morse's companies, was the first in a devastating string of bank failures that threatened the
whole fabric of Wall Street and brought the career of the Street's wunderkind
to an ignominious end. On November 14, Charles Barney, his reputation in
ruins, killed himself just six months after the death of Stanford White, who
had called him "the best friend I have." Like White, Barney, once so proudly
successful in finance and society, was buried without fanfare to avoid mobs of
the "morbidly curious."

With the advent of hard times, sentiment against the millionaire class of
reckless speculators and corporate looters—blamed by the masses for the financial mess and its consequences—finds an outlet in attacks against the DA, who
had promised indictments and could not deliver. The anti-Jerome forces are

gathering steam, goaded by the press's relentless harping on Jerome's failure to follow through on his promises. When an investigation by the Public Service Commission of the Metropolitan Street Railway Company, finally wrecked and thrown into bankruptcy, exposes the facts behind the scandal—the enabling bribes and brazen thievery that had enriched William Whitney, Thomas Fortune Ryan, and their ruthless collaborators—the public is out for blood. Whitney is dead and out of reach, but public rage focuses on Ryan, who has suffered no consequences for stealing investors' money and leaving the transit system in shambles. Jerome has been presenting evidence of Ryan's unscrupulous acts to grand juries for months but with nothing to show for his efforts. His explanation for his failure to act—that the laws on the books have not caught up with the kind of criminality practiced by Ryan—falls on deaf ears. Not even Isidor Kresel, Jerome's "digger-in-chief," could find anything to work with.

In September, shortly before the collapse of the market, two of Jerome's most vociferous critics had gone so far as to file a demand with Governor Charles Evans Hughes for Jerome's removal from office, citing his failure to bring about the conviction of any high insurance officials or to indict a single transit system manipulator. They had accused Jerome of having deliberately whitewashed the Metropolitan's chief looters.

It is with this cloud hanging over him that Jerome enters the courtroom on January 6 to take charge of the prosecution for the second time in *People v. Harry K. Thaw*. Aware that his performance in the first trial had not shown him at his best, he is anxious not to repeat his mistakes this time around. Though he is suffering from a bad cold, he will need to play at the top of his game against a far more skillful and steely advocate than the bombastic Delmas. To defend Harry this time, Mother Thaw has hired the redoubtable Martin Littleton, who will be a fearsome adversary. In his last courtroom encounter with Jerome, Littleton's defense of the dishonorable Colonel William D'Alton Mann had been so effective that a sobbing jury had acquitted the saintly old swindler.

Anyone hoping that this second trial will be conducted in a less circuslike atmosphere than the first is disappointed. Mobs arrive at the Criminal Courts

Building whenever Evelyn is expected, and she seems pleased this time to play her role. Arriving in a new electric brougham, she obliges reporters with the news that she has had 122 proposals of marriage should her present husband get the electric chair, and she denies that she has been paid handsomely by the Thaw family to stick by Harry. Reporters also note a change in Harry's demeanor after the long summer and fall in the Tombs. He is thinner, grayer, less agitated in general, and oddly unaffectionate toward Evelyn, prompting rumors that the two are not getting along.

There is the usual attention to sartorial details when Mother Thaw and her entourage make their entrance, but it is Alice, Harry's ill-used sister, traded on the marriage market for a title, whose presence has the press in a flurry. Only days before the trial opened, newspapers had confirmed the rumors; the Countess of Yarmouth has filed suit in London to annul her marriage. Insanity, bigamy, or non-consummation being the only grounds for annulment in England, the latter choice surprises no one who ever saw Yarmouth perform as a female impersonator.

When Justice Victor J. Dowling gavels the courtroom to order and the trial gets underway, it is is clear that Littleton has assumed full responsibility for the strategy and will brook no interference from the family. He has apparently convinced Mother Thaw that the only way to save Harry's life is to concede that he is insane and accept that he will have to be hospitalized. Evelyn is to tone down the schoolgirl garb this time, and there are to be no histrionics. In his opening statement, Littleton steers clear of any reference to brainstorms or unwritten laws. The defendant, he says, "must plead that he was insane at the time he committed the crime. He need not claim that he was sane or insane before he committed the crime, that he was insane the moment he committed the crime and then, a moment after, sane again. No, he must make the simple claim that at the time he killed Stanford White he was insane."

Jerome, saving his voice, made hoarse by his cold, has Assistant District Attorney Francis Garvan deliver the opening statement for the prosecution. Garvan implores the jury "to be mindful only of the enforcement of the law" and not to be swayed by "the great publicity this case has obtained, or by what you have learned or read of the celebrities involved in the case." After reciting what Thaw had told the arresting officers immediately after the murder—his calm explanation of his plan and his reasons—Garvan states the prosecution's contention that Thaw was sane when he committed the crime, "a premeditated, cowardly murder." In fact, with the compromise plea of temporary insanity abandoned by the defense in favor of a full insanity plea, Jerome is hopeful that Thaw's obsession with White and its violent expression will be interpreted by a jury as the act of a lunatic and that any chance that Thaw will be acquitted and freed has been greatly reduced. It is his duty to argue for first-degree murder, but he is no closer to accepting the idea that death is a just punishment for an irredeemable mental case than he ever was. The urgency now is to convince the jury that, if freed, Harry will always be a danger to society and that he must be locked up for the rest of his life. Since Littleton, too, is working toward that end, the trial will lack the drama of the one that preceded it and offer little glory for the combatants. A conviction of murder would reflect poorly on Jerome, and, for Littleton, it would be an embarrassing defeat. They both need the jury to agree that Harry is insane, although they are approaching it from different angles and want it for different reasons.

Littleton has little trouble lining up witnesses who will attest to Harry's mental instability. A parade of old schoolmasters, servants, and psychologists is followed by the appearance on the stand of Mother Thaw, who has risen from a sickbed to save her son. Instead of protecting the family honor as she had labored mightily to do at the first trial, she is called upon to testify not only to her son's aberrant behavior in childhood but to the Thaw family's astonishing record of mental disorders—Harry's uncle Henry, who was "weak-minded from the age of six," his uncle Josh, who had "brain fever" as a child and had to be institutionalized, an aunt who was epileptic. Anthony Comstock takes the stand with hopes of testifying at length on Stanford White's sex life but is quickly steered to the subject of Thaw's sanity. Prodded by Littleton, Comstock testifies that after listening to Thaw's complaint of being constantly shadowed by sinister spies, he has concluded that Thaw's mind is "unbalanced."

Once again, Evelyn is the star of the show and the defense's main prop. Relieved of the exaggerated childishness and pity-prompting dramatics that Delmas had insisted upon, she strikes the Sob Sisters as having "a new radiant self instead of the wan, pinched girl of the first trial." Less stirring than the first time around, her testimony is nearly a word-for-word repetition of her earlier appearance. When Littleton's questioning seems headed toward a heartrending portrayal of Evelyn's underprivileged childhood, Jerome's hackles are again raised and he objects persistently and annoyingly, arguing that such testimony is irrelevant. He explodes when Evelyn describes Harry's reaction to the story she told him in Paris of her seduction by White and adds something she had failed to mention before—that Harry had been so depressed at the time that he had attempted suicide. In his frustration at her deviousness in picking and choosing her facts, Jerome falls into the same pattern of witness-badgering that had done him no good in the original trial.

His animosity toward Evelyn aroused, he takes a venomous tone, demanding that she account for her original omission of such an important fact.

> Jerome: Did you at the first trial give any account of Harry Thaw's attempted suicide?
> Evelyn: I did not. Mr. Delmas told me not to because it would make Harry out to be too crazy.
> Jerome: Well, insanity was the defense at the last trial, wasn't it?

Littleton responds to this last exasperated and unnecessary question with an angry objection and is sustained.

There is another flashpoint during the DA's two-hour cross-examination of Evelyn when Jerome concedes with undisguised bitterness that Evelyn had been "wronged" by Stanford White but adds that he doubts that White needed any drugs to achieve his purpose.

There is a collective gasp from the Sob Sisters, and Littleton jumps to his feet to denounce Jerome for his "savagery." The DA, he says, is "like a lion in a den," pacing menacingly before his witness.

Later, when her ordeal in the witness chair is over, Evelyn regales reporters with her take on Jerome's harsh treatment. "All that is left for Jerome to do is to tear my little Buster Brown collar to pieces," she tells them with a smile that suggests mockery rather than terror. Once again she feels she has bested her tormentor.

On January 27, just as closing arguments are about to begin, Jerome, who has already been called from the courtroom several times to defend himself from his critics, is summoned away from the criminal court to the Court of General Sessions, where he is severely criticized by Judge Otto A. Rosalsky, a former political ally. Rosalsky accuses Jerome of having conducted his grand jury examination of Thomas Ryan of the Metropolitan Street Railway Company in such a way as to probably invalidate any indictments that body might have found against Ryan. He orders that the whole case against Metropolitan be submitted to another grand jury, an order that Jerome will grudgingly carry out without satisfying his critics, who want nothing short of impeachment.

The day after this dressing-down by Judge Rosalsky, both sides rest their cases. In his summation, Littleton stresses "the hereditary insanity which, working its way to the blood and brain of this defendant, made him nervous, made him mentally unstable, and made him liable to a breakdown under great strain." Most of his argument is ground already well plowed and draws a smaller crowd than Jerome does on the following day, when more people jam into the courtroom than on any previous day of the trial. Among the celebrities spotted by reporters is Richard Harding Davis, the dashing journalist who had publicly protested the campaign of slander against his friend White and had himself come under attack.

Still hoarse, but displaying some of the fire spectators had come hoping to see, Jerome, in his summation, makes no excuses for White's behavior. Nor does he dwell on Evelyn's duplicity except to suggest that as the breadwinner of a family and with legions of suitors, she is perhaps not the helpless victim her besotted fans believe her to be. Instead, he reserves all his contempt for Thaw. How, he asks, did Thaw react after his first proposal to Evelyn when she, "poor little waif of the theaters," declined in order not to "drag him down to her level"? Pointing a finger at the accused, Jerome provides the answer: "This miserable creature, this pervert, this degenerate took the poor little waif from her mother and he flaunted her through the capitals of Europe as his mistress. That was what you did for her, you miserable creature."

This is too much for Harry, who has to be restrained by one of his lawyers.

Though he has neither hope nor the desire at this point to convict Thaw of first-degree murder, Jerome recites the obligatory arguments against a plea of insanity, relishing the opportunity to pour scorn on the malleable medical "experts" with their paid-for theories. "Did you ever hear of a lawyer who couldn't get some expert to take any side of a question?" he asks.

On January 31, the case goes to the jury, which remains in continuous session for thirteen hours before reaching a verdict of not guilty on the ground of the defendant's insanity. As the Thaws dramatize their relief, Jerome strides across the room to embrace Littleton.

"I'm glad it turned out the way it did, old man," he says. "It was a proper verdict." The *Times* reports that Jerome appears "well satisfied with the verdict" and adds that "to set Thaw free again would be in itself a monstrous crime against society."

After thanking the jury, Justice Dowling reads a prepared statement ordering that Harry be taken to the Asylum for the Criminal Insane at Matteawan in the custody of the sheriff. As Thaw reaches the street where his car is waiting to take him to Grand Central Station, he is lustily cheered by a crowd waiting to hail the brave defender of womanly virtue. An even bigger crowd is waiting for him when he arrives at the station where a police guard has to clear a passage for his party. Aboard the train, the mood is festive. A select group of reporters has been invited to join the lawyers accompanying Thaw, who has engaged a private car for the trip and stocked it with whiskey.

Jerome had called it a proper verdict, and it was, but there are no cheers for him as he leaves the courtroom. The defense had enjoyed enormous advantages, dipping liberally into the Thaw fortune to pay for favorable coverage in the corrupt press and buy off potential witnesses for the prosecution. Even so, Jerome had broken through with occasional flashes of the canny courtroom warrior people had come expecting to see. He has actually won the outcome that he sought, but the trial has not been the crowning achievement, the front-page triumph that would have moved his critics to the back pages and hailed him as the man who brought justice to the slayer of one of the city's most brilliant and beloved celebrities.

Instead, because Thaw had faced the death penalty, Jerome could not in good conscience have made a wholehearted case for conviction, which, had it ended in a win, would have made him responsible for sending an obvious lunatic to the electric chair. Arguing for the execution of a defendant not of sound mind would not only have violated his own code of ethics but it also would have been politically disastrous. His prosecutorial duty and his personal ethics had been at odds in this case, and the conflict had put him off his game.

The world's attention had been riveted on the "trial of the century," antic-ipating a thrilling performance by the prosecutor known as a "tiger in the courtroom," but the world had been disappointed. Lacking a cold-blooded perpetrator of premeditated murder, a villain he could have torn into with the full force of his powerful intellect and righteous wrath, Jerome had focused his prosecutorial might on Evelyn. He had looked like a bully, grilling her relentlessly, losing his composure and showing himself capable of abusing the witness who was looked upon by so many as a fragile child, abused by one man in the past and now suffering abuse by another. Jerome had underesti-mated the hold that maudlin sentimentality had on the culture, its worship of pure womanhood requiring manly protection. In the first trial he had been contemptuous of Delmas's suave solicitude, refusing to coddle witnesses and court the jury. He had not felt it necessary to play the game, and his arrogance had cost him sympathy in the jury box and beyond.

He had not adjusted his rational approach to the climate of irrationality, and even more damaging was his underestimation of Evelyn, his failure to anticipate that a showgirl for whom he had so little respect would turn out to be his equal as a sparring partner—and on his own turf. Others had rec-ognized her courage and cleverness and cheered for the brave little wife who had stood up to the coldhearted DA. It seemed to them that she had a point when she complained to reporters that Jerome had become so obsessed by his animus toward her that he had "seemed to lose sight of Harry Thaw completely."

Now, at the end of this second trial, as Harry leaves the courthouse, he is hailed by the mob waiting outside as a hero, and the train ride to Matteawan is more like a triumphal procession than a trip to oblivion.

42

FINISHED AT FIFTY

After all the years he stands out like a mountain peak in personality, and if he missed greatness as a man, it was by a very narrow margin.
—Assistant DA Augustin Derby

Jerome's emboldened critics ratchet up their pressure on Governor Hughes (who now occupies the office Jerome had aspired to), demanding the DA's impeachment. But instead of removing him, the governor appoints a commission to look into the charges of misconduct in office. Of the eight counts of misconduct, one—a testament to the desperation of his enemies—charges that by joining in the ritual flipping of the dice at the entrance to Pontin's restaurant to determine who would pay for the noonday drinks, Jerome had been guilty of gambling in a public place. On May 9, the last day of the hearing, Jerome, acting in his own defense, takes the defiant tone he has used throughout to address the gambling charge. He recalls that it had happened during the first Thaw trial, when he had ducked out of court seeking relief from Delmas's long-winded summation.

Like so many others among Jerome's enemies in the establishment and the press, President Roosevelt is relishing the DA's troubles. Hearing of his "confession" to gambling, Roosevelt professes the same puritanical shock and outrage that had so irritated Jerome earlier in Roosevelt's career when, as police commissioner, he had been hounding Sunday drinkers.

"He shook the dice for drinks!" Roosevelt is said to have exclaimed in horror. "How could he so far forget his dignity?"

The *World*, delighted by Jerome's reversals, is ready to write his political obituary. "Mr. Jerome is one of the tragedies of American politics," writes one of Joseph Pulitzer's editors. "No man of his generation ever had more brilliant opportunities. No man of his training and talents ever rendered a sorrier account of his stewardship…" The *Globe*, a minority voice, comes to Jerome's defense, declaring that "there is no falling away in the belief in his integrity."

In the end, the commission clears Jerome of all charges, but it is something less than a ringing endorsement. Suggesting that Jerome had brought much of the criticism on himself, the referee offers a list of his provocations: "A certain self-confidence and contempt of the opinions of other men, a certain rashness of expression to the verge of recklessness, a certain delight in the exercise of his astuteness of mind and vigor of expression and a certain impatience with criticism have combined, I think, to make men far more eager to attack than they would otherwise have been." A few more voices are heard in support of Jerome once the charges against him are dismissed. The *New York Evening Post* announces that it had always believed in Jerome, and the *New York Sun* declares that the charges against Jerome had been motivated by "malice, mercenary interest and yellow sensationalism."

But at the age of fifty, Jerome's political rise is over. He has offended the party heads by winning without them, and he has antagonized the newspapers by characterizing them as "carrion seekers." He has lambasted the captains of industry, calling them the "criminal rich," and then, by failing to successfully prosecute them, he has angered even his liberal supporters. He has remained true to his principles but has been too quick to assert them, too swift on the attack, too aggressively honest, too much the boat-rocker. In the courtroom contest, pitted against the Thaw millions spent in unlimited amounts to corrupt justice, Jerome's qualities were of little use, his flaws all too evident. He had allowed Evelyn Nesbit to get under his skin, making the once-revered crusader for justice look like a ranting inquisitor. With his outsize faith in his own right-thinking, Jerome had been so ruthless in his pursuit of what he believed to be true that he had looked heartless and arrogant. In the days following the trial, the opinion is widespread that the DA had been curiously inept at this peak moment in his career. The electorate that had once flocked to the polls to vote for the swashbuckling DA has lost faith not in his integrity but in his effectiveness, and it is clear to Jerome that any thoughts of running for governor will have to be abandoned.

Writing later of his friend's fall from glory, Arthur Train recalled that Jerome "shot across the sky at a psychological moment, hung blazing for a brief period of almost unparalleled adulation and then, unable to fulfill the exaggerated hopes which his personality and his own declarations aroused, faded from the public firmament."

A century later, if Jerome is remembered at all, it is as a bit player in the "trial of the century," while the name Stanford White is known all over the world. Born into New York's upper class within a few years of each other, Jerome and White came of age just as the values of the old republic—piety, frugality, moral prudery, and personal rectitude—were bumping up against new, less inhibited attitudes toward money, morals, and sex. The city was seething with cultural, economic, and sexual ferment, and White and Jerome saw themselves as avatars of modernity. Their boldness in pursuing their vision of New York's transformation from a provincial city to a dazzling modern metropolis, swept clean of its 19th-century squalor and drabness, brought them adulation and fame but both men crossed the line between audacity and arrogance and sowed the seeds of their fall from grace—White's descent into posthumous ignominy, Jerome's slide from public favor that put an end to his political career. In his eagerness to kick over every political convention and make his own rules, Jerome alienated the very people he most needed with his impolitic outbursts and unshakable belief in his own freedom from error. White, willing captive of the arrogant notion that as an artist and a modern anti-puritan he was not bound by conventional morality, refused to recognize any limits on his sexual freedom and believed he was entitled to ravish young girls.

A tangible legacy of stunning buildings saved White from future obscurity and ensured that respect for his brilliance as an architect and designer would in time be restored, though his personal reputation remains permanently tainted. Jerome left no such visible monuments to his accomplishments, and there are few who could name the man who made it his mission to save the city from sin and injustice and changed forever the way the work of weeding out crime and corruption is done. His introduction of modern methods to the fight against crime and corruption, the example he set of high-spirited, passionate commitment to good government and justice for all are the legacy he left to future reformist combatants when he slipped from the battlefield.

EPILOGUE

WILLIAM TRAVERS JEROME

No longer the people's hero, Jerome accepts that the path to higher office is closed to him. During the remainder of his term his enemies in the press continue to attack, he endures merciless heckling when he attempts to defend his record, and the reform groups who had once been his most enthusiastic backers have lost confidence in him. Despite the dismissal of all charges against him, there are lingering suspicions that, for Jerome, there are two kinds of law—one for the rich, another for the poor. His plans to run for governor are dashed, but never one to dwell on defeat or self-doubt, he throws himself into plans to run for a third term as DA.

It is a miscalculation. The reformers nominate someone else to run on the Fusion ticket, and on January 1, 1910, an inside page of the *Times* carries a story headlined JEROME SLIPS OUT OF OFFICE.

Jerome enters private practice immediately, but for the next six years, with the support of New York State, he continues to pursue what he still considers his duty: to thwart the continuing efforts to get Harry released from the asylum. Four times during those years Harry, backed by his delusional mother, petitions to be declared sane and released. Each time, Jerome is present to vigorously oppose his release, and each time Harry's insanity is affirmed. When in 1913 Harry succeeds in slipping past the lax guards at the asylum and is spirited away to Canada in a Packard driven by three Hell's Kitchen characters, Jerome follows him there and stays on the case to see Harry finally returned to the Tombs in December 1914.

It is only when Jerome finally withdraws from the fight after nearly a decade devoted to the Thaw case that Harry succeeds in getting a jury to declare him sane in July 1915. He is released, and Jerome has had enough. The public is obviously anxious to see Harry freed, and Jerome's patience is not limitless. Once he no longer feels duty-bound to act as Thaw's nemesis, he is free to enjoy the relatively quiet life of a lawyer in private practice, apparently without bitterness or regret. His domestic life with Ethel Elliot, however irregular, is presumed to be a happy one. (According to a descendant, his "most interesting letters" and early diaries were destroyed by his daughter-in-law, who judged them unworthy of the mature man.) His wife in all but name, Ethel lives with Jerome in Manhattan, while Lavinia, his legal wife, lives with her brothers in a comfortable home in Yonkers and raises no objections. Jerome prospers in his legal practice but joins the ranks of the truly rich when he invests everything he has in Technicolor, the pioneer color process for movies, and the gamble pays off royally. Money, his real opponent in the Thaw trials and the obstacle he so often faced in his efforts to punish the criminal rich, fills his pockets—a sweet triumph that arrives while he still has time to enjoy it. Robust to the end, Jerome contracts pneumonia in New York and dies in February 1934 at the age of seventy-four in the home shared with Ethel. While his political ambitions were thwarted, his fearless anticorruption crusade succeeded in lifting the city from its complacent acceptance of a corrupt political system dependent on rampant vice. Optimistic, energetic, and innovative, he deserves much of the credit for rescuing New York from its ignominy as a capital of vice, igniting a real demand for change and putting it on course as a world capital in the 20th century.

STANFORD WHITE

White's murder and the lurid newspaper stories exposing—and embellishing on—his immoral behavior leave his family bereft and disgraced, his legacy tainted, and his partners anguished by the loss of their brilliant colleague and friend. Even as the trials were in progress, White's indebtedness to dealers, friends, and his firm was being addressed. An auction sale of furnishings from White's Gramercy Park residence was held with an offering of more than four hundred items, including the dining room ceiling, which William Randolph Hearst purchased for $3,000. A week later, White's paintings were put up for sale, and in December another sale of his treasures was held. The three sales brought in more than $260,000, which covered a sizable chunk of his debts. There were to be several more sales of items that White had assembled and stored in various places around the city, with proceeds that came close to satisfying—if not totally covering—his debts to creditors. For years after the murder trials, the unsavory excesses of his personal life overshadow his artistic genius in the public mind. More recently, he has recovered the respect he is due for the beauty of his buildings and the role he played in transforming New York City from a drab provincial town to a dazzling metropolis rivaling the great capitals of the modern world.

HARRY K. THAW

No sooner have the gates closed behind Harry at Matteawan than Mother Thaw and her legal troops go to battle, fighting to have him declared sane and released from the asylum. His journalistic advocates take up the cause, with Hearst's papers depicting him as a martyr imprisoned in an asylum through the efforts of Stanford White's friends and their legal mercenary, William Travers Jerome. The *Journal* reminds readers that in killing White, Thaw "rendered a considerable service to the community," while the Boston *American* complains that Thaw is being "persecuted," a miscarriage of justice more egregious even than what can be found in the "annals of the Middle Ages."

When Thaw finally gives up on his chances for official release, he simply walks past guards at the asylum on August 17, 1913, and is whisked off to Canada in a car driven by hired goons. On his arrival, he is greeted by the Canadian public as a heroic fugitive from "American justice." A *New York Times* correspondent reports from Canada that "men and women almost trampled upon each other in a mad rush to shake his hand. When he went to the courtroom he rode in an open carriage, acclaimed by the populace, lifting his hat and bowing right and left like an emperor."

Extradited from Canada through Jerome's efforts, he spends more than a year in New England before Jerome wins again in 1914, hauling him back to the Tombs. Harry will not be free again until after Jerome, his interest and patience exhausted, has withdrawn from the case. Only then, in July 1915, does Thaw succeed in getting a jury to declare him sane and order him released. His first steps across the Bridge of Sighs as a free man are cheered by a crowd of thousands, causing the New York *Sun* to comment, "In this nauseous business we don't know which makes the gorge rise more, the pervert buying his way out or the perverted idiots that hail him with wild huzzas."

Mother Thaw tells reporters on the eve of Harry's release that she is looking forward to having her Harry home again, living "very quietly" with her in Pittsburgh. In this, too, Thaw manages to disappoint her, speeding off to Atlantic City with his cronies immediately after his release without stopping to visit his mother. A less devoted mother would likely have washed her hands of such a son but not Mother Thaw, who refuses to give up on him, wherever he is and whatever he does. After binging in Atlantic City, Harry's first act as a free man is to put through a divorce from Evelyn on grounds of adultery. In 1917 he is charged with viciously whipping a teenage boy, testing even Mother Thaw's tolerance. After reportedly spending another million of the family fortune to buy Harry's freedom, she comes to the conclusion, as Jerome had a decade earlier, that her son should be locked up and never turned loose, but she can never turn her back on him. He is returned to the asylum, but in 1924 he manages to convince doctors of his sanity and is again released. By then in her eighties, Mother Thaw is presumably ready to give her 53-year-old son another chance. She dies in 1929 at the age of eighty-six, and when Harry dies of a heart attack eighteen years later, aged seventy-six, he leaves an estate of some $1 million, and there is a bequest in his will to Evelyn of 1 percent of his financial worth.

EVELYN NESBIT

Evelyn, who has played her role faithfully, is no match for Mother Thaw, and once she is of no further use to the family after Thaw is sent to the asylum, the money dries up. In 1910 she gives birth to a son she names Russell William Thaw, though Thaw denies paternity. The Thaw family's refusal to compensate her for her heroism on the stand also liberates her from any loyalty, and when reporters descend on her for a comment after Harry's 1913 escape from Matteawan, she responds with stunning truthfulness. "He hid behind my skirts at two trials and I won't stand for it again, I won't let lawyers throw any more mud at me."

Obliged to support herself and her son, she returns to the stage and is a success dancing the new ragtime dances with her partner, Jack Clifford. In 1914, she writes *The Story of My Life*, the first of her two memoirs. Divorced by Thaw in 1915, she marries Clifford in 1916, but when he can no longer stand being known as "Mr. Evelyn Nesbit," they divorce. Through the teens and the Roaring Twenties, Evelyn continues to survive as a performer but with dwindling audiences and fading beauty. On a downward spiral, she appears in seedy clubs, turns to drugs and attempts suicide. Various valiant attempts to take control of her life end in failure. Then, in 1934, perhaps hoping for a best seller to put her back on her feet financially, she writes a second memoir, *Prodigal Days*, but interest in her story has faded and the book does not have the success she had hoped for. Always an unreliable witness to her own story, as a writer she makes certain changes to the one she told in the witness chair. She writes that it was Harry who insisted that the champagne she drank on the night White seduced her was drugged but that, in fact, it was "simply a matter of too much champagne." And though she had denied in court that she had

ever told Abe Hummel that she had been whipped by Thaw in Schloss Katzenstein, in her book she relates the story substantially as it was told in the
affidavit. She also admits that Delmas had forced her to profess hatred for
White but that she had loved him. In an interview conducted shortly before
her death in a nursing home at the age of eighty-two, she declares, "Stanny
was lucky, he died, I lived."

JACK BARRYMORE

Jack Barrymore, perhaps the only man to inspire in Evelyn a truly romantic
love, abandons his rebellion against the family business and becomes one of
America's greatest actors.

NAN PATTERSON

After her acquittal Nan remains of interest to the press, which links her to several home-wrecking romances and the suicide of a rejected suitor—all untrue,
according to Nan. She is not heard of again until 1910 when reporters learn
that, having apparently divorced the "early husband" whom she had remarried shortly after her release, she has married Captain Summer K. Prescott,
the son of a rich manufacturer. There is a bizarre report in the 1920s that Nan
has turned up as a washerwoman in Yonkers, where she is accused of having
started a violent row with a neighbor. In fact, she is living large with her rich
husband in a house overlooking Puget Sound and the newspapers are obliged
to acknowledge the error. Thereafter reporters leave her in peace.

ABE HUMMEL

As soon as he is released from Blackwell's Island prison, Hummel sails for
Europe and spends the rest of his life in London and Paris, enjoying the theater and café life. Insiders believe he is benefiting from a "retirement plan"
financed by Charlie Morse, payment for having held out against Jerome's
relentless attempts to get him to implicate Morse in the Dodge conspiracy.

Had he yielded, he might have been spared the jail sentence but at the sacrifice of a comfortable European retirement.

CHARLIE MORSE

In the aftermath of his disastrous attempt to corner the copper market, Charlie Morse's fortune is in ruins. Worse, his market manipulations are under scrutiny by the US district attorney. Indictments are handed down, a total of seventy-nine, including some by his old nemesis William Travers Jerome. His efforts to squirm free are impressive, but in November 1908, after two days of deliberation, Morse is found guilty on several counts in the federal case, though not on Jerome's conspiracy charge. He is sentenced to fifteen years in federal prison but does not serve his full term. To President Taft's eternal embarrassment, he is persuaded by Morse's allies that Morse is at death's door and agrees to a pardon, only to watch Morse thrive as a war profiteer, among other lucrative activities, and die peacefully in his native Maine at the age of seventy-six.

COLONEL WILLIAM D'ALTON MANN

In the early years after his exposure as an extortionist, Mann's power dissipates, but he continues to publish *Town Topics*, devoting considerable space to celebrating Jerome's eclipse. With the outbreak of World War I, he offers military advice to the Allied powers and goes on to take political positions, supporting Al Smith for governor of New York, pensions for presidents, and women's suffrage. But he is violently opposed to Prohibition, put forward to "darken the otherwise pleasant eventide of a very eventful life." In his final *Town Topics* editorial, written three days before his death at eighty-one in 1920, he predicts a Republican victory in the coming election, an American return to isolationism, and a second war with the Germans. His funeral is held at the Church of the Heavenly Rest, where his Gettysburg saber rests on his flag-draped coffin. Three colonels and a major general attend, and a sergeant from the Seventh Regiment sounds taps. Accountants declare his estate insolvent, but heirs later fight over funds cannily sequestered in case of lawsuits. Years later it is discovered that his safe, supposedly packed with enough dynamite to blow up high society, actually contained his supply of brandy and cigars.

VICTIMS OF THE 1907 PANIC

Charles Barney pays for his part in Charlie Morse's disastrous scheme with his life. Others hold on to their lives but not their money.

The "King of Gamblers," Dick Canfield, whose fortune was at one time estimated at $12 million, loses most but not all of it in 1907. In 1914, when he dies of a fractured skull after a fall in a subway station, he is still a millionaire.

The Panic pauperizes Stanford White's close friend Henry Poor. A multi-millionaire who had inherited a fortune and then added another $5 million in the 1890s by playing the market, he loses everything in 1907—the town house White had so lavishly remodeled, his palace in Tuxedo, his collection of rare books and manuscripts, his stable with its secret room, and the rest of his treasures. At his death in 1915, he is some $2 million in debt.

Jimmie Breese takes a big hit in 1907 but takes it in stride. He is obliged to sell his New York townhouse/studio and rent out his summer home in Southampton. With the proceeds he buys a run-down estate in Maryland and embraces farming with characteristic enthusiasm, proposing to "live on the land." He allows himself some time, however, to play the stock market and succeeds in recovering a good portion of his losses. He returns to New York and Southampton, indulges his passion for fast cars, and develops a new interest in experimenting with radios. Widowed in 1917, he takes a much younger bride in 1919. When his finances take another dive in 1926, he sells the big house in Southampton, is divorced in 1927, and after taking a world tour settles into his radio studio in Southampton, never lacking for female companionship. Two days after celebrating his eightieth birthday, he dies peacefully in Southampton, and his grief-stricken female companion commits suicide.

WORKS CITED BY CHAPTER

PROLOGUE

The New York Herald, 3 November 1901.

The New York Times, 5 January 1901.

The New York Times, magazine supplement, "William C. Whitney," 20 November 1898.

Broderick, Mosette. *Triumvirate: Art, Architecture, Scandal, and Class in America's Gilded Age.* Alfred A. Knopf, 2010.

O'Connor, Richard, *Courtroom Warrior: The Combative Career of William Travers Jerome.* Little, Brown and Company, 1963.

Andrews, Wayne. *Architecture, Ambition and Americans: A Social History of American Architecture.* The Free Press, 1964.

Croly, Herbert David, *The Promise of American Life,* Macmillan, 1911.

Hawley, Walter L., "The Politician Militant," *Ainslee's Magazine,* Vol. 8, No. 6, January 1902.

The New York Herald, 1 April 1894.

CHAPTER 1—"THE JUDGE WITH THE AX"

O'Connor, Richard, *Courtroom Warrior: The Combative Career of William Travers Jerome.* Little, Brown and Company, 1963.

The *New York Times,* 19 February 1901.

Barry, John D., "The Case of William Travers Jerome." *The New York Times Magazine,* December 1906.

Hodder, Alfred, *A Fight for the City.* The Macmillan Company, 1903. (Google Books).

Dash, Mike, *Satan's Circus: Murder, Vice, Police Corruption and New York's Trial of the Century.* Three Rivers Press, 2007.

Crichton, Judy, *America 1900: The Turning Point.* Henry Holt and Company, 1998.

CHAPTER 2—PASSION SPARKED

Nesbit, Evelyn; Paul, Deborah Dorian, ed., *Tragic Beauty: The Lost 1914 Memoirs of Evelyn Nesbit.* Deborah Dorian Paul edition c.2006. Original publisher: John Long Ltd., 1914. Original title, *The Story of My Life.*

Nesbit, Evelyn; Paul, Deborah Dorian, ed. *Prodigal Days: The Untold Story.* Deborah Dorian Paul edition c. 2004. Original publisher: Julian Messner, Inc. 1934.

Baker, Paul R., *Stanny: The Gilded Life of Stanford White.* The Free Press, 1989.

Uruburu, Paula, *American Eve: Evelyn Nesbit, Stanford White, the Birth of the "It" Girl, and the Crime of the Century.* Riverhead Books, 2008.

O'Connor, Richard, *Courtroom Warrior: The Combative Career of William Travers Jerome.* Little, Brown and Company, 1963.

CHAPTER 3—A DIFFICULT LAUNCH

The Chicago Tribune, Morrow, James B., "William Travers Jerome Tells How He Won Success." 1 July 1906.

O'Connor, Richard, *Courtroom Warrior: The Combative Career of William Travers Jerome.* Little, Brown and Company, 1963.

Jefferson, Sam, *Gordon Bennett and the First Yachting Race Across the Atlantic.* Adlard Coles Nautical, Bloomsbury, 2016.

Hodder, Alfred, *A Fight for the City.* The Macmillan Company, 1903. (Google Books).

CHAPTER 4—ON TOP OF THE WORLD

Nesbit, Evelyn; Paul, Deborah Dorian, ed., *Tragic Beauty: The Lost 1914 Memoirs of Evelyn Nesbit.* Deborah Dorian Paul edition c.2006. Original publisher: John Long Ltd., 1914. Original title, *The Story of My Life.*

Nesbit, Evelyn; Paul, Deborah Dorian, ed. *Prodigal Days: The Untold Story.* Deborah
    Dorian Paul edition c. 2004. Original publisher: Julian Messner, Inc. 1934.

Baker, Paul R., *Stanny: The Gilded Life of Stanford White.* The Free Press, 1989.

Lowe, David Garrard, *Stanford White's New York.* Doubleday, 1992.

Mooney, Michael Macdonald, *Evelyn Nesbit and Stanford White: Love and Death in the
    Gilded Age.* William Morrow and Company, 1976.

www.senate.gov.

McCullough, David, *The Greater Journey, Americans in Paris.* Simon and Schuster, 2011.

Lessard, Suzannah, *The Architect of Desire: Beauty and Danger in the Stanford White Family.*
    Dell Publishing, 1996.

White, Claire Nicolas, ed. *Stanford White: Letters to His Family, Including a Selection of
    Letters to Augustus Saint-Gaudens.* Rizzoli, 1997 (Stanford White writing to his mother,
    23 February 1873, 1 September 1878, 6 November 1878, 4 February 1884 and to
    his sister-in-law 20 July 1884), Rizzoli, 1997.

Broderick, Mosette. *Triumvirate: Art, Architecture, Scandal, and Class in America's Gilded Age.*
    Alfred A. Knopf, 2010.

Larkin, Oliver W., *Art and Life in America.* Holt, Rinehart and Winston, revised edition,
    1960.

Homberger, Eric, *Mrs. Astor's New York: Money and Social Power in a Gilded Age.* Yale
    University Press, 2002.

CHAPTER 5—GOO-GOOS AND GRAFTERS

The Chicago Tribune, 1 July 1906.

The New York Times, 20 May 1890.

O'Connor, Richard, *Courtroom Warrior: The Combative Career of William Travers Jerome.*
    Little, Brown and Company, 1963.

Stryker, Lloyd Paul, *The Art of Advocacy: A Plea for the Renaissance of the Trial Lawyer.*
    Zenger Publishing Company reprint; Simon and Schuster original publisher.

Chicago Tribune, 3 November 1901.

Lowe, David Garrard, *Stanford White's New York*. Doubleday, 1992.

The New York Times, 15 November 1900.

CHAPTER 6—SOARING CELEBRITY, SOARING DEBTS
The New York Times, Russell, John, "75 Crates Could Not Confine an Architect's Imagination." 12 March 1998.

Baker, Paul R., *Stanny: The Gilded Life of Stanford White*. The Free Press, 1989.

Lowe, David Garrard, *Stanford White's New York*. Doubleday, 1992.

CHAPTER 7—HERO ON THE HUSTINGS
The New York Herald, 3 November 1901.

Hodder, Alfred, *A Fight for the City*. The Macmillan Company, 1903. (Google Books).

O'Connor, Richard, *Courtroom Warrior: The Combative Career of William Travers Jerome*. Little, Brown and Company, 1963.

The New York Times, 6 Nov. 1901.

Woods, Philip H., *Bath, Maine's Charlie Morse: Ice King & Wall Street Scoundrel*. The History Press, 2011.

CHAPTER 8—"MAD HARRY"
Stern, Robert; Gilmartin, Gregory; Massengale, John Montague, *New York 1900: Metropolitan Architecture and Urbanism 1890-1915*. Rizzoli International Publications, 1983.

Langford, Gerald, *The Murder of Stanford White*. Bobbs-Merrill Company, 1962.

O'Connor, Richard, *Courtroom Warrior: The Combative Career of William Travers Jerome*. Little, Brown and Company, 1963.

Mooney, Michael Macdonald, *Evelyn Nesbit and Stanford White: Love and Death in the Gilded Age*. William Morrow and Company, 1976.

Lowe, David Garrard, *Stanford White's New York*. Doubleday, 1992.

Baker, Paul R., *Stanny: The Gilded Life of Stanford White.* The Free Press, 1989.

Uruburu, Paula, *American Eve: Evelyn Nesbit, Stanford White, the Birth of the "It" Girl, and the Crime of the Century.* Riverhead Books, 2008.

CHAPTER 9—INTO THE FRAY

Stern, Robert; Gilmartin, Gregory; Massengale, John Montague, *New York 1900: Metropolitan Architecture and Urbanism 1890-1915.* Rizzoli International Publications, 1983.

Bentley, James R., "William Travers Jerome, A Unique District Attorney," *Meriden Morning Record,* 5 September 1905.

O'Connor, Richard, *Courtroom Warrior: The Combative Career of William Travers Jerome.* Little, Brown and Company, 1963.

Hodder, Alfred, *A Fight for the City.* The Macmillan Company, 1903. (Google Books).

Logan, Andy, *The Man Who Robbed the Robber Barons, The Akadine Press, 2001.*

The New York Times, 2 December 1902.

The New York Times, 28 September 1902.

CHAPTER 10—PASSIONATE PLAYMATES

Nesbit, Evelyn; Paul, Deborah Dorian, ed. *Prodigal Days: The Untold Story.* Deborah Dorian Paul edition c. 2004. Original publisher: Julian Messner, Inc. 1934.

Uruburu, Paula, *American Eve: Evelyn Nesbit, Stanford White, the Birth of the "It" Girl, and the Crime of the Century.* Riverhead Books, 2008.

Baker, Paul R., *Stanny: The Gilded Life of Stanford White.* The Free Press, 1989.

Lessard, Suzannah, *The Architect of Desire: Beauty and Danger in the Stanford White Family.* Dell Publishing, 1996.

Mooney, Michael Macdonald, *Evelyn Nesbit and Stanford White: Love and Death in the Gilded Age.* William Morrow and Company, 1976.

CHAPTER 11—"THE KING OF GAMBLERS"

The New York Times, 2 December 1902.

O'Connor, Richard, *Courtroom Warrior: The Combative Career of William Travers Jerome.* Little, Brown and Company, 1963.

The New York Times, 12 December 1914.

CHAPTER 12—ERRANT EVELYN

Baker, Paul R., *Stanny: The Gilded Life of Stanford White.* The Free Press, 1989.

Sports Illustrated, S.I. Vault, Ryan, Pat "A River Running Out of Eden," 25 May 1970.

Uruburu, Paula, *American Eve: Evelyn Nesbit, Stanford White, the Birth of the "It" Girl, and the Crime of the Century.* Riverhead Books, 2008.

Lessard, Suzannah, *The Architect of Desire: Beauty and Danger in the Stanford White Family.* Dell Publishing, 1996.

CHAPTER 13—CHARLIE'S FOLLY

Train, Arthur, *True Stories of Crime from the District Attorney's Office.* Wildside Books (reprint of original published in 1908).

O'Connor, Richard, *Courtroom Warrior: The Combative Career of William Travers Jerome.* Little, Brown and Company, 1963.

Woods, Philip H., *Bath, Maine's Charlie Morse: Ice King & Wall Street Scoundrel.* The History Press, 2011.

CHAPTER 14—HEADING FOR TROUBLE

Nesbit, Evelyn; Paul, Deborah Dorian, ed., *Tragic Beauty: The Lost 1914 Memoirs of Evelyn Nesbit.* Deborah Dorian Paul edition c.2006. Original publisher: John Long Ltd., 1914. Original title, *The Story of My Life.*

Mooney, Michael Macdonald, *Evelyn Nesbit and Stanford White: Love and Death in the Gilded Age.* William Morrow and Company, 1976.

Nesbit, Evelyn; Paul, Deborah Dorian, ed. *Prodigal Days: The Untold Story.* Deborah Dorian Paul edition c. 2004. Original publisher: Julian Messner, Inc. 1934.

Baker, Paul R., *Stanny: The Gilded Life of Stanford White.* The Free Press, 1989.

Uruburu, Paula, *American Eve: Evelyn Nesbit, Stanford White, the Birth of the "It" Girl, and the Crime of the Century.* Riverhead Books, 2008.

Lessard, Suzannah, *The Architect of Desire: Beauty and Danger in the Stanford White Family.* Dell Publishing, 1996.

MacColl, Galil; Wallace, Carol McD.; *To Marry an English Lord, Or How Anglomania Really Got Started.* Workman Publishing, 1989.

CHAPTER 15—"THE DODGE-MORSE TANGLE"

Murphy, Cait, *Scoundrels in Law: The Trials of Howe & Hummel, Lawyers to the Gangsters, Cops, Starlets, and Rakes Who Made the Gilded Age.* Smithsonian Books, Harper-Collins Publishers, 2010.

Woods, Philip H., *Bath, Maine's Charlie Morse: Ice King & Wall Street Scoundrel.* The History Press, 2011.

O'Connor, Richard, *Courtroom Warrior: The Combative Career of William Travers Jerome.* Little, Brown and Company, 1963.

CHAPTER 16—THAW UNMASKED

Nesbit, Evelyn; Paul, Deborah Dorian, ed. *Prodigal Days: The Untold Story.* Deborah Dorian Paul edition c. 2004. Original publisher: Julian Messner, Inc. 1934.

Lowe, David Garrard, *Stanford White's New York.* Doubleday, 1992.

Mooney, Michael Macdonald, *Evelyn Nesbit and Stanford White: Love and Death in the Gilded Age.* William Morrow and Company, 1976.

Baker, Paul R., *Stanny: The Gilded Life of Stanford White.* The Free Press, 1989.

CHAPTER 17—JEROME'S SECRET

O'Connor, Richard, *Courtroom Warrior: The Combative Career of William Travers Jerome.* Little, Brown and Company, 1963.

Interview, William Travers Jerome IV, great-grandson of WTJ, 19 September 2017.

CHAPTER 18—SPIRALING DOWNWARD

Lowe, David Garrard, *Stanford White's New York.* Doubleday, 1992.

The New York Times, 3 February 2004.

Baker, Paul R., *Stanny: The Gilded Life of Stanford White.* The Free Press, 1989.

O'Connor, Richard, *Courtroom Warrior: The Combative Career of William Travers Jerome.* Little, Brown and Company, 1963.

White, Claire Nicolas, ed. (Stanford White writing to his wife, June 1904).

CHAPTER 19—DEATH IN A HANSOM CAB

Levy, Newman, *The Nan Patterson Case,* Simon and Schuster, 1959. (Included in Best-in-Books compilation, Nelson Doubleday, 1959)

CHAPTER 20—EVELYN ASCENDANT

Baker, Paul R., *Stanny: The Gilded Life of Stanford White.* The Free Press, 1989.

Sports Illustrated, 25 May 1970.

Mooney, Michael Macdonald, *Evelyn Nesbit and Stanford White: Love and Death in the Gilded Age.* William Morrow and Company, 1976.

CHAPTER 21—HARD WORK AND HEADACHES

O'Connor, Richard, *Courtroom Warrior: The Combative Career of William Travers Jerome.* Little, Brown and Company, 1963.

Levy, Newman, *The Nan Patterson Case,* Simon and Schuster, 1959. (Included in Best-in-Books compilation, Nelson Doubleday, 1959)

Rovere, Richard, *Howe & Hummel: Their True and Scandalous History.* Farrar, Straus and
   Giroux, 1947.

CHAPTER 22—KEEPING UP APPEARANCES
Baker, Paul R., *Stanny: The Gilded Life of Stanford White.* The Free Press, 1989.

CHAPTER 23—CORPORATE SCANDAL AND A CAUTIONARY CASE
The New York Times, 16 June 1905.

Lord, Walter, *The Good Years: From 1900 to the First World War,* Harper & Brothers,
   1960.

The New York Journal, 16 February 1905.

CHAPTER 24—COMING TO TERMS
Nesbit, Evelyn; Paul, Deborah Dorian, ed., *Tragic Beauty: The Lost 1914 Memoirs of
   Evelyn Nesbit.* Deborah Dorian Paul edition c.2006. Original publisher: John Long
   Ltd., 1914. Original title, *The Story of My Life.*

Baker, Paul R., *Stanny: The Gilded Life of Stanford White.* The Free Press, 1989.

White, Claire Nicolas, ed. (Stanford White writing to his wife, February 7 and 17, 1905).

Nesbit, Evelyn; Paul, Deborah Dorian, ed. *Prodigal Days: The Untold Story.* Deborah
   Dorian Paul edition c. 2004. Original publisher: Julian Messner, Inc. 1934.

CHAPTER 25—"THE BIG SPIDER"
The New York Times, 16 June 1905.

O'Connor, Richard, *Courtroom Warrior: The Combative Career of William Travers Jerome.*

Little, Brown and Company, 1963.

Levy, Newman, *The Nan Patterson Case,* Simon and Schuster, 1959. (Included in Best-in-
   Books compilation, Nelson Doubleday, 1959)

Logan, Andy, *The Man Who Robbed the Robber Barons, The Akadine Press, 2001.*

CHAPTER 2—A SHOPPING SPREE

Baker, Paul R., *Stanny: The Gilded Life of Stanford White.* The Free Press, 1989.

The New York Times, 12 March 1998.

CHAPTER 27—MORE CHALLENGES

Logan, Andy, *The Man Who Robbed the Robber Barons, The Akadine Press, 2001.*

The New York Times, 1 August 1905.

The Times Magazine, Barry, John D., "The Case of William Travers Jerome," January, 1907. (Google Books).

O'Connor, Richard, *Courtroom Warrior: The Combative Career of William Travers Jerome.* Little, Brown and Company, 1963.

The New York Times, 8 November 1905.

Murphy, Cait, *Scoundrels in Law: The Trials of Howe & Hummel, Lawyers to the Gangsters, Cops, Starlets, and Rakes Who Made the Gilded Age.* Smithsonian Books, Harper-Collins Publishers, 2010.

CHAPTER 28—PARADISE LOST

Nesbit, Evelyn; Paul, Deborah Dorian, ed. *Prodigal Days: The Untold Story.* Deborah Dorian Paul edition c. 2004. Original publisher: Julian Messner, Inc. 1934.

McCullough, David, *The Greater Journey, Americans in Paris.* Simon and Schuster, 2011.

White, Claire Nicolas, ed. (Stanford White writing to Saint-Gaudens, 11 May 1906).

Baker, Paul R., *Stanny: The Gilded Life of Stanford White.* The Free Press, 1989.

Nesbit, Evelyn; Paul, Deborah Dorian, ed., *Tragic Beauty: The Lost 1914 Memoirs of Evelyn Nesbit.* Deborah Dorian Paul edition c.2006. Original publisher: John Long Ltd., 1914. Original title, *The Story of My Life.*

Langford, Gerald, *The Murder of Stanford White.* Bobbs-Merrill Company, 1962.

CHAPTER 29—ANOTHER PROBE, A NEW HERO

O'Connor, Richard, *Courtroom Warrior: The Combative Career of William Travers Jerome.*

Little, Brown and Company, 1963.

Myers, Gustavus, *The History of Tammany Hall.* Making of America digital library of
   primary sources, MLibrary, originally published in 1917.

CHAPTER 30—GATHERING SHADOWS

Baker, Paul R., *Stanny: The Gilded Life of Stanford White.* The Free Press, 1989.

The New York Times, 23 February 1906.

The New York Times, 1 January, 1903.

The New York Times, 23 February 1906.

White, Claire Nicolas, ed. (Stanford White writing to Saint-Gaudens, 25 October
   1905).

Baker, Paul R., *Stanny: The Gilded Life of Stanford White.* The Free Press, 1989.

Miller, Frances, *"Tanty": Encounters with the Past,* Sandbox Press, 1979.

Logan, Andy, *The Man Who Robbed the Robber Barons, The Akadine Press, 2001.*

O'Connor, Richard, *Courtroom Warrior: The Combative Career of William Travers Jerome.*
   Little, Brown and Company, 1963.

CHAPTER 31—A HIGH-WIRE ACT

Logan, Andy, *The Man Who Robbed the Robber Barons, The Akadine Press, 2001.*

O'Connor, Richard, *Courtroom Warrior: The Combative Career of William Travers Jerome.*
   Little, Brown and Company, 1963.

CHAPTER 32—JUNE 25, 1906

Nesbit, Evelyn; Paul, Deborah Dorian, ed. *Prodigal Days: The Untold Story.* Deborah
   Dorian Paul edition c. 2004. Original publisher: Julian Messner, Inc. 1934.

Uruburu, Paula, *American Eve: Evelyn Nesbit, Stanford White, the Birth of the "It" Girl, and the Crime of the Century.* Riverhead Books, 2008.

Baker, Paul R., *Stanny: The Gilded Life of Stanford White.* The Free Press, 1989.

CHAPTER 33—BEFORE THE STORM
The New York Times, 5 July 1906.

O'Connor, Richard, *Courtroom Warrior: The Combative Career of William Travers Jerome.* Little, Brown and Company, 1963.

Nesbit, Evelyn; Paul, Deborah Dorian, ed. *Prodigal Days: The Untold Story.* Deborah Dorian Paul edition c. 2004. Original publisher: Julian Messner, Inc. 1934.

Troytaylorbooks.blogspot.com, Taylor, Troy, "Harry Thaw and the Girl in the Red Velvet Swing." posted by Whitechapel Press, 11 April 2014.

CHAPTER 34—A DISCREET FAREWELL
Baker, Paul R., *Stanny: The Gilded Life of Stanford White.* The Free Press, 1989.

The New York Times, 29 June, 1906.

CHAPTER 35—THE PRESS POUNCES
Nesbit, Evelyn; Paul, Deborah Dorian, ed., *Tragic Beauty: The Lost 1914 Memoirs of Evelyn Nesbit.* Deborah Dorian Paul edition c.2006. Original publisher: John Long Ltd., 1914. Original title, *The Story of My Life.*

O'Connor, Richard, *Courtroom Warrior: The Combative Career of William Travers Jerome.* Little, Brown and Company, 1963.

GallerySink.com, Augustus Saint-Gaudens letter to *Collier's Magazine,* 1906.

CHAPTER 36—GIRDING FOR BATTLE
O'Connor, Richard, *Courtroom Warrior: The Combative Career of William Travers Jerome.* Little, Brown and Company, 1963.

CHAPTER 37—*PEOPLE V. HARRY K. THAW* I: THE PRELIMINARIES

Chiasson, Lloyd, Jr. ed., *The Press on Trial: Crimes and Trials as Media Events.* Greenwood Press, 1997.

O'Connor, Richard, *Courtroom Warrior: The Combative Career of William Travers Jerome.* Little, Brown and Company, 1963.

Uruburu, Paula, *American Eve: Evelyn Nesbit, Stanford White, the Birth of the "It" Girl, and the Crime of the Century.* Riverhead Books, 2008.

Langford, Gerald, *The Murder of Stanford White.* Bobbs-Merrill Company, 1962.

Samuels, Charles, *The Girl in the Red Velvet Swing,* reprinted by Aeonian Press, original copyright 1953.

CHAPTER 38—*PEOPLE V. HARRY K. THAW*: THE "ANGEL CHILD" TESTIFIES

O'Connor, Richard, *Courtroom Warrior: The Combative Career of William Travers Jerome.* Little, Brown and Company, 1963.

Samuels, Charles, *The Girl in the Red Velvet Swing,* reprinted by Aeonian Press, original copyright 1953.

law2.umkc.edu/faculty/projects/trials, Linder, Douglas O., "The Trials of Harry Thaw for the Murder of Stanford White."

Langford, Gerald, *The Murder of Stanford White.* Bobbs-Merrill Company, 1962.

Chiasson, Lloyd, Jr. ed., *The Press on Trial: Crimes and Trials as Media Events.* Greenwood Press, 1997.

CHAPTER 39—*PEOPLE V. HARRY K. THAW* I: JEROME, THE INQUISITOR

Langford, Gerald, *The Murder of Stanford White.* Bobbs-Merrill Company, 1962.

Mooney, Michael Macdonald, *Evelyn Nesbit and Stanford White: Love and Death in the Gilded Age.* William Morrow and Company, 1976.

Samuels, Charles, *The Girl in the Red Velvet Swing,* reprinted by Aeonian Press, original copyright 1953.

Law2.umkc.edu, Linder.

O'Connor, Richard, *Courtroom Warrior: The Combative Career of William Travers Jerome.* Little, Brown and Company, 1963.

CHAPTER 40—CLOSING ARGUMENTS

Law2.umke.edu, "Summation of William T. Jerome, D.A., Harry Thaw Trial, 10 April 1907."

Law2.umke.edu, "Summation of Delphin Delmas for the Defense, Harry Thaw Trial, April 1907."

O'Connor, Richard, *Courtroom Warrior: The Combative Career of William Travers Jerome.* Little, Brown and Company, 1963.

Langford, Gerald, *The Murder of Stanford White.* Bobbs-Merrill Company, 1962.

Baker, Paul R., *Stanny: The Gilded Life of Stanford White.* The Free Press, 1989.

Samuels, Charles, *The Girl in the Red Velvet Swing,* reprinted by Aeonian Press, original copyright 1953.

CHAPTER 41—*PEOPLE V. HARRY K. THAW* II: A "PROPER" VERDICT

Langford, Gerald, *The Murder of Stanford White.* Bobbs-Merrill Company, 1962.

The New York Times, 15 November 1907.

O'Connor, Richard, *Courtroom Warrior: The Combative Career of William Travers Jerome.* Little, Brown and Company, 1963.

CHAPTER 42—FINISHED AT 50

O'Connor, Richard, *Courtroom Warrior: The Combative Career of William Travers Jerome.* Little, Brown and Company, 1963.

Logan, Andy, *The Man Who Robbed the Robber Barons,* The Akadine Press, 2001.

EPILOGUE

William Travers Jerome: *The New York Times,* 1 January 1910.

Harry K. Thaw: O'Connor, Richard, *Courtroom Warrior: The Combative Career of William Travers Jerome.* Little, Brown and Company, 1963.

Evelyn Nesbit: Nesbit, Evelyn; Paul, Deborah Dorian, ed. *Prodigal Days: The Untold Story.* Deborah Dorian Paul edition c. 2004. Original publisher: Julian Messner, Inc. 1934.

INDEX

A

abortion, 97–98, 243–244
Ahle, Charles, 168–169, 176–177, 180
American aristocracy, 34, 37
anti-vice society, 13
architecture, 33
Armstrong Committee, 187–188, 222
Astor, Caroline, vii–viii, 69
Atwell, Ben, 215

B

Barker, James, 41–42
Barney, Charles, x, 55–58, 131, 151, 191–192, 261, 282
Barney, Helen, vii, viii, 54
Barney, Lily, viii, 56, 191
Barney mansion, 191–192
Barrymore, Ethel, 30–31, 84
Barrymore, Jack, 30–31, 84–85, 94–98, 106–107, 243–244, 280
Barrymore, Lionel, 84
Beale, Truxton, 203, 231
"Beauty Dinner," 70
Bedford (butler), 119, 208–209
beer, 47
Belmont, Frances, 72
Belmont, Oliver H. P., 197
Benedick, 37
Bennett, James Gordon, 23, 25, 26, 36–37, 172, 215
Bentley, James, 77
Bergoff, P. L., 161, 171, 193
Bigelow, Annie, 36
Bigelow, William Blake, 35–36
blackmail, 14, 15, 41, 71, 167, 169, 176

Blocher, Jesse, 112
blue laws, 47, 62–63
Board of Public Works, 6
Bowery district, 43
Box Hill, 39–40
Bracken, Edward, 111
breach-of-promise blackmail, 15
Breese, Jimmie, 30, 57, 131–132, 137, 151, 159, 161, 193, 214, 282
brothels, 8, 13, 43
Bryan, William Jennings, 31
Bucklin, David, 89, 90
Butler, Prescott Hall, 38

C

Caine, J. J., 203
Canfield, Richard, 3, 64, 81, 87–91, 101–102, 142–143, 282
Carnegie, Mrs. George, 228
Casino Theatre, 18, 67–68
Century Association, 32
Cheever, Jack, 116
Churchill, Jennie, 22
Churchill, Lady Randolph, 70
Churchill, Lord Randolph, 22
Churchill, Winston, 22
Citizens Union, 60, 113, 178–179
Clarke, Thomas B., 116, 214
Cleveland, Clement, 162
Clifford, Jack, 279
Cobb, Irvin S., 142, 207, 210, 217, 230, 238–239, 253
Collier, Bobby, 86, 143–144, 167, 170, 177, 180
Collier, Mrs. Robert, 197

Collier, Peter, 144

Collier's Weekly, 144, 167, 170, 179–180, 196, 216

Committee of Fifteen, 51

Comstock, Anthony, 13, 138, 192

Countess of Yarmouth, 108–109, 228, 263

Court of Special Sessions, 47, 59

Croker, Richard, 8–10, 25–26, 44, 48, 49,
    59–60, 62, 64

Cryder triplets, viii

Cutting, Robert Fulton, 178–179

D

Davis, Richard Harding, 216, 225–226, 266

Delahunty, John, 89

Delmas, Delphin, 220, 226, 229–231,
    234–238, 243, 246–256, 268

DeMille, Cecil B., 105

DeMille, Mathilda, 105

Democratic Party, viii, 244

Depew, Chauncey, 179

Derby, Augustin, 77, 271

Deuel, Joseph M., 168, 170, 179–180, 197

Devery, William "Big Bill," 4–5, 7–8, 49,
    59–60, 64, 81, 179

Dey Street raid, 3–7

district attorney's office, 26–27, 41–42, 77–81,
    113–114

divorce
    of Clemence Dodge, 103–104, 111–112,
        157, 181
    of Evelyn and Harry, 278
    of Lederer, 84
    societal views of, 125

Dodge, Charles, 103, 104, 111–114, 133,
    145–147, 157, 181–182

Dodge, Clemence, 102–104, 111–112, 157, 181

Dowling, Victor, 101, 102, 263

Drake, A. W., 213

Dunn, Robert, 9

Dunne, Finley Peter, 144, 196

E

Earl of Yarmouth, 108–109, 228, 263

elites, Jerome and, 9–10

Elliot, Ethel Stewart, 124–125, 208, 276

Equitable Life Insurance Society, 155–157, 187

Evans, Britton D., 237

F

Farragut, David, 35

Fields, Andrew C., 187

Fitzgerald, James, 196–197, 228, 233, 243,
    250, 252, 253

Flood, Bernard, 168, 180

Florodora, 11–12, 67–68, 84

Fulton, Maude, 202, 205, 206

G

gambling dens, 3–9, 51, 78, 81, 87–91

Garden Theater, 202

Garland, James, 241, 242

Garvan, Francis, 135, 144, 199, 217, 230,
    263–264

Gelshenen, Katherine, 103, 111, 146, 147, 177

Gelshenen, William, 103

Gibson, Charles Dana, 144, 216

Gilder, Richard Watson, 38

Gleason, John, 230, 231

Goff, John, 43–44, 198–199

Goodrich, Edna, 11–14

Goo-goos, 42–44, 48, 60

Gould, Jay, 23

graft, 8–9, 41, 44, 49

Grant, Hugh, 46

Greeley-Smith, Nixola, 238, 249, 254

H

Hapgood, Norman, 144, 167, 170, 177,
    179–180, 188, 195–199

Hearst, William Randolph, 50, 113–114,
    131, 157, 169, 175–176, 180, 181, 215,
    221–222, 277

hideaways, 54–55, 131, 138

Hodder, Alfred, 24–25, 60, 79

Holahan, Maurice, 6

Holman, Charles, 138, 229

Holman, Mrs., 138, 139, 229, 237–238,
    241–242

Horse Show, 150–151, 155–156
Howe, Gus, 80
Howe, Lavinia Taylor, 27
    See also Jerome, Lavinia
Howe, Nick, 80
Hughes, Charles Evans, 187, 188, 222, 262,
    271
Hummel, Abraham
    disbarment of, 220–221
    Dodge and, 145–146, 157
    Evelyn's affidavit to, 120–121, 137, 227
    indictment of, 157, 177–178
    Morse and, 103–104, 111–112, 133
    retirement of, 280–281
    Thaw trial and, 244–246, 249–251
    trial of, 181–182
    White and, 15
Hyde, James Hazen, 155–157, 160
Hyde Ball, 156–157, 160, 170

I
ice market scandal, 49–50, 56, 64, 102
insanity defense, 219–220, 226–227, 231, 247,
    249, 252, 263–264, 267
insurance companies, 155–157, 175, 187–188
Interborough Rapid Transit (IRT), 191–192
Irwin, Wallace, 3

J
Jacobs, Joseph, 88, 90, 91, 142–143
Jerome, Catherine, 21–25
Jerome, Clara, 22
Jerome, Lavinia, 80, 124, 125, 276
Jerome, Lawrence, 22, 23, 25–26, 124
Jerome, Leonard, 22, 88
Jerome, Lovell, 22
Jerome, Roswell, 22
Jerome, William Travers, xi–xii, 21
    affair of, 124–125
    on blackmail, 41
    candidacy for governor of, 221
    Canfield and, 87–91, 101–102, 142–143
    celebrity of, 9–10
    childhood of, 21–23

college years for, 23–24
criticism of, 24–25, 81, 87, 101–102,
    155–157, 169, 175–176, 187–188, 226,
    261–262, 266, 271–272, 275
Croker and, 8–10
cross-examination of Evelyn by, 241–252
Devery and, 7–8
as district attorney, 77–81, 113–114
downfall of, 271–274
early legal career of, 25–27, 41–42
election as district attorney, 60–65
elites and, 9–10
enemies of, 65, 271–272
health issues of, 21, 24
judicial career of, 4, 46–47
Mann and, 167–170, 176–177, 179–180,
    195–199
marriage of, 27, 63, 80
misconduct charges against, 271–272
Morse and, 102–104, 112–114, 177–178
Patterson case and, 134–135, 141–142,
    144–145, 165–167
political work of, 44–45
popularity of, 123–124
in private practice, 275–276
raids by, 3–7, 9, 51, 89–91
reelection of, 178–181
reform movement and, 41–48, 51
Thaw case and, 207–208, 210, 219–222,
    226–231, 233–239, 241–258, 261–269,
    272–273, 275–276
Whitney and, 113–114
Jerome, William Travers, Jr., 27, 80
Journal-American, 157, 215, 226

K
Kasebier, Gertrude, 173
King, Leroy, 201
Knickerbocker Trust Company, x, 55, 56, 261
Kresel, Isidor Jacob, 78–79, 262

L
LaFarge, John, 33
Lawrence, Lionel, 202, 206

Lederer, George, 84
Levy, Abraham, 142, 144–145, 165, 166
Levy, Newman, 133, 141
Lexow, Clarence, 43
Lexow Committee, 43–44, 49, 51
liquor sales, 47
Littleton, Martin, 198, 199, 261–266
Longfellow, Frederick W., 250
Lonsdale, Lord, 70
Lorraine Hotel, 202–203, 208
Low, Seth, 48–49, 63, 113, 123
Lower East Side, 62, 79

M
MacKenzie, May, 203, 208, 228
Madison Square Garden, 53, 150–151,
    201–202, 204–206
Madison Square Garden Tower, 30
Mamzelle Champagne, 202
Mann, William D'Alton, 14–15, 19, 143–144,
    167–170, 175–180, 195–199, 216, 262,
    281–282
Marbury, Elizabeth, 117, 120
mayoral elections, 45–46, 48–49, 63, 114,
    180–181, 221
Mazet Committee, 49
McCaleb, Thomas, 203
McClellan, George, 114, 123, 180, 181
McKim, Charles, 16, 33–36, 94, 160, 173,
    192, 208, 214
McKim, James Miller, 33
McKim, Mead & White, 16, 18, 29, 36–37,
    184
McKinley, William, 31, 48, 59
Mead, William Rutherford, 35, 36, 214
Metropolitan Club, 10, 53
Metropolitan Street Railway Company, viii, xi,
    62, 64, 113, 129, 130, 262, 266
Monk Eastman Gang, 138, 139, 203
Montague, James I., 195
Morgan, J. P., 7, 177
Morrow, James, 21, 41
Morse, Charlie, 49–50, 55–56, 64, 102–104,
    111–114, 133, 146–147, 177–178, 261, 281

Morse, Jim, 177
Morton, Levi P., 31
muckrakers, 8
municipal elections, 59–65, 180–181
    See also mayoral elections
Mutual Life Insurance Company, 187

N
Nesbit, Evelyn, xi, xii, 11, 29
    abuse of, by Thaw, 119–120, 227,
        244–246, 250–251
    affair between White and, 18–19, 29–31,
        53–54, 73, 83–86, 93, 97, 109–110, 137,
        162, 208, 233–239
    Barrymore affair and, 94–98, 243–244
    career of, 11–12
    childhood of, 18
    cross-examination of, 241–252
    European trips of, 115–121, 138–139, 150
    Harry Thaw and, 68, 72–73, 115–121,
        137–139, 150, 162–163
    health issues of, 162
    initial meeting of Stanford White and,
        11–19
    life after trial for, 279–280
    marriage to Thaw of, 163, 185–186,
        202–203
    memoirs of, 279–280
    murder of White and, 208–209
    at Pamlico School for Girls, 105–107
    pregnancy of, 97–98, 106, 108, 243–244
    rape of, by White, 17–18, 120
    as showgirl, 67–68, 85, 279
    society life and, 30–31
    Thaw's pursuit of, 107–110
    trial of Thaw and, 209–210, 227–228, 231,
        233–239, 255–258, 263, 265–266, 268–269
Nesbit, Howard, 29, 139, 229
Nesbit, Mrs., 13, 16, 69, 96, 107–108, 110,
    116, 139, 217
    See also Holman, Mrs.
Nesbit, Winfield, 18
Newport Casino, 37
New Woman, 13

New York City
  politics, viii
  post-Civil War, 34
  transformation of, into modern city, 273
New York City Police Department, 43
New York Coaching Club, 156
New York Herald, vii, xiii, 23, 25, 26, 36, 59
New York Journal, 50
New York Life, 187
New York Times, 87, 178, 215–216
New York World, 50, 57, 87, 272
Nicoll, Delancey, 181–182
Northern Pacific Railroad, 58

O
Osborne, James W., 180
Osborne, John W., 195

P
Palmer, Potter, 70, 156
Pamlico School for Girls, 105–107
Panic of 1907, 282
Parade Turf Club, 3, 5–6
Parkhurst, Charles H., 43
party bosses, 61
Patterson, Nan, 133–135, 141–142, 144–145,
  157, 165–167, 175, 255, 280
People v. Harry K. Thaw, xii–xiii
  closing arguments in, 253–258, 266–267
  cross-examination of Evelyn by Jerome in,
  241–252
  defense strategy in, 219–220, 226–227,
  230, 231, 247, 248, 263
  Evelyn's testimony in, 233–239, 255–258,
  265–266, 268–269
  Hummel testimony in, 244–246, 249–251
  insanity defense and, 219–220, 226–227,
  231, 247, 249, 251–252, 263–264, 267
  jury deliberations in, 257, 267
  mistrial in, 257–258
  Mother Thaw testimony in, 248–249
  preliminaries in, 225–231
  publicity about, 225–226, 228, 233–234,
  236–237, 246, 268

second trial, 261–269
  verdict in, 267–268
People v. Mann, 198–199
People v. Nan Patterson, 144–145, 165–167
Philbin, Eugene, 4–5
"Pie Girl Dinner," 57, 95
Piper, Deputy Police Commissioner, 89
Platt, Thomas Collier, 61
police corruption, ix, 4–8, 41, 49
politicians, viii, 31, 41, 47
Poor, Henry, 54–55, 57, 58, 282
Post, Edwin, 168–169, 176, 199
Potter, Henry Codman, 50–51
Potter, Nathaniel, 97, 108
Prescott, Summer K., 280
presidential election (1896), 31
prostitution, 8, 43
Pulitzer, Joseph, 50, 55, 57
puritanism, 25

R
Racquet Club Boys, 85–86
Railroad Manual, 54, 58
railroads, 58
Rand, William, 135, 144, 145, 165, 166
Reading Room, 36–37
reform movement, 41–48, 50–51, 64
Republican Party, 48, 60
Restigouche Salmon Club, 94, 131–132, 149,
  193
Richardson, H. H., 33, 34, 36
Rochefoucauld, Charles de la, 70
Ronalds, Reginald, 11, 15
Roof Garden Theater, 30, 204–206
Roosevelt, Alice, 143–144, 155–156, 167
Roosevelt, Theodore, 47–49, 59, 143, 271–272
Rosalsky, Otto A., 266
Russell, John, 53
Russo-Japanese War, 113, 144
Ryan, Thomas Fortune, viii, 62, 130, 262, 266
S
Saint-Gaudens, Augusta, 35
Saint-Gaudens, Augustus, 30, 33–35, 38,
  183–184, 192–193, 216

Schiff, Mortimer, 91

Sewer Club, 55

Shearn, Clarence J., 180

Shepard, Edward M., 195, 198

Sherry, Louis, 131

Short, Harry, 205

Sin City, xi

Sinclair, Upton, 63

slums, ix

Smith, Bessie, x, 37–40

    See also White, Bessie

Smith, James Clinch, 250

Smith, J. Lawrence, 37, 38

Smith, Sarah Nicoll, 37–38

Society for the Suppression of Vice, 13, 138

Sousa, John Philip, 70

Spanish-American War, 49

Stanchfield, John, 181

Steffens, Lincoln, 8, 44, 59

Stevens, Harry, 205

Stewart, A. T., 38

Stewart, Cornelia Clinch, 38, 40

stock market speculation, x, 57–58, 149

Strong, William, 45–47, 48

Sullivan, "Big Tim," 62

Sweetzer, William, 112

T

Tammany Hall, viii

    1890 elections and, 42

    campaign against, 45–47, 61

    corruption, 4, 7–8, 26, 41, 44, 49, 64

    crackdown on, 44–45

    Croker leadership of, 8–10, 44, 49, 59–60

    Jerome and, 178–179

    resurgence of, 48–49

Taylor, Henry, 131

Tenderloin, ix, 43, 44, 49, 107

tenements, 50, 62, 80

Thaw, Alice. *See* Countess of Yarmouth

Thaw, Harry K., xii, 98

    arrival in New York of, 18–19

    background of, 68–72

    character of, 255–256

    death of, 279

    defense strategy for, 219–220, 226–227, 230, 231, 247, 248, 263

    escape from asylum by, 278

    Evelyn and, 68, 72–73, 115–121, 137–139, 150, 162–163

    hatred of Stanford White by, 71–72, 137–139, 161

    imprisonment of, 209–210, 277–278

    marriage of, to Evelyn, 163, 185–186, 202–203

    mental status of, 219–220, 226–227, 231, 247–248, 251–256, 263–264, 267–268, 275–276

    murder of White by, 204–211

    Patterson case and, 255

    publicity about, 215–217

    pursuit of Evelyn by, 107–110

    release of, 276, 278

    second trial of, 261–269

    social life of, 69–71

    statement by, 248

    surveillance of White by, 161, 192, 202

    threats against White by, 193

    trial of. *see People v. Harry K. Thaw*

    troubling behavior of, 71, 107, 138–139

Thaw, Mary Copley

    death of, 279

    Evelyn and, 108, 138, 163, 185–186, 203

    Holmans and, 229, 238

    protection of Harry by, 68–69

    release of Harry and, 278

    trial of Harry and, 209, 210, 215, 217, 220, 229, 248–249, 262

Thaw, Russell William, 279

theater district, 13

Thomas, T. Gaillard, 97–98

Tower Studio, 84

Town Topics, 14–15, 18–19, 69, 72, 93, 143–144, 167, 168, 170, 180, 197–199, 216, 281

Train, Arthur, 24, 26, 61, 63, 77, 79, 101, 123, 220, 273

Twain, Mark, vii, 30, 65

Tweed dictatorship, viii

U

Unger, Henry, 142
Union Club, 71
unions, 81
United States Postal Service, 13
University Club, 45
"unwritten law," 231

V

Vanderbilt, Reginald Claypoole, 81, 90
Van Wyck, Robert, 48–50, 64, 65, 103, 133
vice, 43, 44, 49, 50

W

Wagner, Charles, 237
Washington Square arch, 53
Wector, Dixon, 129
Wharton, Edith, x
Whist Club, 71
Whistler, James McNeill, 88, 101, 201
White, Alexina, 32
White, Bessie, 132, 161, 191, 229
White, Lawrence Grant, 39
White, Richard Grant, 31–32, 39, 214
White, Stanford, vii–xii, 183
     affair between Nesbit and, 18–19, 29–31,
        53–54, 73, 83–86, 93, 97, 109–110, 137,
        162, 208, 233–239
     architectural projects of, 53–57, 106, 173,
        184–185, 191–192, 201–202
     attitude toward women of, 32
     Barney and, 191–192
     childhood of, 31–32
     early career of, 32–37
     European trips of, 34–36, 171–173
     financial problems of, x, 54, 55, 57–58,
        93–94, 115–116, 130–132, 149–151,
        160–161, 172–173, 184, 277
     Florida trip of, 159–160
     funeral of, 213–214
     at Garden Theater, 201–202
     health issues of, 94, 159, 173, 184,
        210–211
     on Hyde ball, 160
     initial meeting of Evelyn Nesbit and,
        11–19
     legacy of, 273–274, 277
     marriage of, 37–40
     murder of, 206–208
     parties thrown by, 30–31
     philandering by, xi, 14–15, 116, 138
     public image of, 95, 120–121, 215–217,
        225–226, 277
     rape of Evelyn by, 17–18, 120
     stock market speculation by, x
     success of, 53–54
     surveillance by Thaw of, 161, 192, 202
     Thaw's hatred of, 71–72, 137–139, 161
     threats by Thaw against, 193
     Whitney and, 130
Whitney, Harry Payne, 91, 144
Whitney, Helen, 171–173, 184–185
Whitney, Payne, 106, 130, 171–173, 184–185
Whitney, William, vii, viii, 54, 61
     business practices of, viii–ix, 62, 262
     death of, 129–130
     Jerome and, 113–114
     mansion of, vii, ix
Whittier, John Greenleaf, 91
Wild Rose, The, 84, 85, 94
Wolfe, Elsie de, 117, 120

Y

yellow journalism, 6–7, 50, 215–217
Young, Caesar, 133–135, 141–142, 144–145,
     165–166